Sixth Edition

The World News Prism

Sixth Edition

The World News Prism

Global Media in an Era of Terrorism

William A. Hachten
James F. Scotton

Iowa State Press
A Blackwell Publishing Company

WILLIAM A. HACHTEN is professor emeritus of journalism and mass communication at the University of Wisconsin-Madison.

JAMES F. SCOTTON is associate professor of journalism at Marquette University.

©2002 Iowa State Press
A Blackwell Publishing Company
All rights reserved

© 1999, 1996, 1992 William A. Hachten
© 1987, 1981 Iowa State University Press

Iowa State Press
2121 State Avenue, Ames, Iowa 50014

Orders: 1-800-862-6657
Office: 1-515-292-0140
Fax: 1-515-292-3348
Web site: www.iowastatepress.com

∞ Printed on acid-free paper in the United States of America

First edition, 1981
Second edition, 1987
Third edition, 1992
Fourth edition, 1996
Fifth edition, 1999
Sixth edition, 2002

Library of Congress Cataloging-in-Publication Data

Hachten, William A.
   The world news prism: global media in an era of terrorism / William A. Hachten and James F. Scotton.—6th ed.
      p. cm.
   Includes bibliographical references and index.
   ISBN 0-8138-2788-4
   1. Foreign news. 2. Communication, International. 3. Journalism—Political aspects. I. Scotton, James Francis, 1932- II. Title.
   PN4784.F6 H3 2002
   070.4'332—dc21

                                             2002003497

The last digit is the print number: 9 8 7 6 5 4 3 2 1

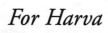
For Harva

Contents

Preface ix

Introduction xiii

1 News Communication for a New Global System 3

2 War on Terrorism Challenges News Media 15

3 International News System 29

4 Internet, Comsats, and New Media 41

5 The Impact of Great News Events 57

6 Globalization of Media 73

7 New Media and the Developing World 89

8 Public Diplomacy and Political Warfare 101

9 New Ways to Report the World—or Not 115

10 Covering the World's Hot Spots 129

11 Changing Ideologies of Press Control 147

12 Western Media to World Media 167

Selected Bibliography 183

Index 187

Preface to the Sixth Edition

In modern times, a few major global news events have had a profound impact on the lives of Americans as well as on the news media that report the "first draft of history." The attack on Pearl Harbor, the nuclear bombing of Japan that ended World War II, wars in Korea and Vietnam, the sudden cessation of the Cold War, and the rise of a global economy have all been major foreign news stories that have changed our lives and the way we view the world.

On September 11, 2001, another ominous global upheaval, the terrorist attacks on New York's World Trade Center and on the Pentagon in Washington, D.C., abruptly altered the lives of Americans and sharply affected international news communication. With the collapse of those two skyscrapers and about three thousand lost lives, Americans (and many others) no longer felt secure and personally safe from the perils of a dangerous world beyond our borders. Terrorist hijackings and bombings were not new: from 1983 to 2001, ten attacks had claimed the lives of one hundred or more Americans. But the 9/11 attacks were the largest violent taking of life on American soil since the Civil War and had a traumatic impact on the American psyche. Most Americans agreed that the nation was at war with terrorism—our first war of the twenty-first century.

So, after a decade of looking inward and ignoring news about the outside world, frightened and stunned Americans suddenly began taking a serious interest in world affairs again, trying to comprehend the threat of terrorism and the complex politics of the Middle East and Central Asia. Osama bin Laden became a subject of intense public interest.

On September 11, the news media responded quickly, professionally, and at times magnificently. Global television, with up-to-the minute and nonstop coverage in vivid color video (without commercial interruptions), reported the horrifying details of the tragedy to every corner of the world. The horrific but awesome images of the two airliners crashing into the twin towers of the World Trade Center were etched into the minds of millions. Supplemented by radio, the Internet, and print, much of the world saw the same video and reports as Americans. This shared experience elicited unprecedented responses of sympathy and empathetic support from many nations and, in some places of the Muslim world, elation and celebration.

The reporting of the horrific events along with the world's response were reminders of how much we have become a global society. Not just in trade and economic affairs but also in social and political ways, we are increasingly coming together. But such acts of terrorism also were grim reminders that deep divisions between rich and poor countries remain. Democratic societies, with their open borders and individual freedoms, were indeed vulnerable to stealth attacks. Radical terrorism was indeed the dark underside of globalization.

In this revised edition, we discuss how the news media responded to this great national crisis. Both at home and abroad, journalists and their editors sprang into action even as the armed forces mobilized. Only subsequent events and time will determine how significant the events of the year 2001 will become in modern history. But there is no doubt that the year 1989 was historic. Then, the world watched on television in dazzled amazement as communist regimes were toppled in Poland, East Germany, Hungary, Czechoslovakia, Bulgaria, and Romania. Two years later, the Soviet Union itself, after a right-wing coup had failed, went through a convulsive revolution of its own, outlawing the Communist Party and its media as well as dismantling the Soviet Union itself. With the collapse of communist political economies came the withering away of the Communist theory of the press and the disappearance of many communist news media. The communist concept of journalism in Eastern Europe and the Soviet Union became a remnant of history rather than a viable way to organize news and mass communication. These historic events also heralded the end of the Cold War and the demise of the propaganda or information "wars" that had enlivened international communication for forty-five years. (New propaganda wars, now focused on terrorism, have resumed since September 11, 2001.)

The post-Cold War world of the 1990s proved to be a harsh and forbidding place. The forces of intense nationalism and unleashed ethnic animosities led to civil wars, genocide, terrorism, political instability, and economic and social chaos starkly evident in the prolonged and agonizing strife engaging the Bosnian and Kosovo Muslims, Croatians, and Serbs of the former Yugoslavia. Elsewhere, various experiments in democracy and market economies sputtered and foundered.

The decade was one of great global economic expansion. In China and throughout East and South Asia, economies grew at spectacular rates and world trade expanded as a new phenomenon, *globalization*, was elaborated. *Globalization* is an inexact expression for a wide array of worldwide changes in politics, communications, business and trade, life styles, and culture. But despite great expansion of world trade, many of the economies of Asian nations have had serious trouble: Plummeting currencies and stock markets in free fall sent shock waves around the world. (Nations with market economies are not free of market forces.) Even Japan's economy had severe problems. In our new post-Cold War world with its increasingly globalized economy, economic concerns often took precedence over political concerns.

Elsewhere, more than 120,000 innocent civilians died in an irrational six-year civil war in Algeria, a half dozen nations fought a nasty regional war over the Congo, genocide flared up again in Rwanda and Burundi, and in the Middle East, bitter violence continued between the Palestinians and the Israelis—peace seemed farther away than ever. Saddam Hussein's Iraq managed to annoy and vex the United States and United Nations; North Korea's erratic and starving communist regime worried the West, and in Bosnia and Kosovo, an uneasy truce continued. Other global headlines: President Suharto was overthrown in Indonesia; India and Pakistan tested nuclear devices; peace was tantalizingly close in Northern Ireland. But these events were perceived as mainly regional, not global, problems, and none of those hot spots made America's top ten news stories.

Until the terror attacks of 2001, there were clear indications that Americans had much less interest in what was happening abroad, and the news media themselves responded by reporting a good deal less foreign news and much trivia. With a diminished nuclear threat and little fear of global warfare, polls showed that Americans were comfortable with the post-Cold War era. But as much of twentieth-century history reminds us, the world can change very quickly, as indeed it did on September 11, 2001.

International communication in the 1990s was affected by world events as it continued to expand; international broadcasting became less propagandistic and more informative and entertainment minded. In most countries, journalists enjoyed greater access to news. New independent and outspoken publications and broadcast outlets sprouted like mushrooms in spring. Communication satellites transmitting news and pop culture proliferated, and media audiences greatly expanded, especially in Asia.

Further, personalized media—videos, VCRs, audio cassettes, personal computers with modems, cell phones, and fax machines—have continued their rapid global penetration, as have cablevision and the Internet. Western Europe has been going through its own regional communication revolution with transnational competition between commercial cable and satellite systems as it moves haltingly toward economic integration.

The ongoing rush of technological developments in international communication has accelerated. Direct broadcasting from portable transmitters to satellites and then back to dish antennas—bypassing complicated, expensive ground installations—has become commonplace. Small portable earth terminals, for example, have enabled broadcast journalists reporting remote news events to send their video reports directly to satellites and thus to the whole world. The cell phone and the videophone have played unexpected roles in news dissemination: A report of an event in Afghanistan or, for that matter, in almost any faraway troubled area, can instantly become a global news event. In just a few years, the Internet has become a player in international communication of great and ominous potential for both journalism and as a device that lets people share ideas freely on a global network.

The rush to media consolidation has accelerated as well. Multibillion-dollar mergers involving major American media companies surprised Wall Street and the world. Time Warner and Turner Broadcasting (owner of CNN) combined forces and then was bought out by America Online. The Disney Company bought Capital Cities/American Broadcasting Co., and Westinghouse Electric bought out Columbia Broadcasting System, only to be purchased later by Viacom. With the constant buying and selling of media properties, newer brand names such as Vivendi and Viacom became more visible. The communications giants are now positioning themselves to compete for the expanding overseas markets for news, television, motion pictures, and recordings. At a time of global crisis, a continuing concern is, where does independent and reliable journalism fit into these media behemoths?

In this age of information, communications systems are at the leading edge of social, economic, and political changes. With the unprecedented growth in global telecommunications, an informed public has developed a more immediate concern with both world news and the symbiotic relationship between events and those who report them.

For this sixth edition, the text has been thoroughly revised, with new material added to every chapter. A new second chapter focuses on the journalistic aspects of September 11. A new co-author, Professor James F. Scotton, has come aboard for this edition. His insights, knowledge, and editing skills, honed through long involvement with international communications and the foreign press, including a recent Fulbright fellowship in Shanghai, are found here. My wife, Harva Hachten, a skilled writer, edited the manuscript of the earlier editions. For this edition, I am responsible for any errors or bad judgments.

—W.A.H.

Introduction

After years of global fretfulness about the brute effectiveness of modern armaments, it turned out during one of the most pervasively revolutionary years of the 20th century, if not of all recorded history, that the most potent single weapon in nearly every conflict was the video camera. In nation after nation, vastly superior military forces were stood off and frequently compelled to retreat before the symbolic and testimonial power of televised images.

—William A. Henry III

As our tragic and war-stained century (and millennium) came to an end and then the world faced up to the threat of global terrorism, we were reminded both of the changes as well as continuities that have marked journalism and international communications in our times. In 1900, all the elements were in place—great metropolitan newspapers, rotary presses and linotypes, the typewriter, the telegraph and the underseas cable, the Associated Press and cooperative news gathering—as building blocks for the changes to come. News was recognized as a valued and useful commodity in itself and as an essential means of comprehending and coping with a strange and distant world. At the same time, sensationalism and trivia had long been standard fare in the press.

But no one could have foreseen the political and social changes to come in our tumultuous times as a result in part of the greatly enhanced speed, volume, and reach of international news and "public knowledge." Journalists and broadcasters jetting about the globe with camcorders, Comsat phones, and laptop computers reported great events instantly via satellite networks and, in so doing, often became participants and catalysts in global news stories.

From the Spanish-American War to the war on terrorism, the press has reported news from abroad, but it has been only in the last three decades that we have seen how great events abroad vividly illustrate the technotronic age, the melding of technology and electronics, that planet Earth has entered. It is a new era of information whose potential we but dimly perceive; whose complicated gadgetry only a few of us totally grasp; whose social, political, and economic consequences are accelerating change and cleavages among the nations of the world.

For the world we live in today is changing rapidly, in no small part because worldwide television, communication satellites, high-speed transmission of news and data, and other computer and electronic hardware and software, including the Internet, have transformed the ways that nations and peoples communicate with one another. The fact that a news event can be transmitted almost instantaneously to newsrooms and onto television and computer screens around the world can be as important as the event itself. Long-distance mass communication has become a rudimentary central nervous system for our fragile, shrinking, and increasingly interdependent world.

Yet there can be disconcerting side effects. The accelerating speed and efficiency of news media technology have often created severe strains on the standards and ethics of responsible journalism. The same system can report trivia and sensation. The news eruptions that followed the auto-crash death of Princess Diana or the Gary Condit/Chandra Levy story illustrated how news now breaks around the clock instead of at the more leisurely pace that prevailed before the rise of twenty-four–hour cable television news and news on the Internet. As fierce competitors such as MSNBC, the Fox Channel, and CNN and other talk shows have proliferated on cable and online, some news organizations have relaxed their rules on checking and verifying sources. There is a growing sense that getting it first is more important than getting it right. A result is journalism that is sometimes shaky, or worse. With it has come a loss of public trust in news media.

High among the various factors contributing to the collapse of communist regimes (and their press) was certainly the global impact of Western communications in all their diversity and seductive appeal. For throughout the 1980s, two great groundswells rolled through the seas of international communication. On an incoming tide, the methods of organizing and distributing news and mass culture developed in Western democracies have washed inexorably over the globe, driven by innovations in media technology and expanding audiences along with a resurgence of market economies on a global scale.

On an outgoing tide, the theory and practices of communist or Marxist/Leninist public communication have become widely discredited by the many millions living under communist regimes, as well as by their own journalists and rulers. The resounding rejection was directly related, of course, to the worldwide failures of socialist political economies and, particularly, the rejection of communist political rule in Eastern Europe. The crowds that protested communist regimes in Warsaw, Beijing, East Berlin, Prague, Budapest, Sofia, and Moscow in 1989 were also calling for more open and free media systems, the kind they knew about from images and sounds from the West. Expanding waves from these astonishing events radiated to the former Third World. Even Africa felt pressures for multiparty democracy.

So far, such high hopes have generally not been realized. Africa—beset by economic stagnation; drought and famine; political unrest; and brutal civil wars in Sudan, Somalia, Mozambique, Liberia, Congo, and Rwanda—has in fact retrogressed. Hopes for meaningful democracy in Kenya, Zimbabwe, and Congo have all been dashed recently. Today's unipolar world, with the United States as its uncertain and often indecisive leader, is challenged not only by terrorism but also other related problems, such as resurgent nationalism, poverty, racism, and religious fundamentalism. To these can be added the ups and downs of a recently faltering global economy.

This book analyzes the changing role of transnational news media in our evolving globalization and its impact on rapidly changing news events. In the current crisis over terrorism, Western news media have played a major role both in informing the world and in organizing and facilitating responses to terrorism. (The media are also an unwilling accomplice of terrorism by publicizing the atrocities.) Throughout this book, the focus is on the role of American news organizations, yet I acknowledge that news media of many other nations contribute to this cooperative activity of reporting the world to itself.

News has increasingly become a powerful political and diplomatic force. For example, U.S. television shows stark pictures of starving Somali mothers and children, American public opinion becomes concerned, and the White House watches, hesitates, and then sends in the military to help feed the starving and keep the peace. A few months later, a dozen American soldiers are killed in an ambush, and the U.S. public is outraged at seeing on television the body of an American soldier dragged through the streets of Mogadishu. Soon the White House announces that troops will be withdrawn.

In late 1995, after unrelenting media coverage of Bosnia's bitter civil war, the United States and its NATO allies finally intervened with a bombing campaign that led to a tenuous peace accord. With American troops involved in enforcing the peace, the public's perceptions on how well or how badly things were going in Bosnia were influenced by the news coverage. During NATO's air war with Yugoslavia in 1999, vivid television reports of the brutal treatment of Kosovo refugees created widespread sympathy for the victims and gained support for NATO's aerial bombing of Serbia. News, instantaneous and vivid, speeds up history as it directly influences diplomacy and government policy. At the same time, in this age of satellites, the Internet, and shortwave radio, tyrants find it impossible to keep unflattering news about their regimes from reaching their own people.

On the one hand are the technological and operational changes taking place in the international news media, with their enhanced capability for global communication that is reshaping "spaceship Earth." Wider communication often seems to exacerbate political and cultural conflicts between the West and Islam, and between rich and poor nations. Also, there are the frictions and the problems these changes have wrought, including conflicts over transnational news gathering and the impact of television programming, motion pictures, videos, radio broadcasting, and other aspects of mass culture, much of it coming out of the United States and Europe.

Another source of concern is that, when no crisis intrudes, serious international news seems often to be shunted aside for more profitable content. "Infotainment"—scandal, sensation, celebrities—has become more and more the staple of many American and British media.

Before September 11, network television news programs, from which most Americans get their news, had sharply cut back on the amount of foreign news. Similar trends were seen among the news magazines. This reflects (or explains) why Americans have been showing a declining interest in news from abroad. The terrorism crisis of 2001 has reversed this trend, but for how long?

This book deals with various facets of the changing media and their impact on transnational journalism and mass communication. It is intended to provide some insights into how and why international news communication is evolving. Few of us can appreciate, much less fully understand, the meaning of the global information revolution we are living through. The major components of this quiet revolution are the computer and telecommunications, principally the communication satellite plus other sophisticated electronic devices that have become as much a part of our lives as the electric light.

We may not be aware of how our perceptions of the world are being changed by the transformed news system, but we quickly learn to take that system for granted. If there is another terror attack on American cities, or another civil war in Africa, we expect to see live television reports the same day or on a twenty-hour–hour news channel, such as CNN, within the hour via satellite. We are fascinated but not surprised to see detailed, computer-refined pictures of the exploration of planet Mars or the dramatic saga of the space shuttle.

In a broader context, the fact that information of all kinds, including urgent news, can now be communicated almost instantly to almost anywhere has profound implications for international organization and interaction. News of Iraq's invasion of Kuwait, for example, had an almost immediate impact on the price of gas at the pump and initiated an international diplomatic reaction resulting in mass movement of U.S. military forces. And the world's subsequent perceptions of the crisis and war were certainly shaped and, at times, distorted by the flickering images on television screens. Instant information is not necessarily the whole truth or the complete picture and, on occasion, does distort images that people receive.

Still, global news has many uses. The global financial media's close, day-to-day reporting of the recent economic crises in Asian stock markets and currencies and their effects on financial markets and economies of Japan, Europe, and America illustrates how many millions around the world, including small stockholders, rely on fast, accurate information in their daily lives. The global economy simply could not function without the flow of fast and reliable information provided by the growing business media.

A new global society of sorts is emerging rapidly and inexorably, though experts disagree about its extent and nature. (Many nations, especially in the Middle East and Africa, do not feel a part of it.) The media of mass communication, along with global telecommunications, air transportation, and growing interdependence of national economies, are providing the essential linkages that make interaction and cooperation—and stealth terrorist attacks—possible.

Full understanding of the nature of this new society requires that today's students of international communication be conversant with world affairs and politics, including recent history, and be quick to recognize significant trends as they occur. Further, they must understand national and cultural differences and keep up with technological innovations in communication media, such as the Internet, and with changing journalistic practices.

Communication satellites are just one example of the truly revolutionary impact that communication technology has had on the modern world. The earlier role of transistor radios in the Third World is another example, and today, the small hand-held video camcorder is having news effects undreamed of. The Internet is beginning to be perceived as yet another technological marvel that may dramatically alter international communication, but so far, no one seems to know exactly how and when it will happen. FM radio, cell phones, and cable television are each having an unexpected impact in developing nations.

The interplay of these elements makes the study of international communication fascinating and important. The major emphasis throughout this book is on the journalistic aspects of international communication: the new challenges and perils of reporting the news; the important but imperfect and controversial ways that journalists and mass communicators keep the world informed. Further, the cultural and entertainment facets of media are often significant as well. As noted, the emphasis is on the American experience in reporting the world.

Several chapters concern the changing media: the ways that international journalism is adapting to altered global conditions, changing the concepts of news, and utilizing the new hardware of our information age.

Today, for the first time in history, all nations, however remote, have stepped onto the stage of the modern world. What happens in Rwanda or Indonesia, or Afghanistan, can have global significance and often sends repercussions around the world, in part because those events are reported. More important, a much greater degree of interdependence among all peoples and nations has developed. Before the terrorism crisis, Americans were perhaps much slower than others to recognize this. Because our families, jobs, and local communities are of primary and immediate concern, most people, including many leaders, did not perceive the rapid and fundamental changes taking place, changes directly related to our expanded powers of long-distance communication. Since September 11, 2001, Americans and their media have become reengaged with the outside world because they feel worried about it.

The world has been evolving an international news system that moves information and mass culture ever faster and in greater volume to any place on earth where an antenna can be put on a shortwave radio receiver, where dish antennas can receive television programs from a communication satellite, or, increasingly, where there is a personal computer with a modem hooked onto the Internet. Although politics, economic disparities, cultural and linguistic differences, and ideology keep us apart on many issues, the international news system has on occasion made us one community, if only for a few brief moments—as when Neil Armstrong took that "one giant leap for mankind" in 1969. An estimated 600 million people throughout the world watched that first walk on the moon, and they sat before their television sets not as Americans, French, Africans, or Japanese but as earthlings watching in awe as one of their kind first stepped onto spaceship Earth's closest neighbor.

Actually, the reportage of Armstrong's walk has further relevance for this book because the new information age is partly an outgrowth of the exploration of space. The communication satellite, high-speed data transmission, and miniaturized computer technology are by-products of space technology. All are playing integral roles in the transformation of international communication and transnational journalism.

The modern practices of globally collecting and distributing news are only about a hundred years old and were initiated by news agencies of the United States and the great imperial powers, Britain and France. Today, the world agencies—the Associated Press (United States), Reuters (Britain), and Agence France-Presse (France)—are still the principal, but far from only, conduits of transnational news, although they and other media have been transformed by the new space-age technology. Change has been coming so quickly that it is often difficult to stay current with the ways in which news is being moved. And to understand the future potential of, say, the Internet is like trying to perceive in 1905 what the absurd horseless carriage or the telephone would do in time to the cities and lifestyles of the twentieth century.

Furthermore, technology and global reach are modifying some of the institutions of transnational communication. Subtly and almost imperceptibly, various media, including the news agencies, are evolving from national to increasingly international or even to supranational institutions of mass communication. The successful *International Herald Tribune* reaches a sophisticated non-American readership from Paris to Hong Kong; *Time* and *Newsweek* publish special editions truly international in outlook; the *Asian Wall Street Journal* is widely read by Asian business people; and CNN is viewed in almost every country. Some may deplore this trend, but there is no doubt that it is a response to the information needs of a shrinking world and an expanding global economy served by a growing business press. Concomitantly, English is clearly the world's media language.

Modern media, especially shortwave radio, are utilized by many nations for purposes of "international political communication," a polite term for propaganda. The international broadcasters—BBC World Service, Voice of America, Radio Moscow, Deutsche Welle, Radio Cairo, and many others, including small national services in developing nations—use the airwaves to voice their reactions to world crises such as the September 11 events. Propagandistic or not, shortwave radio conveys news and information to untold millions, especially in the poorer nations.

The international news media, furthermore, are unevenly distributed among nations, creating serious frictions between the haves and have-nots in mass communication. The explosion of communication technology has coincided with the post-World War II decolonization of the Third World, and the penetration of Western news and mass culture into the newly independent nations, as well as into the former communist bloc, has been perceived by some as a new attempt to reassert the domination of the former colonial powers. Certainly, the Western media—and the nations behind them—are much resented in many of what are now referred to as "failed nations."

Part of this book focuses on the differences that frustrate and at times inhibit the flow of international news and divide journalists and mass communicators: political and ideological differences, economic disparities, geographic and ethnic divisions. The conflicts and frictions in international communication arise in part from divergent concepts of mass communication. In the concept of the press that has evolved in Western democratic nations, journalists are relatively independent of government, free to report directly to the public that uses the information to understand the world and to assess its governors. This view is unacceptable to authoritarian nations, which control and manipulate their media to serve better the goals of the state and their often unelected leaders. In numerous, mostly impoverished nations, a similar theory—the Developmental concept—has emerged, which holds that mass media must be mobilized to serve the goals of nation building and economic development.

The deep differences between the media-rich and media-poor nations closely parallel other differences between rich and poor nations. Despite the impressive gains in the technical ability to communicate more widely and quickly, the disturbing evidence is that in some ways the world may be growing further apart rather than closer together. Most of the benefits of the communication and information revolution have accrued to the industrialized nations of the West and to Japan and the Pacific Rim nations. For an individual to benefit fully from the news media, he or she ideally should be literate, educated, and affluent enough to have access to a variety of news sources. Unfortunately, in our unfair world, the largest share of such individuals is found in the few industrialized democracies. Technological change in communication seems to race far ahead of our political will to use it for the greatest good of all.

The world's system of distributing news can be likened to a crystal prism. What in one place is considered the straight white light of truth travels through the prism and is refracted and bent into a variety of colors and shades. One person's truth becomes, to another, biased reporting or propaganda, depending on where the light strikes the prism and where it emerges. As we understand the optics of a prism for measuring the spectrum of light, so must we understand and accept the transecting planes of different cultural and political traditions that refract divergent perceptions of our world. Obviously, Islamic terrorists have a radically different view of America than most Europeans have.

We must acknowledge how the light refracts for us. In considering the problems of international communication, we have tried to be sympathetic to the views and frustrations of people in non-Western nations and the enormous difficulties they face. Journalism is a highly subjective pursuit, tempered and shaped by the political conditions and cultural traditions of the particular society where it is practiced; the news and the world do look different from Shanghai, Lagos, or Baghdad than they do from New York City or London.

As products of the Western press tradition, we believe that journalists in their pursuit of the news should be suspicious of, and disagree at times with, political leaders and with other journalists and the owners of the media. For us, the essence of journalism is diversity of ideas and the freedom to express them. We agree with Albert Camus, who wrote that "A free press can of course be good or bad, but certainly without freedom, it will never be anything but bad.... Freedom is nothing else but a chance to be better, whereas enslavement is a certainty of the worst."

And in the dangerous, strife-ridden world of the twenty-first century, we believe that the billions of people inhabiting this planet deserve to know more about the events and trends that affect their lives and well being. Only journalists who are free and independent of authoritarian controls and other constraints can begin the difficult task of reporting the news and information we all have a right and need to know.

Sixth Edition

The World News Prism

CHAPTER 1

News Communication for a New Global System

> Globalization is not simply a trend or a fad but is, rather, an international system. It is the system that has now replaced the old Cold War system, and like that Cold War system, globalization has its own rules and logic that today directly or indirectly influence the politics, environment, geopolitics and economics of virtually every country in the world.
>
> —Thomas L. Friedman, *The Lexus and the Olive Tree*

The rapid integration of the world's economy, loosely called globalization, has been facilitated by an information revolution driven by communication technologies that provide a nervous system for our world today. Globalization is a broad and inexact term for a wide array of world-wide changes in politics, economics, trade, finance, life styles, and cultures. To its critics, globalization is trendy and controversial; they see the world becoming a consumer colony of America, led by Coke, McDonald's, Nike, and the vast pop-culture output of Hollywood. How people feel about globalization often depends a lot on where they live and what they do.

With just a visit to a mall, one is struck by the plethora of products and services from many distant lands. In the past twenty years, much of the world's economy has become increasingly integrated; direct foreign investment has grown three times as fast as total domestic investment. From 1980 to 1995, the value of world trade rose sharply with the total value of world exports estimated at U.S. $5.1 trillion, up from U.S. $2 trillion in 1980. But globalization is more than buying and selling; some see it as a profound interchange of cultures—a communication revolution that is dissolving our sense of boundaries, our national identities, and how we perceive the world.

Deregulation of telecommunications systems and computerization have been called the parents of globalization. Three technologies in particular—

computers, satellites, and digitalization—have converged to produce a global communications network that covers the earth as completely as the atmosphere. Today's era of globalization is based on falling telecommunications costs, thanks to microchips, satellites, fiber optics, and the Internet.

The popular culture of the West—movies, television shows, music CDs, video and audio cassettes, books, magazines, newspapers—have been increasingly flowing about the world. It can be argued that the world is beginning to share a popular culture, based only in part on that of the West. Critics differ about what happens when cultures meet.

Rather than fight, cultures often blend. Frederick Tipson noted in 1999, "More like a thin but sticky coating than a powerful acid, this cosmopolitan culture of communication networks and the information media seems to overlay rather than supplant the cultures it interacts with."[1] When cultures receive outside influences, it is said, they ignore some and adopt others, and soon begin to transform them. An example can be something called *bhangra pop* in India—music that sounds like Jamaican reggae but is played on Indian instruments and then amplified.

Critics of this global media market castigate globalization for several reasons: the centralization of media power; and heavy commercialism, which is linked to declines in public broadcasting and public service standards for media performance. Media are seen as a threat to democracy because of lessened public participation and concern with public affairs. Press critics have other concerns about these corporate giants. The news media, they argue, risk becoming submerged and neglected inside vast entertainment conglomerates that are primarily concerned with entertainment profits.

Others see globalization in more positive terms. It is argued that many millions more people than ever before now have access to news and information, especially in such countries as China and India. Globalization means multitudes now have many newfound choices: how they will spend their leisure time; what they will watch or read; what to buy with newly acquired personal income from rapidly rising standards of living. Anthropologist James Watson wrote in 1999, "The lives of Chinese villagers I know are infinitely better off now than they were 30 years ago. China has become more open because of the demands of ordinary people. They *want* to become part of the world—I would say that globalism is the major force for democracy in China. People want refrigerators, stereos, CD players."[2]

Journalist Thomas Friedman wrote that globalization is essentially about change, which is a reality and not a choice. "Thanks to the combination of computers and cheap telecommunications, people can now offer and trade services globally—from medical advice to software writing to data processing—services that could never be traded before. And why not? A three-minute call (in 1996 dollars) between New York and London cost $300 in 1930. Today it is almost free through the Internet."³

The primacy of the issue of globalization reminds us of the extent to which most of us all now think and act globally—as a matter of course.

A Big, Cloudy, Blue, Agate Marble

Perhaps one of the most significant photographs of modern times was taken during the Apollo 11 mission to the moon. The astronauts photographed the earthrise as seen from the moon, and there was our planet, like a big, cloudy, blue, agate marble. The widely reprinted picture illuminated the fragility and cosmic insignificance of our spaceship Earth.

That stunning image coincided with the worldwide concern about ecology and global pollution; even more, it made it easy to grasp why many scientists already treated that cloudy, blue marble as a complete biological system in which change in one part will inevitably affect other parts.

Certainly in the years since, concerned persons around the world have become more aware of our global interdependence. Although some experts disagree, an important trend of our times is that the world is becoming a single, rudimentary community. Today's world must grapple with an agenda of urgent and complex problems, most of them interrelated: overpopulation; poverty; famine; depletion of natural resources (especially energy); pollution of the biosphere; regional political disputes; continuing arms buildup, including the nuclear threat; and the widening gap between rich and poor nations, which seems exacerbated by economic integration. The attack on the World Trade Center and the Pentagon has pushed terrorism high up on this agenda. The September 11 attack on America was a somber reminder of how much hate and anger divides our diverse societies.

These and other global crises ebb and flow on the world's news agendas, but they are truly international in scope; the amelioration, much less solution, of any of them requires cooperation and goodwill among nations. To achieve that, there first must be information and understanding of these challenges, for these are crises of interdependence. No one nation or even combination of nations can deal effectively with such global concerns as international monetary crises, pollution of the air and oceans, population control, terrorism, regional warfare, and widespread famine and food shortages, yet the blinders of nationalism and modern tribalism continue to influence political leaders everywhere to react to international problems with narrow and parochial responses.

Lester Brown, an authority on global needs, described the problems of the late twentieth century as "unique in their scale." Previous catastrophes—famines, floods, earthquakes, volcanic eruptions—were local and temporary. But now, the world's more pressing concerns can be solved only through multinational or global cooperation, yet the institutions to cope with them are largely national. And because each technological innovation seems to create new problems but not the political will capable of resolving them, Brown sees global conditions worsening in the years immediately ahead. Brown's view of world problems, although shared by many, is still not truly understood by any great numbers of people. We Americans, for example, periodically turn inward and become self-absorbed, failing to comprehend how domestic problems have roots in events that may occur thousands of miles away.[4]

Americans and some leaders of developing countries are becoming aware that population growth is putting intolerable pressures on the earth's land, water, and energy resources as well as its economies.

Pressures of Population

On September 11, 2001, the world's population had passed 6,176, 921,171, according to the U.S. Census Bureau. (In 1950, the world had 2.5 billion people.) The Population Reference Bureau projects the world's population in 2025 will be 7.818 billion, and in 2050, it will be 9.036 billion. At least 74 countries, including Nigeria, Iran, Ethiopia, Iraq, and Guatemala, will probably double their populations in 30 years; and in addition, thirty-three countries, twenty of them in Africa, still have a fertility rate of six children per woman; and that three billion women—the equivalent of the world's population in 1960—will enter their childbearing years in the next few years.

Thomas Merrick, president of the Population Reference Bureau, a private, nonprofit group, said, "For the developing nations it is a question of whether they will evolve into a kind of permanent underclass at the bottom of a two-tiered world economy. For the more developed nations, now approaching population stabilization, it may be difficult to continue to be islands of prosperity in a sea of poverty in a world made smaller by modern transportation and communication."[5] This separation of rich and poor will be more difficult to maintain if these imbalances generate waves of immigration, as indeed they have. Even without these ominous developments, the very nature of the problems of the early twenty-first century— transnational in scope and beyond the ability of this or any single nation to solve—are changing America's traditional provincialism.

The world's political structures, many believe, must be reshaped to enable us to cope with these global challenges. Hence, the great importance, despite their shortcomings, of international organizations such as the United Nations and its attendant agencies. After the 2001 attacks on New York and Washington, the U.S. government was encouraged by the promises of collective action against terrorism by not only Western nations but also China, Russia, and some Muslim nations. It remains to be seen how long such unity will persist.

Public opinion polls have long shown that many Americans are uninformed about international affairs. For example, a Gallup Poll found that half of all Americans did not know that the United States had to import petroleum to meet its needs. The extent of our current neglect of international education at all levels is shocking. Before September 11, most American news media paid little attention to news from abroad. What worries experts is that ignorance and apathy about the world beyond America's borders may undermine this country's political, diplomatic, and economic influence. The next generation of Americans will be ill prepared to grapple with global problems.

As important as formal education is, its influence sometimes does not change attitudes or improve understanding until a generation or two later. In immediate terms, the media flow of information and news throughout the globe will have a greater impact than education on the world's ability to understand its problems and dangers. Since World War II, an intricate and worldwide network of international news media has evolved, providing an expanded capability for information flows. This relationship between the capacity and the need to communicate rapidly has resulted from the interaction of two long-term historical processes: the evolution toward a single global society and the movement of civilization beyond four great benchmarks of human communication—speech, writing, printing, and electronic communications (telephone and radio)—into a fifth era of long-distance instant communication based on telecommunications (mainly satellites) and computer technology.

Harold Lasswell believed that the mass-media revolution has accelerated the tempo and direction of world history. What would have happened later has happened sooner, and changes in timing may have modified substantive developments.[6]

The toppling of President Ferdinand Marcos from power in the Philippines in 1986 provided a cogent example of the power of international news media to influence international politics. From the assassination of opposition leader Benigno Aquino through the election campaign, the U.S. news media took a close interest in Marcos' affairs, reporting extensively on Marcos' "hidden wealth," including New York City real estate, as well as his dubious war record. This scrutiny helped the cause of candidate Corazon Aquino and galvanized U.S. public opinion and the Congress. The Reagan White House in turn was pushed to urge Marcos to step down after full media glare showed his election victory to be a fraud. As Thomas Griffith of *Time* wrote, "The visuals on American TV did Marcos in. It wasn't Dan Rather or George Will. It was the pictures—the nuns, and the crowds wearing a touch of yellow, blocking the path of the armored cars. It was the sight of ballot boxes being dumped. In a few precarious days, it was the total collapse of Marcos' American support that sped the end. TV proved its awesome power."[7]

Commenting on the episode, Walter B. Wriston observed, "This is a brand new situation in the world. The global electronic network that has evolved in the last decade is forcing us to redefine our ideas of sovereignty. The rapid transmission of information has become a radical force for change, encouraging the growth of political and economic freedom. Marcos's demise is not an isolated instance."[8] The revolutionary year of 1989 provided further examples of the power of modern communications in the uprisings from Berlin and Prague to Tiananmen Square. (See Chapter 5, "Impact of Great News Events.") Intense global media attention to Indonesia in May 1998 probably contributed to the bloodless coup that toppled President Suharto.

Paradoxically, even with this greatly enhanced capability of involvement in world affairs, comparatively few people are well informed or even care much about what happens beyond their borders. Many who follow the news on television have only a superficial knowledge of events such as a cancellation of an election in Nigeria or a stock-market crash in Indonesia. But for those comparative few who do follow public affairs closely (and they are found in every nation), perceptions of the world are being formed and reshaped by this revolution in long-distance instant communications.

Our ability, or lack of it, to use the fruits of this technological revolution is directly related to our success or failure to act decisively and in concert as a world community. International experts worry whether the world can organize itself and deal effectively with what have been called the seven major interrelated world problems: mass poverty, population, food, pollution, energy, military expenditure, and the world monetary system. To organize, though, we must communicate, since communication is the neural system of any organization. The extent of its ability to communicate determines the boundaries of any community—be it a primitive tribe in Papua New Guinea or a global society—and only expanded and more effective communication can make possible a viable global community.

The technology to circulate that information exists, but the barriers of illiteracy, poverty, and political constraints keep too many people in the world from receiving it. The illiteracy situation is particularly vexing. However, there has been improvement. The tide of worldwide illiteracy is turning: The illiteracy rate, estimated at 45 percent fifty years ago, had fallen to about 23 percent. This was a remarkable achievement, considering that world population continued to rise during that period. The average rate, however, masked significant disparities. In 1995, nineteen nations had an illiteracy rate equal to or higher than 70 percent, fourteen of them in Africa. Moreover, UNESCO reported that the number of illiterates is rising in Southern Asia, sub-Saharan Africa, and the Arab states.

Literacy is the key skill for modernization, education, and use of mass media. Illiteracy is widespread in Africa, so it is no wonder that there are only about 125 daily newspapers in all of Africa compared with more than 1,770 in the United States. In any country, therefore, the proportion of people able to receive news and information will vary greatly according to the availability of mass media and the ability of people to use the media. Those living in such "information societies" as Japan, Western Europe, or the United States are overwhelmed with information and news, whereas throughout the many poor nations only a tiny fraction of persons is able to participate in the international news flow, due in large part to the lack of news media. Regardless of where they live, however, too few people take advantage of opportunities to acquire and use information in the solution of urgent transnational problems.

Importance of Foreign News

Much of the essential information we need for our personal lives comes from the news media. Our economy, our society, and our government would have difficulty functioning without the flow of reliable news and information. An open, democratic society without independent news media is impossible for Americans to imagine.

Foreign news is a special genre of news. It's not just from afar but also news of widespread significance. The attacks on the World Trade Center were major news everywhere. Serious journalists and editors have long held that important information from overseas should be reported capably and thoroughly, even though most people are primarily concerned about what happens in their own communities or to themselves personally.

Throughout our turbulent times, events beyond our borders have directly affected, and disrupted, many American lives: World War I, a global depression, the rise of Hitler and Stalin, World War II, the Korean and Vietnam wars and the Cold War, and, more recently, our interdependent global economy. In an open, democratic society, the public must know what is happening in the outside world in order to judge how well our government and leaders respond to challenges from abroad. The history of American journalism clearly shows that the best and most responsible news media have always given high priority to foreign news. This is still true today, especially for a handful of great daily newspapers.

Yet for many Americans, until September 11, 2001, foreign news did not seem as important and relevant as it was before the Cold War ended and the nuclear threat receded. Who is to blame: the press, our political leaders, or the public? Perhaps all three. Without a crisis demanding our attention—famine and civil war in Sudan, genocide in Rwanda, civil war and aerial bombing in Bosnia and Kosovo—the average daily paper carries usually only about six short items from abroad—unless American soldiers are involved, as in Somalia, Bosnia, or Afghanistan.

Most Americans rely on television for their news, yet anyone regularly watching network news is aware that foreign news has been typically reduced to several short items ("And now the news from abroad…") unless some video with violent footage is available. (Fifty percent of television's foreign coverage does portray violence.) Critics say that serious foreign news on television has been pushed aside in favor of either scandal or the so-called "you news"—self-help and advice stories.

The public apparently does not mind. A recent survey of the American public by the Pew Research Center found that among regular users of the news media, the topics of most interest were, in this order, crime, local news about people and events, and health news. International news ranked ninth, well behind sports, local government, science, religion, and political news. Another 2001 poll (before 9/11), by Andrew Kohut, found that fewer than one in five Americans were strongly interested in serious news programs and publications—international, financial, government, and politics. Gender, generation, and education are keys: College-educated men over forty years of age and older have the most interest; lesser-educated, younger women have decidedly the least.[9]

Other surveys conducted by the Pew Research Center in 1997 found that the percentage of people following foreign news dropped from 80 percent in the 1980s to 20 percent in 1990. The decline was most precipitous among young people, who were turned off by such traditional categories as international politics, security, war, and peace. The relatively few serious news stories that attract the attention of adult Americans are those that deal with national calamities or the use of American military force.

We agree with Stephen Hess of the Brookings Institution, who argues that we have become a nation with a two-media system, especially in regard to foreign news. Hess wrote, "Our society is awash in specialized information (including foreign news) available to those who have the time, interest, money, and education to take advantage of it. The other society encompasses the vast majority of Americans, who devote limited attention to subjects far removed from their necessary concerns (again, foreign news). They are content to turn to the top stories of television networks' evening news programs and their community's daily newspapers for the information."[10]

Yet perhaps this diminished interest in international events is not as significant as it would seem. Recent polls show that although the public is turned off by some foreign news, the public does crave engagement in the world's crises, but not in ways defined by government, academics, and the media. For example, a University of Maryland poll found that 74 percent of people wanted a sharing of power internationally, whereas only 13 percent wanted the United States to assert itself as the only superpower. Also, although Congress refused to approve $1.5 billion in overdue assessments for the United Nations, a Pew Center survey found that Americans hold the organization in high regard. The Pew survey found broad support for cooperative action to halt global warming, even if it meant applying fuel consumption standards leading to higher U.S. gasoline prices.

In short, the public seems highly concerned about issues they see as directly affecting their lives. Americans clearly felt their lives threatened by the September 11 attacks. They are also concerned about immigration and trade negotiations that could have an impact on their jobs and taxes, as well as environmental issues such as resource depletion, health threats, drug trafficking, and other cross-border crime.[11]

Moving Together or Apart?

Whether the problem is pollution of the seas or proliferation of nuclear weapons, the fact remains that international society is marked by the absence of effective collective procedures, by competition rather than cooperation, and by the lack of a commitment to a common goal. The world is ruled by nation-states, not by an effective international organization, and each state will usually act according to its own interests and needs. In several African nations, such as Somalia, Liberia, and Sierra Leone, an even more discouraging trend has emerged: the complete breakdown of a nation into warring camps without a coherent central government. Some academics argue that the apparent thrust toward global unity and globalization is actually misleading. Political scientist Steven Krasner of Stanford believes that the idea that the world has fundamentally changed lacks historical perspective. The international transfer of ideas, trade, and capital has been going on for four hundred to five hundred years, he says. Others agree that the idea of global integration has been overblown and that we are not yet up to the late-nineteenth-century standard of integration. They argue that the current globalization is a return to a process interrupted by two world wars.[12] From the mid-1880s to the Great Depression, the world experienced a similar age of globalization. The volumes of trade and capital flows across borders and the flow of labor across borders, relative to populations, in the pre-World War I era of globalization was similar to what we are living through today. But today, powerful communications, including the media, drive our current globalization.

Others feel that the world is both converging and diverging at the same time. In 1993, the *New York Times* listed forty-eight nations where long-suppressed ethnic, religious, and sectional conflicts had surfaced. Policymakers say the ethnic conflicts are actually the third wave of this century, with the first having taken place after World War I and the second with the explosion of anticolonial movements in Africa and Asia after World War II. Most of these nations' ancient rivalries and bigotry have remained largely unaffected by communication technology. The rise of international terrorism to the top of the world's agenda is further strong evidence of global divisiveness.

On the other hand, powerful technotronic forces are binding the world together—circulating news, ideas, and information faster and in greater volume than ever before. These technologies are transforming many economic enterprises into truly global businesses. Further, countless more individuals are, through education and media participation, joining the modern world. So, although global integration may seem both real and illusory, there may be encouragement in the futuristic views of science-fiction writer Arthur C. Clarke expressed more than 25 years ago regarding the communication satellite:

> What we are now doing—whether we like it or not—indeed, whether we wish it or not—is laying the foundation of the first global society. Whether the final planetary authority will be an analogue of the federal systems now existing in the United States or the USSR I do not know. I suspect that, without any deliberate planning, such organizations as the world meteorological and earth resources satellite system and the world communications satellite system (of which INTELSAT is the precursor) will eventually transcend their individual components. At some time during the next century they will discover, to their great surprise, that they are really running the world.
>
> There are many who will regard these possibilities with alarm or distaste and may even attempt to prevent their fulfillment. I would remind them of the story of the wise English king, Canute, who had his throne set upon the seashore so he could demonstrate to his foolish courtiers that even the king could not command the incoming tide.
>
> The wave of the future is now rising before us. Gentlemen, do not attempt to hold it back. Wisdom lies in recognizing the inevitable—and cooperating with it. In the world that is coming, the great powers are not great enough.[13]

Some signs of this trend are visible; a slow but perceptible movement toward internationalization of the world's news media is taking place. The world's news agencies, a few newspapers and magazines, and both radio and television broadcasting (CNN and BBC World in particular) are transcending the national states from which they arose and are serving international audiences. With this has come from the West a pervasive popular culture. Such a transition will be welcomed by some as a contribution to better world understanding or resented by others as efforts by some nations to impose their models of mass communication and pop culture on everyone.

The technological capability for worldwide communication has never been greater, but then never have truly global problems and challenges seemed more urgent. Not enough people anywhere understand these problems or are in a position to cooperate with others in resolving them. Serious questions can be posed about the quality and adequacy of today's system of global news communication, but no doubts exist about the importance to the world of the newspapers, news agencies, and broadcasters that report the world's news to itself.

Notes

1. Erla Zwingle, "Goods Move. People Move. Ideas Move. And Cultures Change," *National Geographic*, August 1999, 12.
2. Ibid., 13.
3. Thomas Friedman, *The Lexus and the Olive Tree* (New York: Anchor Books, 2000), xviii.
4. Lester R. Brown, *World Without Borders* (New York: Vintage Books, 1973), 10–12.
5. United Nations Population Fund, as reported in the *New York Times*, August 18, 1994, A4.
6. Harold Lasswell, "The Future of World Communication: Quality and Style of Life," Papers of the East-West Communication Institute, Honolulu, no. 4 (September 1972), 3.
7. Thomas Griffith, "Newswatch," *Time*, March 17, 1986, 72.
8. Walter P. Wriston, "Economic Freedom Receives a Boost," *New York Times*, April 15, 1986, 31.
9. Andrew Kohut, "Balancing News Interests," *Columbia Journalism Review*, July/August 2001, 58.
10. Stephen Hess, *International News & Foreign Correspondents* (Washington, D.C.: Brookings Institution, 1996), 8.
11. Barbara Crossette, "U.S. Likes its Foreign Affairs in Nontraditional Terms, Polls Say," *New York Times*, December 28, 1997, 8.
12. Susan Wels, "Global Integration: the Apparent and the Real," *Stanford Magazine*, September 1990, 46–50.
13. Arthur C. Clarke, "Beyond Babel: The Century of the Communication Satellite," in *Process and Effects of Mass Communication*, W. Schramm and D. Roberts, eds. (Urbana: University of Illinois Press, 1971), 963.

CHAPTER 2

War on Terrorism Challenges News Media

> The news media rank as one of the big winners of Sept. 11: Terrorism gave us a huge story and restored our seriousness of purpose. Before Sept. 11, the press was caught in a prolonged process of self-trivialization. We seemed to live in an era dominated by the personal, the small and the titillating. The summer's big stories were Gary Condit and shark attacks. Now that has changed dramatically. Here is a story that truly matters. It's about good and evil, life and death, war and peace, religion, technology, the clash of cultures—our future as a society.
> —Robert J. Samuelson, *Washington Post*

The news of a single day rarely has had a profound effect on history. December 7, 1941—the surprise attack on Pearl Harbor that brought America into World War II—was such a memorable day. September 11, 2001—the terrorist crashes by hijacked airliners into the World Trade Center in New York and the Pentagon in Washington, D.C.—was another historic day that set off a global upheaval with repercussions we cannot foresee. After the collapse of the two skyscrapers, the scarring of the Pentagon, the crash of four airliners, and about three thousand lives lost, Americans (and many others in the West) no longer felt personally secure and safe from the threats of a dangerous world beyond our borders.

Terrorist hijackings and bombings were not new. The tactic of using planes as bombs was used by 3,913 Japanese pilots who killed themselves flying kamikaze attacks against U.S. warships near the end of World War II. Just between 1995 and 2000, the State Department reported, there had been more than 2,100 international terrorist attacks. But just fifteen of them occurred in North America, causing just seven casualties. The sheer enormity of the 9/11 assaults on American soil were rightly considered acts of war. Aside from the loss of life, some estimates have placed the total damage of 9/11 events at about $350 billion. The United States and its allies promptly embarked on a war against terrorism.

The news coverage of the many facets of 9/11 can only be described as comprehensive and magnificent. In New York and Washington, D.C., journalists reported a local story of great national and international import. Global color television—nonstop and constantly updated—carried unfolding details to every corner of the earth. Supplemented by radio, print media, the Internet, and the ubiquitous cell phone, much of the world saw and heard nearly the same video images and news reports as Americans received. And the American audience was huge: 79.5 million viewers were watching news coverage on broadcast and cable TV networks in prime time on September 11, according to Nielsen Media Research.[1]

On September 14, three days later, 39.5 million viewers tuned in to television news coverage in prime time. The Internet audience (which is international) was huge as well. The number of page views that CNN.com normally experiences on an average weekday is fourteen million; on September 11, the number of page views on CNN.com jumped to 162.4 million.

Moreover, that vast audience approved of the way both the U.S. government and the media had responded. According to a Pew Research poll, 89 percent of people felt the media had done a good or excellent job in covering the September 11 attacks.[2] Professional journalists agreed.

Global news reports of 9/11 elicited unprecedented responses of sympathy and support for America from other nations. The reporting and widespread response were reminders again of how much of the world has become a global society. Not just in trade and economic affairs but in social and political matters as well, we are increasingly coming together. Yet the sobering reality that the 9/11 terror acts were applauded and celebrated in much of the Islamic world were reminders that deep divisions pervade relations between rich and poor nations and that democratic societies with open borders and individual freedoms are indeed vulnerable to stealth attacks. The United States was clearly the prime target of highly organized and skillful terrorists animated by deep hatred for America and much of the Western world.

So, after more than a decade of looking inward and ignoring the outside world, the news media as well as thoughtful Americans began showing a serious interest in world affairs again, in particular, trying to understand radical Islam and the complex politics of the Middle East and Central Asia. The nature and motives of Osama bin Laden became a subject of intense public and media interest.

A poll by the Pew Research Center for the People and the Press, taken in October 2001, found that the terrorist attacks and the war in Afghanistan had created a new internationalist sentiment among the public. There was much more support for a multilateral foreign policy than before September 11, with roughly six-in-ten (59 percent) now saying that interests of allies should be taken into account by U.S. policymakers. By two-to-one margins, the public thought that taking an active role in the world, rather than becoming less involved, would be a more effective way of avoiding problems such as terrorism in the future. And support for assertive U.S. leadership also had grown.[3] The opinion shifts were dramatic but no one could say how long they would last.

Media Scramble for New Kind of War

The U.S. news media seem to operate under three different modes in covering the day-to-day news. Mode One is a routine, normal news day offering a variety of news stories when no one major story or "blockbuster" dominates the news. Mode Two is when a story of major significance breaks: an unexplained crash of an airliner, the assassination of a major world leader, or a terrorist attack somewhere, as on September 11. When this happens, both print and broadcasting throw all their resources into covering these stories. This mode shows U.S. journalism at its best. Mode Three is when a major scandal or sensational story of high public interest (but little real importance) breaks—the O.J. Simpson trial, the Clinton/Lewinsky scandal, and recently, the Gary Condit/Chandra Levy story that monopolized the news before September 11. These stories attract audiences and often dominate much of cable and broadcast television, news magazines, and talk radio for weeks or months on end. A few serious media avoid or downplay these kinds of stories.

Press critics have argued that for years now the media, especially television and news magazines, have been preoccupied with the sensational Mode Three stories that have attracted huge audiences and advertising revenue. At such times, serious foreign news is ignored. In retrospect, we can ask: Why have local newspapers and television stations been so indifferent to international news during an era in which ethnic conflicts have killed millions and globalization has touched nearly every American community? Part of the reason Americans were so shocked and disoriented by the terror attacks was that they had become so complacent and uninformed about the threat of foreign terrorism to what is now called the "homeland."

They certainly did not learn much from their local media or network television (or from the federal government, either) about the possible dangers of such devastating attacks striking close to home.

Since September 11, the major national news media have been given a chance for redemption and are clearly operating in Mode Two—reporting with great competence a complex global news story with many facets and dimensions. Because of budget cuts and fewer overseas reporters and foreign bureaus, the broadcast networks—ABC, NBC, FOX, and CBS—were the least prepared for this new "asymetrical" war against terrorism, which has no standing armies to confront; the enemies are hidden, subversive, and of differing nationalities but are found in "training camps" in remote areas of the Third World—in Afghanistan and maybe in Iraq, Sudan, or Somalia. Or probably some terrorists have been living among us for many years in deep cover and waiting for the chance to strike—a new challenge for reporting as well as for government counter-terrorism efforts.

The news media have been challenged to report adequately on both the international and national aspects of a new kind of "war." In Central Asia, media covered the more conventional war against the Taliban and Al Qaeda in Afghanistan along with efforts to hunt down Bin Laden, as well as diplomatic efforts to maintain a coalition of nations against terrorism. At home, the press followed various counter-terror efforts to protect airliners, airports, and other public facilities; the press also reported on other government efforts to prepare the nation for possible biological or even nuclear attacks in the homeland. As one journalist said about his colleagues, "We are all war correspondents now!" How well and effectively the news media reports any of these ongoing stories could very much affect the public's understanding and support of the war effort. But all agreed that the war will be difficult, dangerous, and expensive to report. Obviously this would be a very different war to report than, say, the Persian Gulf war of 1991. Sometimes the news was about air strikes and special forces; sometimes it was about seeking out terrorist cells. Commandos and secret agents don't take journalists along; the Pentagon warned that much of what happens may not be reported. And there would be times when no war news occurred at all.

The 9/11 events thrust CNN back into a clear leadership among the 24-hour cable services because of its wide reception overseas. CNN was expected to report on American retaliation to terrorism wherever and whenever it occurred. In the first weeks after 9/11, CNN's audience, normally about six to eight hundred thousand, jumped to three million U.S. listeners. (As time went on, these totals slipped.)

The coverage on network television was important, unprecedented, remarkable, and revealing about television news itself. Network news showed that it could still mount a powerful system of coverage; no U.S. network or cable system did badly. Viewers depended on Tom Brokaw, Dan Rather, and Peter Jennings not only for news but also for reassurance and solace. In the first weeks, television coverage was unabashedly patriotic with U.S. flags much in evidence, but the public apparently didn't seem to mind. In the first days, television ran up huge costs but carried few commercials. No one could see how the broadcast industry could bear such expenses for very long.

The *New York Times, Washington Post, Time, Newsweek,* and other print organizations dispatched platoons of reporters and photographers to cover whatever could be found out in Pakistan, Afghanistan, or wherever. Despite remote and difficult conditions of Afghanistan and in the face of Pentagon warnings that scant news would be divulged and that access to troops would be denied, U.S. and British reporters, as well as journalists of other nations, did a remarkable job of keeping the world informed. The war was also very dangerous to report. Eight journalists were killed in the first weeks in the Afghan campaign—at the time more fatalities than U.S. forces had suffered.

In this first war in an age of globalization, despite a lack of Pentagon help, a steady torrent of 24/7 coverage went out to the world. Vastly improved communications enabled journalists in Central Asia to send out a flood of information and images. Satellite telephones greatly facilitated the news flow. But for television, the most important new reporting tool was the video telephone, which enabled a war correspondent to send an on-camera television report via satellite from a obscure corner of Afghanistan onto an evening news show in New York City.

Americans were also getting their news from other sources: BBC television reporters scored several major news scoops because the British government was more forthcoming with news. Early in the war against the Taliban, the Arab broadcast service, Al-Jazeera, from Qatar, had the only video available—including an interview with Osama bin Laden and showing bombing damage—from inside Afghanistan. Al-Jazeera itself became controversial but for a short time was the best source of war news and pictures.

Political analysts have argued that Arab public opinion has undergone a major change since the emergence of satellite broadcasting and some privatization of media. The "Arab street," once all but powerless, may be taking on a new importance. The "street" (that is, views of Arab public opinion) has become a real force: now exposed to more sources of information that repressive governments do not control; harder to rein in once inflamed; and more susceptible to radical Islam. Arab rulers no longer have a monopoly on information and can no longer shape public opinion. Particularly with the existence of Al-Jazeera, an explosion of information has occurred that has defined the debate. This trend was seen as a threat to the stability of more moderate governments in the Arab world.[4]

Although the American press received high marks for its initial war coverage, the news media still faced controversy when reporting war news from the "homeland." Some thought that some members of the press had foregone their traditional skepticism and were too willing to be a pawn of government and accept only the government versions of events. But other critics argued that the press was unpatriotic at times—too sympathetic to war protestors, and tending to overplay stories about collateral damage to civilians and atrocities from our side.

A more serious charge was that the press, in reporting the early stories on the anthrax fright in New Jersey and Washington, D.C., had become unwitting accomplices of terrorism by causing unnecessary fear and even panic among the public. Despite the few anthrax cases found, the news media had treated anthrax as a lurking menace that might quickly strike all of us. Similarly, regarding the reporting about security breaches at airports, the nation's vulnerability to other bioterrorism or possible nuclear threats, and the shortcomings of security agencies such as the FBI and CIA, it was argued that media created unfounded fright and confusion among some of the public. The media had become, it was said, the silent allies of terrorists. But, of course, such stories must be reported and the public must be informed of all possible dangers. Most hyping came from the highly competitive cable channels: CNN, MSNBC, and Fox News. No one was quite sure where to draw the line.

Apropos of this, a Gallup Poll for November 16, two months after the 9/11 attacks, found that the vast majority of Americans approved of the way top administration officials and major government institutions were handling the war on terrorism, but that a majority of Americans disapproved of the news media's performance. President Bush received 89 percent approval; Colin Powell, 87 percent approval; Congress, 77 percent; but the news media had only 43 percent approval. Some of the public thought the press had overreacted to the anthrax scare.

As the bearer of bad news during a crisis, the press was seen as being in conflict with government at a time when public officials were highly regarded. The news media would have their ups and down as the many-faceted story continued to unfold.

All agreed that this was a different kind of war to report. There was no Soviet Union of terrorists to face nor were there standing armies to confront. There was no end in sight and it was unlikely there would be a day when victory could be declared. Ending terrorism was considered to be a goal without a goal line. No one knew what would happen next and some important news would perhaps not be reported because of security concerns. Yet there were parallels with the Cold War against communism. People wondered whether Americans have the patience for another 40-year war—what President Kennedy termed a "long twilight struggle." Communism in the 1950s was not seen as a rival state but as a fearsome, state-sponsored, international conspiracy that threatened us from within and without. The American response, according to journalist Bill Keller, was called "containment," a kind of global gopher hunt aimed at countering communist influence wherever it surfaced, using diplomacy, economic power, and armed proxies more often than American military might.[5]

The emerging war on terrorism shares many of these similarities, and already the U.S. government has been gearing up for a long struggle. For the first time since the end of the Cold War, the press has an international story to focus on—one with real staying power. For journalism and the news media, the war has meant adapting once again to what has been termed the "twin arms of political warfare: censorship and propaganda."

Censorship and Control of Information

Whenever America goes to war, the press recognizes that it has a crucial responsibility to tell the public as much as it can—accurately and responsibly—about the conflict and the fate of its armed forces. As in the past, the needs of the press and the military will inevitably come in conflict. Reporting a war requires a degree of cooperation from the military. In recent conflicts—in Grenada in 1983, Panama in 1989, and the Gulf War in 1990–1991—different administrations have reduced the access of reporters to the battle zones and placed obstacles in the path of timely, independent reporting.

In the current war on terrorism, press restraints have so far been even stricter than in the past.

Secretary of Defense Donald Rumsfeld seems committed to controlling information and has warned the public that because of the clandestine nature of the "long thin war," much information about the location and activities of troops will not be divulged until well after operations are concluded. Releasing classified information, he said, is not only dangerous but against federal law.

Veteran communicators from other wars were amazed at the limited information and limited access to the battlefield in Afghanistan. Barry Zorthian, chief spokesman for the U.S. war effort in Vietnam from 1964 to 1968, said this conflict in Afghanistan was much tighter than Vietnam and that Saigon was almost wide open compared to the current war. He said that in Vietnam, the military gave out much more information and had no trouble with the press revealing anything that harmed U.S. troops. In contrast, during the first months of the war against Afghanistan, almost all the important news about the U.S. military came out of the Pentagon.

It soon became apparent that, perhaps more than usual, press-military relationships would be at times strained and even abrasive. At a Pentagon podium, Rumsfeld told reporters he did not want to be quoted when he cited Winston Churchill's words that "in wartime truth is so precious that she should always be attended by a bodyguard of lies"—even as he was appearing live on CNN and being heard around the world. He also said he did not "intend to" lie to the press.

In October, the White House requested that broadcast network executives not air in full the prerecorded statements of Osama bin Laden carried on Al-Jazeera, the Arab television network. The White House expressed concern about giving the terrorists unchecked outlets for their propaganda; the White House also feared that such appearances might contain coded messages for bin Laden operatives around the world. The six major television news organizations agreed jointly to abridge future videotaped statements. But some in the press criticized this action, arguing that the American people should have unfettered access to the terrorist leader and his views.

Conservative press critics also criticized the news media for being too neutral or "balanced" in reporting and not sufficiently patriotic and outspokenly antiterrorist. But the problem for the news business was to make the public and its critics understand that the press expresses its patriotism by aggressively defending the public's right to know what's going on. That's the job of a free press, even in wartime.

That ethic was at the heart of the press's efforts to gain more access to the war in Afghanistan and elsewhere. News organizations believe they need to have reporters with all sizeable military units: aircraft carriers, Air Force squadrons, regular Army and Marine ground units, as well as some form of access to special forces units. In Afghanistan, the press had little such freedom of movement. Yet in the past, American journalists have been highly responsible in responding to sensible guidelines on real operational security, and no serious breaches of military security have occurred. On some occasions, the press has held back on sensitive information when requested by the administration.

A Pew Research Center poll in late November 2001 showed the quandary the press faced regarding censorship and public support. By and large, Americans continued to praise the press for its coverage on terrorism at home and abroad. Yet at the same time, the public showed strong support for government control of news for the sake of national security. The survey of fifteen hundred adults found that the number who think the media usually gets the facts straight had risen from 35 percent in early September to 46 percent in late November—the best grades for media accuracy since 1992. The press also had higher grades for professionalism, morality, patriotism, and compassion. Yet the poll respondents favored tight government control over national security information, indeed for military censorship as high as in the Persian Gulf War. By 54 percent to 39 percent, the poll said it is more important that the government be able to censor stories it believes could threaten national security than for the media to be able to report news it sees as being in the national interest. By a comparable margin, Americans say the military should exert more control over news about the war rather than leave most decisions to the media.[6]

Early in 2002, a review of news coverage of the war showed that as time went on, the public had been getting fewer facts and more opinion from the news media. One reason for the decline of factual coverage was that the U.S. government had imposed the most stringent censorship in history.[7] The study by the Project for Excellence in Journalism found that during the opening four months, straight factual reporting in the media dropped to 63 percent of coverage in November and December, compared with 75 percent in mid-September. The rest of the coverage was analysis, opinion, and speculation—the kind of content that people consistently tell survey takers they resent. Further, the study found that the spectrum of viewpoints in media commentaries was remarkably limited in its political range. Less than 10 percent of opinion offered any dissent from administration policy.

Kovach and Rosenstiel said the findings help explain why polls in mid-November found only 30 percent of the public rating the news media's performance as excellent, as compared with 56 percent ratings in

September. Other reasons for the drop in public esteem included network cutbacks that left television news hard pressed to maintain sustained in-depth reporting. Further, cable networks had substituted talk for reporting, and local newspapers, the study reported, had taken reporters off the story.[8] Also, of course, major domestic stories, such as the high-profile collapse of the Enron corporation in January, certainly diverted the media's attention from the war on terrorism.

Nonetheless, the best of the press will always find ways to cover an American war. If the military restricts information, reporters will find other sources and ways to get the story. (In Afghanistan, much news came from British journalists, the BBC, and journalists of other nations.) But as Michael Getler of the *Washington Post* wrote: "The public's best interests are served by an enlightened relationship between the military and the media, when both sides make an honest stab at solving some of the problems that naturally arise in a way that does not interfere with military operations and security but allows an independent account of America at war to be recorded."[9] (See Chapter 10, "Covering the World's Hot Spots," for more on press-military relations in wartime.)

The Propaganda War

From the beginning of 9/11, the conflict was seen in part as a propaganda war—a battle for the "hearts and minds" both of Americans and people everywhere. The second strike to the World Trade Center, displayed on live television, was seen as a horrific shock to the psyches of millions and a profound propaganda statement by Islamic terrorists—greatly amplified by the world's impressive media system. And yet Bin Laden's 9/11 attacks may have backfired because after two decades of absorbing terrorism attacks without sustained counterattacks, a stunned and horrified America recognized such terrorism as "acts of war" and subsequently has geared up for a many-faceted war against terrorism or, as some said, a war against Islamic totalitarianism.

Along with mobilizing its armed forces and something new, a "homeland" security apparatus, the White House began to mobilize its resources and tools for political warfare and propaganda. With the global impact of the attacks—applauded and hailed in much of the Muslim world—and subsequent television statements by Bin Laden, it was a war of words in which, many said, the United States and the West were at best playing catch-up and at worst losing. For America, the heart of the problem was a broad chasm between the way Americans see themselves and the way they are seen by others.

Part of the struggle is over something that has long troubled traditional societies: the invasion of their cultures by powerful outside influences such as social mobility and cosmopolitan thinking that can undermine the traditional ways of clans, religious elders, and dictators. Western mass media and consumer products, although widely used and enjoyed, are also seen in Islamic nations as corrupting and seditious influences to be eradicated. In the West, information is seen as a key to deflecting the hatred aimed at the United States. And, of course, one person's "information" is another person's "propaganda"—and vice versa.

Two main sources conveyed "information" from America: the independent news media, particularly global television, and the official government agencies: Voice of America and other ad hoc efforts. CNN, BBC World, and other private broadcast and print media reached a far greater global audience than U.S. government efforts could. But the global audience had most of its news (or propaganda) filtered through its own national media and, in the crucial Middle East, Muslims were happy to get their news from Al-Jazeera, the independent CNN-like satellite television service from Qatar, which provided a steady diet of radical Islamist-flavored news and commentary. (See Chapter 7, "New Media and the Developing World," for more on Al-Jazeera.) Before 9/11, most Arab governments, who tightly controlled their own broadcast services, were opposed to the independent Al-Jazeera, but after the attacks, they welcomed it. For the West, the worrisome feature of Al-Jazeera was that it often slanted its news with a vicious anti-Israel and anti-American bias. Islamic radicals dominated its talk shows. For example, Al-Jazeera reported that four thousand Jews were told not to go to work in the World Trade Center on September 11 thus promoting the rumor widely believed by Muslims that Jews were behind the attack. These biases mirrored public opinion in the Islamic world and reinforced the region's anti-American views.

During the first weeks of war, the White House efforts at global PR were hit and miss. To reach Islamic audiences, the State Department brought in Charlotte Beers, a former advertising executive, to use her marketing skills to make American values as much a brand name as Ivory soap. The department's efforts were also intended to counter Bin Laden's propaganda.

Clearly the message was not getting out. So, the White House and Britain's 10 Downing Street set up a joint publicity operation to respond, campaign-style, to charges by the Taliban and the terrorists. Working with Prime Minister Tony Blair, the "Coalition Coordination Center" tried to make quick responses on a 24-hour basis. For example, on November 22, 2001, the center issued in Islamabad a twenty-two–item catalog of atrocities committed by Al Qaeda and the Taliban.

Already on duty since World War II was the Voice of America, which currently broadcasts nine hundred hours of original programming every week in fifty-three languages to some one hundred million people around the world. Before 9/11, VOA's top five countries in numbers of listeners were China, Bangladesh, Ethiopia, Nigeria, and Afghanistan. VOA research found that in 2000, 80 percent of men in Afghanistan listened to VOA news at least once a week in Pashto or Dari, the principal languages. (The Taliban would not permit a survey of women.) Sanford Ungar, former VOA director, said "The Voice of America wins listeners because it is not propaganda—because people around the world know they can count on it for fair and balanced coverage when their own news outlets are often slanted to protect the government in power."[10]

Credibility has been seen as essential to effective short-wave broadcasting. But this long-term policy came under attack soon after 9/11. The Voice of America had broadcast a rare interview with the leader of the Taliban four days after outraged State Department officials argued that he should not be given a taxpayer-financed platform. Some one hundred VOA employees protested in a letter to newspapers that their work was being censored. Soon after that, the Bush administration appointed a new VOA director—someone with strong conservative credentials.

Congress seemed to second the White House actions by voting on November 7 to create Radio Free Afghanistan to beam American news and entertainment to Afghans in their native languages. The vote was 405 to 2 and was hardly a vote of confidence in the VOA. The bill was sent on to the Senate. The broadcasts were to be modeled after Radio Free Europe of Cold War days.

Implied in all of this was the realization by elected officials that the nation must do a better job of explaining itself to the Muslim world. Within Afghanistan, two propaganda efforts considered useful were the dropping of leaflets and radio broadcasting from roving aircraft.

Sometimes, a well-known maxim of political warfare—"propaganda of the deed will always trump propaganda of the word"—will come into play. As Taliban forces fell back in retreat and disarray after the bombing onslaught, images coming out of Afghanistan did much to advance the war against Islamic extremism. Global television viewers saw joyous Afghans in

Kabul shaving their beards, dancing to music, women's faces appearing in public, the reopening schools for girls, and people making clear their delight with the end of harsh Taliban rule. Claims by Islamic propagandists that the U.S.-led military campaign had done great damage to the Afghan people were discredited. But these propaganda coups for the United States had little to do with the "public diplomacy" policies of the government to market and control information. (See Chapter 8, "Public Diplomacy and Political Warfare," for more on this topic.)

By January 2002, the conventional war against the Taliban and Al Qaeda was winding down and a clandestine and difficult stage beginning —that of locating the fleeing leaders of the Taliban and of Bin Laden's top leaders. Yet the long-term need to influence global public opinion against terrorism remained. The evolving war on terrorism will offer new challenges for the news media. Will the press continue to report fully and responsibly after the shooting stops and the media audiences turn back to lighter and more frivolous fare? As ratings and advertising revenues fall, will the media managers cut back on foreign news and look for more sensational and trivial ways to hold onto their audience? The war on terrorism is only in its opening stages. Stay tuned.

Notes

1. "Add It Up," *American Journalism Review,* November 2001, 11.
2. Ibid., 11.
3. "America's New Internationalist Point of View," Pew Research Center for the People and the Press, October 24, 2001, Online report.
4. John Kifner, "The New Power of Arab Public Opinion," *New York Times,* November 11, 2001, sec. 4, 1.
5. Bill Keller, "The 40-Year War," *New York Times,* October 6, 2001, 23.
6. "Terror Coverage Boosts News Medias' Image But Military Censorship Backed," Pew Research Center for the People and the Press, November 28, 2001, Online report.
7. Kovach, Bill and Tom Rosenstiel, "In Wartime, People Want the Facts," *New York Times,* January 29, 2002, 29.
8. Ibid.
9. Michael Getler, "Challenges: The Press and the Pentagon," *Columbia Journalism Review,* November/December 2001, 26.
10. Sanford J. Ungar, "Afghanistan's Fans of American Radio," *New York Times,* October 5, 2001, A23.

CHAPTER 3

International News System

> What we are building now is the nervous system of mankind, which will link together the whole human race, for better or worse, in a unity which no earlier age could have imagined.
>
> —Arthur C. Clarke

On September 11, 2001, the horrendous events were proclaimed in that day's various newspaper headlines:

U.S. ATTACKED: HIJACKED JETS DESTROY TWIN TOWERS AND HIT PENTAGON IN DAY OF TERROR (*New York Times*)

TERRORIST ATTACKS HORRIFY NATION (*Seattle Times*)

"NONE OF US WILL EVER FORGET THIS DAY" (*St. Louis Post-Dispatch*)

ACTS OF WAR (*San Jose Mercury News*)

"TODAY OUR NATION SAW EVIL" (*Orlando Sentinel*)

Throughout that long day, before those banner headlines appeared, most Americans, and many millions abroad, had watched the unfolding events on television, whose global reach mainly through CNN and BBC World relentlessly carried the vivid and horrifying images to every corner of the world. Others got the news via radio or the Internet, including e-mail and cell phones. In Shanghai, all Chinese papers carried stories; journalism students there heard the news from friends in the media and clustered around TV sets in classrooms to learn more. Across the world in Cairo, a friend of the writers heard the news on her car radio and drove home, where she found that both Egyptian channels 1 and 2 were carrying CNN coverage. Many people would long recall where they first heard the news. Most people, whether in Asia or America, followed developments from their local media, which received news from a complex system connected to newsrooms and broadcast stations around the world. (See Chapter 9, "New Ways to Report the World—or Not.")

This story, like most major news stories, was essentially reported by journalists working for the news organizations of Western nations. To Americans, Western Europeans, the Japanese, and some others, news has—like electricity, water, and gas—become an essential service that is taken for granted. By merely turning on a radio or television set or picking up a newspaper at the door, people expect to find the latest news, whether it be from the Middle East, Europe, Africa, or wherever. (Such is not the case, however, in most nonindustrialized nations.)

Indeed, most people in the industrialized world cannot remember when important breaking news was not available immediately (like any other public utility) at the flick of a switch; the technicalities of news delivery are of little public concern and only dimly understood at best. The fact is, however, that global news communication is of fairly recent origin. The far-flung apparatus or "system" through which news flows around the world has evolved and expanded greatly since World War II, along with our modern information society. We learned, for example, about the important battles of World War II many hours or often several days after they began—and then only through radio or newspapers. About thirty years later, the daily clashes in Vietnam were brought to us in full color on our home television screens at dinner time, sometimes on the same day they occurred.

Naturally, the public's perceptions of a war have always been colored by the way journalists have reported them, but color television pictures of Vietnam, including U.S. dead and wounded, had an unusually strong impact on public attitudes. And today, with the ongoing war on terrorism, the public follows many dramatic news events while they are taking place.

In this century, and particularly since 1945, an intricate web of international communications has been spun about the planet, greatly expanding the capability for news and political interaction at a time when the need for information has become so much more urgent. This rapid growth of what Colin Cherry termed an "explosion" in mass communication around the world has had widespread significance: for international relations and world politics; for the flow of news and information; for the cultural impact abroad of motion pictures, television, and video from the West; and for the institutions of international communication, including news agencies, broadcast networks, and international newspapers, magazines, and other publications. Further, today the world reacts politically much more quickly and perhaps emotionally to events than ever before.

As we become, in various ways, a more interdependent world community with common problems, if not common values and goals, the world's ability to communicate effectively with all its parts has been greatly expanded. We now have a global economy, and we are trying to develop institutions to deal with it. Doing so requires reliable news and adequate communications.

This communication explosion has three broad dimensions: geographically, vast areas of Africa, South and East Asia, and Latin America have been drawn into the global communication network for the first time; the amount of traffic and the number of messages carried in the system have multiplied geometrically; and the technical complexity of both the new hardware and the skills and specialized knowledge needed to maintain and run the network has become increasingly sophisticated.

"For two thousand years and more the means of distant communications were various postal services, derived from the Roman cursus publicus, working at the speed of the horse (up to and including the Pony Express); and then the explosion hit us, not immediately upon the invention of the telegraph, but nearly a century later," Cherry wrote. "It is the sheer suddenness of the explosion which is of such profound social importance, principally following the Second World War."[1]

Advancing from crystal sets in 1920 to a television service in 1937 took, as Cherry pointed out, only seventeen years. The first transistor appeared in 1948, and electronic memory chips, the silicon brains of microcomputers, came soon after that. The first Sputnik went up in 1957, and only eight years later Early Bird, the first generation of the global INTELSAT system of communication satellites, went into operation in 1965 and brought television pictures from Europe. Just twenty-five years later, INTELSAT VI was in the heavens and, compared with Early Bird, had fifty-five times more power and a total communications capacity that had increased 170 times. Comparing the communications capacity of Early Bird INTELSAT I to INTELSAT VI, a major carrier of international news, is like comparing the height of a toolshed with a skyscraper in New

York City.[2] And today, the Internet has added a whole new dimension to international news.

The International News System

The expanded international news system is largely an outgrowth of Western news media, especially those of Britain, the United States, and, to a lesser degree, France and Germany. A world news system exists today because the peoples of Western democracies wanted world news, and the great independent newspapers, newsmagazines, news agencies, and, later, broadcast organizations have cooperated and competed to satisfy those wants and needs. Editors and correspondents, working for independent (that is to say, nongovernmental) and profit-making news organizations, have developed the traditions and patterns of providing the almost instantaneous world news upon which people everywhere have come to rely. The credibility and legitimacy that such news generally enjoys rests on its usually unofficial and independently gathered nature as well as its informational or generally objective content. The enduring ethic of Western journalism was summed up more than one hundred years ago by an editor of the *Times* of London:

> The first duty of the press is to obtain the earliest and most correct intelligence of the events of the time, and instantly, by disclosing them, to make them the common property of the nation. The duty of the journalist is to present to his readers not such things as statecraft would wish them to know but the truth as near as he can attain it.

That nineteenth-century statement represents a journalistic ideal; actual practice is often much different. Some transnational media have close, compromising ties to their governments, and all independent media are subject to varying kinds of controls and influences from the corporate interests that own them. Nonetheless, the news media of Western nations have more freedom and independence to report world news, and hence more credibility, than media of other nations. And because of greater financial resources and technology, Western media have a greater capability to report world news.

Some newspaper and broadcasting organizations use their own correspondents to report foreign news, but the global workhorses and the linchpins of the world news system have long been the so-called world news services: AP, UPI (United Press International), Reuters, AFP, and TASS, which are in effect "newspapers for newspapers." It is no coincidence that they come from the United States, Britain, France, and the former Soviet Union. (With the breakup of the USSR, TASS, now Information Telegraph Agency of Russia, or ITAR-TASS, has slipped considerably in importance.) In a general sense, great powers have been great news powers. Today, however, the continued importance of France and Britain in world news may owe more to relationships developed during their imperial pasts than their geopolitical importance today.

What made these five organizations world agencies is their capability to report news from almost anywhere to almost anywhere else. Although they are sometimes perceived as dominating world news flow, the Western agencies are definitely not in an economic class with such powerful multinational corporations as Mitsubishi, Exxon, or Shell. UPI, for example, has been in a shaky financial condition for more than two decades and has been teetering on the edge of collapse, its operations drastically cut back. AFP has been losing money for years and depends on subsidies from the French government. Reuters is a major news service yet is only a part of a successful larger organization that specializes in business and financial information.

The Associated Press, with 241 bureaus (95 abroad), a total editorial staff of 2,700, and more than 6,000 subscribers, processes 20 million words and 1,000 photos daily. Yet, with an annual budget of $570 million, AP is small potatoes indeed compared with the scope of the giant oil companies such as Exxon, which has reported $4 billion in profits for a single year. Yet, AP, a cooperative mainly owned by U.S. newspapers, is the dominant institution in the world news system.

News organizations in two great economic powers, Deutsche Press Agentur (dpa) in Germany and Kyodo News Service in Japan are approaching world-agency status. Other second-tier agencies are ANSA in Italy, efe in Spain, and Mena in Egypt. In addition, there are numerous national agencies that serve as important vital links, especially in the developing nations, between the major world agencies and the "retail" newspapers, broadcast stations, and other recipients of the reports of AP, Reuters, and AFP. The world services sell their reports to the national agencies, which in turn distribute the news reports to local media that otherwise might not receive them. Finally, the national agencies stand as key gatekeepers (and potential censors), deciding which news can and cannot be distributed to the local media within their own nations.

Some of the great newspapers of the world—the *Times, Daily Telegraph, Financial Times*, the *Independent*, and the *Guardian* of London; *Le Monde* of France; *Frankfurter Allgemeine* of Germany; *Neue Zürcher Zeitung* of Switzerland; *Asahi* of Japan; *New York Times, Washington Post, Los Angeles Times, The Wall Street Journal*, and others in the United States—maintain their own correspondents abroad. The same is true of the extensive broadcasting systems BBC, CBS, NBC, ABC, CNN, and others, as well as the leading newsmagazines such as *Time, Newsweek*, the *Economist, L'Express*, and *Der Spiegel*, among others.

Several newspapers, such as the *New York Times, Washington Post*, and *Los Angeles Times*, as well as the *Guardian* of London, syndicate their news and sell it to other newspapers at home and abroad. As a result, their news stories and features supplement as well as compete with the world news agencies. It is well to remember that once a news event is reported—the death of a king or a major earthquake—it becomes the common property of journalism and can be repeated anywhere; only the precise wording of a news story can be copyrighted, and this rarely becomes a factor in news flow.

A survey in 2002 reported on the foreign bureaus of major U.S. papers. *The New York Times* had forty reporters in twenty-six bureaus; the *Washington Post* had twenty reporters in twenty-six bureaus; and the *Los Angeles Times* had twenty-one reporters in twenty-six bureaus. Knight-Ridder had fourteen reporters in fourteen bureaus. *USA Today* had four reporters in four bureaus. Regional papers with five or more bureaus included the *Chicago Tribune* (10), *Newsday* (5), the *Dallas News* (5), the *Baltimore Sun* (5), and the *Boston Globe* (5).

The expansion in overseas coverage has happened, in part, because of the expanded interest in overseas business and financial news, a key aspect of the global economy. This interest explains the 119 reporters in forty bureaus of *The Wall Street Journal* with its business focus and overseas editions. Reuters and Bridge News (formerly Knight-Ridder financial news) have hundreds of overseas staffers to report specialized business news. Bloomberg News, another financial news service, had 226 reporters in sixty-two countries.

With the growing importance of broadcast media, people receive more and more of their news from electronic sources, especially television. As a result, two television news services, Reuters TV (formerly Visnews) and Worldwide Television News (WTN), as well as the great Western networks, have been playing an increasingly important role in the international news system. Live feeds from another continent are usually identifiable as the work of the network involved, but the source of the news on tape or film is not as evident. Most viewers are unaware that much of the foreign news viewed on television is supplied by two television news agencies dominated by American and British interests.

Reuters TV, the biggest and best known, is the world's leading supplier of international news video and film for television, servicing more than 409 customers in eighty-three countries, and is distributed by both satellites and air-mailed videocassettes. Reuters TV says it reaches 1.5 billion people daily. In 1992, Reuters bought out its co-owners, NBC and BBC, and changed its name from Visnews. Reuters TV staffs thirty-eight bureaus and works with contract crews in about seventy countries.

The Avis of these services is WTN, also located in London, which remains a center and clearinghouse for international news exchanges. WTN is 80 percent owned by ABC and cooperates with ABC and CNN in distributing video news. WTN has fifteen overseas bureaus and contracts with film crews in about seventy countries.

Both services also have exchange agreements with the U.S. networks, ABC, CBS, NBC, and CNN, all of which maintain several bureaus overseas. The U.S. networks sell some of their news products abroad and thus contribute to the interchange that makes the international news system work.

Eurovision, the regional television exchange system in Western Europe, gets about 40 to 50 percent of its material from Reuters Television and WTN. The majority of television systems around the world depend on these two services for all of their world news on television. In numerous small African nations, often a lone television service depends on a five-minute package of world news from Reuters TV for its entire evening news show.

It has been said with some but not much exaggeration that an American's right to know is the world's right to know. For any news story that gets into the American news media can and often does flow rapidly around the world and can appear in local media anywhere if it gets by the various gatekeepers that select and reject the news of the day. Stories about civil war in Chechnya, riots in Algeria, an anthrax terrorism scare in America, or any other report prepared for the U.S. news media can and often will be read or viewed or listened to in Africa, Asia, and Latin America.

The domination of international news by AP and other Western news organizations is often resented in other nations. The poorer nations particularly are dependent on the Western agencies and media to find out about themselves and their neighbors. They criticize what they consider a one-way news flow from North to South, from the rich to the poor. They resent the fact that Western journalists with Western values set the agenda for the world's news.

There is some basis to complaints about this Western-dominated system. But the West does not enjoy a closed monopoly of world news; any news organization is free to report world news, but few have the capability and credibility for so doing. Moreover, far ranging and technically sophisticated as it is, the world's present news system is not as pervasive and efficient as it might be, considering the world's diversity and its need for information. Western journalists do an imperfect job, and most operate under a variety of constraints, which are discussed later.

CNN and Global Television News

The successful establishment of the twenty-four–hour Cable News Network (CNN) has been a major innovation in international news as well as in competitive U.S. cable television news. Ted Turner, the Atlanta, Georgia, broadcaster, launched the around-the-clock news service to attract viewers to cable television and to compete in news with the three major U.S. networks. Started in 1980, its growth and success have been impressive—and imitated. Most important, CNN is seen in more than two hundred countries, so when a world crisis such as the 9/11 terror attacks occurs, CNN plays a major role in informing the world quickly. CNN has two twenty-four–hour daily news channels, a Spanish-language service (two thirty-minute newscasts daily), as well as CNN International, the worldwide channel put together from the two domestic services plus other programming. CNN and its companion cable service, Headline News, have an estimated value of $1.5 billion. CNN employs 1,800 staffers in nine domestic and nineteen overseas bureaus, all feeding their reports through Atlanta to CNN's widening global audience. In the 1990s, when CBS, NBC, and ABC were cutting back on overseas operations, CNN was opening new bureaus in such places as Nairobi, New Delhi, Frankfurt, Paris, and Beijing—at a cost of about $6 hundred thousand to open and staff each additional office overseas.

During an international crisis, CNN plays a special global role. Whereas ABC, CBS, and NBC will issue news bulletins and then go back to scheduled programming and perhaps do a late-evening wrap-up, CNN stays on the air for long stretches of time, continually updating the story. The networks' version of the story will be seen in the United States; CNN's version will be seen all over the world. Overseas, travelers often can watch

CNN in their hotel rooms, foreign television services pick up the whole service or some news programs from CNN, and individual television viewers can get it off their satellite dishes or subscribe to the service locally.

During prolonged crises, such as the Gulf War and now the terrorism war, CNN can play a key role with its extensive coverage of all facets of the story. Indeed, CNN's international position often makes it a player in diplomacy as well as a reporter of major events. With its reports available in all world capitals, political leaders and diplomats watch closely and are willingly interviewed on CNN in order to get their views widely known. (CNN recognizes its near-diplomatic status, and reporters are aware of the danger of being manipulated by their interviewees, whether they be George W. Bush or a spokesman for Osama bin Laden.)

Recently, CNN has not been without its problems and its critics. When there is not an international crisis or a Gary Condit-type story, viewership of CNN drops off sharply, and recently revenues from advertising have declined as well. As the Gulf War ended, nearly eleven million of CNN viewers switched back to the big three networks and CNN's audience was reportedly down to about normal, which is six hundred thousand to eight hundred thousand households.[3] During the O.J. Simpson trial, CNN audiences soared when it provided gavel-to-gavel coverage, often to the neglect of foreign news coverage.

It can be argued that CNN is primarily a technological innovation in international news by reason of its ability to interconnect so many video sources, newsrooms, and foreign ministries to so many television sets in so many remote places in the world. In this regard, CNN has undoubtedly had a major impact on diplomacy as well as global news. Nonetheless, a television news channel of true global reach was an innovation whose time had come and, as proof of that, CNN now has serious competition at home and abroad.

In 1991, the BBC began its own World Service Television (WST), now called BBC World, and has been expanding it rapidly. Since 1997, BBC World has been challenging the dominance of CNN International, which according to CNN company figures, reaches 113 million homes in 210 countries and territories outside the United States. CNN's domestic services reach another seventy-one million homes. After two years in Europe, BBC World had gained an audience of thirty million homes outside of its worldwide viewership in fifty million homes in 174 countries and territories.

In what has been called our newest public utility, the 24/7 cable-news-television industry, CNN has been bucking stiff competition from

MSNBC and Fox News Channel (FNC). MSNBC, owned jointly by NBC and Microsoft, recently for a three-month period averaged a higher daily audience than CNN for the first time in its eleven-year history. Fox News Channel, which appeals to a more conservative audience than the other two cable channels, had been making large gains. Since September 11, the cable channels have been competing fiercely. During the first week of coverage, CNN pulled in a near-record number of viewers. CNN was first among all cable networks for the week of September 10–16, pulling in 3.07 million cable and satellite households. That was one million more households than second-place FNC. However, in early 2002, FNC pulled ahead of CNN for a time.

Both Rupert Murdoch, owner of FNC, and NBC have had their sights on global networks similar to CNN International and BBC World. Some experts argue that in normal times the overwhelming interests of audiences everywhere are not about global news per se but, in a more focused way, about their own region and locality. Yet as the most recent global crisis shows, global television news takes center stage once again by reporting, explaining, and influencing the world's response to great events.

The success of CNN and BBC World illustrates the ways that media technology can shape the contours and impact of international news—and will continue to do so. Further, with the merger of Turner Broadcasting with Time Warner and later America Online, the future financial support of CNN seems assured.

With the greatly enhanced technological reach of international communication, the location of a sender or receiver is no longer as important as it once was. The key gatekeepers of the world news system are still concentrated in New York City, London, Paris, and similar metropolitan centers, but it is not necessary to be in those cities to follow the news of the world. A shortwave radio or a satellite dish and now a computer with Internet connections can keep a person almost anywhere in touch with the day's principal events. Furthermore, distance has become increasingly less a factor in the cost of long-distance news communication, whether it takes place through a private telephone, computer or fax messages, television reception, or news reports bounced off satellites. Essentially the same technological process (and at the same cost) is required to send a news flash via satellite from London to Paris as from London to Tokyo. And the greater the traffic on the system, the lower the unit cost of messages sent. International communication is tied to computer technology, and in that explosive field the costs of computers are dropping as rapidly as their efficiency is increasing. In addition, the capacity of communication satellites to carry information is expanding.

Cracks in the Conduits

If technology is the good news, then performance in recent years is the bad news. In earlier years, the American "national media"—particularly the *New York Times, Washington Post, Los Angeles Times, The Wall Street Journal,* CBS, NBC, ABC, *Time,* and *Newsweek* — which set the news agenda for other media, did much of the gathering of news from abroad with the help of news agencies.

But that situation changed around 1989 when the Cold War ended. The television networks and the newsmagazines gave much less attention to serious foreign news. One indicator: In its heyday, CBS maintained twenty-four foreign bureaus; by 2002, it had nine reporters in only four capitals: London, Moscow, Tel Aviv, and Tokyo. Dan Rather admitted to Harvard students, "Don't kid yourself, the trend line in American journalism is away from, not toward, increased foreign coverage."[4]

Max Frankel, former editor of the *New York Times,* wrote, "A great shroud has been drawn across the mind of America to make it forget that there is a world beyond its borders. The three main television networks obsessively focus their cameras on domestic tales and dramas as if the end of the Cold War rendered the rest of the planet irrelevant. Their news staffs occasionally visit some massacre, famine, or shipwreck and their anchors may parachute into Haiti or Kuwait for a photo op, but these spasms of interest only emphasize the networks' apparent belief that on most evenings the five billion folks out there don't matter one whit."[5]

Foreign news is expensive to gather and often not of interest unless American lives—as soldiers or terrorism victims—are at stake. Instead, network television and the newsmagazines shifted their resources and considerable talents into high-profile stories of scandal, celebrity, and sensation, such as stories of White House sex scandals, the violent death of Princess Diana, the O.J. Simpson trial, and most recently the travails of Congressman Gary Condit.

The content of *Time, Newsweek,* and *U.S. News and World Report* reflected the declining interest in global news. Throughout 1995, *Time* devoted 385 pages, or 14 percent of the magazine, to international news. *Newsweek* used 388 pages, or 12 percent of its coverage, and *U.S. News* had 386 pages of foreign news, or 14 percent. For all three magazines, this was a significant decline from ten years earlier. In 1985, *Time* had run 670 pages, or 24 percent, of foreign news; *Newsweek* had 590 pages, or 22 percent; and *U.S. News* 588 pages, or 22 percent.[6]

However, a few major daily papers still report the world. The best and most comprehensive foreign reporting, some of very high quality, comes from just six daily newspaper groups, those owning the *New York Times, Washington Post, The Wall Street Journal, Chicago Tribune* (including *Los Angeles Times*), *Christian Science Monitor,* and *Baltimore Sun,* all of which maintain overseas news bureaus. These papers, whose total daily circulation is about eleven million, represent only about 20 percent of newspaper circulation of all U.S. dailies. This small group plus AP and Reuters are the prime sources for foreign news. It should be noted that a good deal of serious foreign news is available to radio listeners of National Public Radio's two daily programs, "All Things Considered" and "Morning Edition."

But as the events of September 11, 2001, demonstrated, the news media of America and other Western nations responded, and responded magnificently, to the challenges of the new war on terrorism.

The elaborate international news system is still in place and fully capable of handling any major news that breaks anywhere in the world. But a small, nagging question remains: How well do the global news media do when there is not a major crisis? Or when there is a long lull in the war on terrorism?

Notes

1. Colin Cherry, *World Communication: Threat or Promise?* (New York: Wiley Interscience, 1971), 57–58.
2. Joseph Pelton, "Heading for Information Overload," *Inter-Media,* Autumn, 1988, 19.
3. Tom Rosenstiel, "The Myth of CNN," *New Republic,* August 22–29, 1994, 27.
4. Stephen Hess, *International News & Foreign Correspondents* (Washington, D.C.: Brookings Institution, 1996), 61.
5. Max Frankel, "The Shroud," *New York Times Magazine,* November 27, 1994, 42.
6. Ibid.

CHAPTER 4

Internet, Comsats, and New Media

> We are laying the foundations for an international information highway system. In telecommunications we are moving to a single worldwide information network, just as economically we are becoming one global marketplace. We are moving toward the capability to communicate anything to anyone, anywhere, by any form—voice, data, text, or image— at the speed of light.
>
> —John Naisbitt

The presidential election of 1920 holds a place in communications history as the first in which election results were broadcast on radio. A crackling KDKA in Pittsburgh kept a small number of devotees of the newfangled wireless in a small area of the country up-to-date on the tabulations as they slowly were counted. But for large numbers of interested voters in remote rural regions of America far from telegraph lines, without telephones or electricity and beyond large population centers with daily newspapers, it was two weeks before the news reached them that Warren K. Harding had defeated James M. Cox for the presidency.

Eighty-two years later, there is not a place in the United States—nor in much of the world—where one cannot follow a U.S. presidential election tabulation instantaneously and, indeed, be told the winner's name even before the polls close. But sometimes, as in the election of November 2000, the media can be wrong in proclaiming a winner.

The drastic differences between then and now dramatize the reality that the mechanics of delivering the news to an interested public is a significant factor in the communication process. New technologies have been shaping and changing editorial content in diverse ways. News, particularly international news, has over the years been directly affected by each new invention. The postal service, telegraph, cable, telephone, and radio in turn have each greatly extended the reach of foreign correspondents and world news agencies and the speed with which they can deliver news, each innovation supplementing rather than replacing earlier methods of communication.

41

Like many other institutions and organizations, the news media—newspapers, news services, radio stations, television, cable channels and networks, and newsmagazines—are being strikingly altered by the information revolution. News communication is being dramatically affected by ongoing revolutionary changes in communication satellites, computers, digitalization, miniaturization, and the Internet.

Stuart Loory pointed out that information was once transferred from one power center to another in Washington, D.C., by newspapers but that recently, television news, mainly CNN, has been doing the job: "The executive and legislative branches increasingly exchange news and views via live, ubiquitous coverage."[1] Now, new technologies make it possible for international journalists to do for the entire world what domestic television and, to a lesser extent, print media do in Washington. "The corollary," Loory said, "is that television will have increasing significance for foreign policy making. Programs like ABC's 'Nightline' and 'Capital to Capital' and events like the 'spacebridge' [two-way live conversations between nations] have demonstrated the possibilities."[2] Here again we see the steadily increasing importance of CNN, MSNBC, BBC World television, and other global news media.

To these media must now be added the Internet, which has been playing a facilitating and supplementary role in the rapid dissemination of a fast-breaking story—either a trivial Gary Condit scandal or the ominous events of September 11. Online news junkies have quick access not only to more news but also to a heady mix of unconfirmed rumor, conjecture, commentary, discussion, and conspiracy theories. Sometimes, rumor and conjecture find their way into the legitimate news media. Further, the Internet and twenty-four–hour cable news cycle can greatly accelerate a story, often to the detriment of traditional journalistic practices such as verifying sources. More and more Americans are getting their news from cable and the Internet.

The Key Role of Satellites

In our immediate concern with how international news moves about the globe, the significant changes initiated by communication satellites, a major by-product of the space age, must be recognized. Recently there has been a quantum jump in the ability of people to talk to and see one another. Marshall McLuhan once wrote that we were experiencing a "global electronic village" being created by television. John Naisbitt countered that it is in fact the communication satellite that is "creating a super tribal community unlike any environment previously known to mankind since the Tower of Babel."[3]

In the past thirty years, global telecommunications by satellite have achieved remarkable results. Joseph Pelton pointed out that "trillions of dollars of electronic funds transfers and hundreds of millions of dollars of airline reservations flow through global networks each year. Billions of conversations carry on international business, diplomacy, finance, culture, and recreation as a matter of routine."[4] Included in these vast communication flows are, of course, the world's news in pictures, sounds, data, and words.

Our interest is with the impact of telecommunications on international news flow. And the most immediate short-term effect of Comsats (that is, communication satellites) is a reduction in the cost of long-distance communications and a corresponding increase in the amount of words, data, and images exchanged. In other words, more news is flowing at less expense. We have seen dramatic changes in long-distance telephone calls, which form the bulk of traffic on the INTELSAT system; that system is operated by a multinational consortium controlling long-distance point-to-point Comsat communications.

Arthur Clarke dismissed the notion that Comsats are merely an extension of existing communication devices and do not engender much change. He placed Comsats in the same class as the atomic bomb and automobile, "which represent a kind of quantum jump which causes a major restructuring of society." Clarke recalled a parliamentary commission in England a hundred years ago when the chief engineer of the post office was asked to comment on the need for the latest American invention, the telephone. The engineer made this remarkable reply: "No Sir. The Americans may have need of the telephone—but we do not. We have plenty of messenger boys."[5]

That telephone, in time, came to have its own revolutionary impact on modern life, and now the personal letter has been replaced by the long-distance call as well as by fax and e-mail. And telephone services, as has been noted, constitute the primary activity today of communication satellites and are the major source of revenue for INTELSAT. (The telephone and its wireless version, it should be noted, is a major tool as well in news gathering—formerly a local tool but now used for global communication as well.)

At the end of the 1970s, the traffic of INTELSAT still consisted mostly of people talking to people, but since the mid-1980s, at least half the information volume has consisted of machines communicating with other machines. The mind-boggling information-carrying capacity of INTELSAT VI is driving this trend, and INTELSAT VII, launched in 1993, followed by INTELSAT VII-A, in 1995, have continued it. Pelton developed a term, TIUPIL, to show the relationship between human capabilities of processing information and the speed of the information machines—present and future. A "TIUPIL" represents the "Typical Information Use Per Individual Lifetime" and was defined as twenty billion bits of information: the total information received by a person who lives seventy years and processes some twenty-seven thousand written or spoken words a day. A TIUPIL can be transmitted on INTELSAT VII in a matter of just seven seconds, or about nine times a minute. "Soon we will have networks of satellites capable of sending up to 100 billion bits of information in a second. This means we will have machines capable of processing information thousands or even millions of times faster than the human brain," Pelton wrote. "If one asks why we need such high-speed machines, the answer is clearly for machine-to-machine communication. Once we have communication satellites and fiber optic cables capable of handling super high-definition, 3-D television, the meeting of telephone or human data requirements will be small potatoes indeed."[6]

Although they have been called microwave relay towers in the sky, Comsats do have broader, unique properties. They do not link just two points, but many. They can simultaneously receive and transmit to many places, sending a panoply of message forms—television, telephone, telex, photo facsimile, fax, and high-speed computer data. For example, an increased mobility of money is a result of the computer revolution.

Today, satellite systems are operational at the international (intercontinental) level, the regional (continental) level, and the domestic (national) level. Satellites extend the range of over-the-air broadcasting systems, but they have a much greater impact on satellite-cable networks. CNN and various other cable services, such as Home Box Office and other pay services, extend their reach dramatically by being tied in with cable services. In addition, numerous specialized satellite systems are functioning, such as those designed for military, data relay, and maritime and aeronautical purposes. As a result of the endeavors of dozens of laboratories and hundreds of scientists and engineers, some 3,300 satellites had been launched as the new century dawned. The numbers are steadily increasing.

INTELSAT is the largest and oldest system, with fifteen satellites (plus backups) over the Pacific, Atlantic, and Indian Oceans. Some 120 nations, each with its own earth segment, belong to the consortium, and any two member countries can communicate directly without going through former colonial capitals. User countries, territories, and possessions total about 170, operating internationally on almost 1,500 preassigned pathways. INTELSAT also functions as the carrier for national domestic services in about thirty countries.

The U.S. space shuttle Challenger launched the Insat 1-B (Indian National Satellite) in 1983. Built by Indian scientists at a cost of $130 million, the Comsat has the capability of land-based telecommunications that would have cost a trillion dollars to construct. Insat 1-B places 70 percent of the Indian population within range of television signals and is being used primarily for telephone services, weather forecasting, nationwide linking of computer services such as transport and tourism, and, interestingly, providing community television services to thousands of Indian villages.

Comsats have greatly expanded the capacity of news media to move international news around the globe, but the ability of the satellites to relay color television signals, giving that medium a global impact, is what has made Comsat technology such a significant mass communication development. This is true even though television use accounts for a comparatively small proportion of the monthly revenue of INTELSAT.

When Early Bird, the first commercial Comsat, was launched in 1965, the principal television use was expected to be for occasional live events such as sports, state funerals, space missions, and the coverage of disasters and wars. Although reportage of such major events still accounts for much television traffic on INTELSAT, the most extensive and consistent use of the global system is for daily television news "packages" sent from one country to another. The U.S. networks—NBC, CBS, and ABC—plus CNN daily incorporate satellite news feeds from their correspondents in various parts of the world or, for special coverage, sporadically purchased from foreign broadcast news services, such as Reuters Television or Worldwide Television News.

Innovations in communication technology are changing both the ways that global news is gathered and disseminated and the ways that individuals receive the news. The speed and scope of foreign news reporting is constantly expanding as the use of laptop computers is increasing. Foreign correspondents have long said that their worst problems are not censorship or other authoritarian restraints, but logistics—getting to the remote news scene, such as an earthquake in Peru or a civil war in Congo, and then getting the story out. The technology to solve part of that problem has been developed and increasingly utilized: especially small portable computers that can transmit stories over phone lines (or by wireless) directly to newsroom systems. Initially, these portables were used to cover golf matches, auto races, football and basketball games, and court trials, but now journalists covering the whole range of news carry them.

A major technological advance for television reporting was the development of new, highly portable "satellite uplinks," which can be disassembled, checked as baggage, and flown to the site of a breaking story in order to feed back live reports. A "flyaway" dish can become a temporary CNN or ABC bureau in just the time it takes to get one on the scene. Other innovations useful to reporters in the field (as well as to individual citizens) are the portable wireless telephone and the video telephone.

This advance means that an editor can telephone a foreign correspondent, whether he or she is covering a conference in Geneva or a war in Central Asia. And that correspondent can, if necessary, send in the story by his or her cordless telephone or by video phone to a television station.

Another significant aid for reporters today are databases, which are collections of text or numbers that are stored in computers. Online databases, of which there are now thousands, are mainly for the retrieval of information by researchers who can tap into a data bank through telephone lines attached to a computer terminal. Increasingly, newspapers and broadcasters have used such sources for investigative and general reporting. Distance is not a factor, for in a matter of minutes a U.S. reporter can gain access to anything printed in a British newspaper or a journal in Japan. Closer to home, the reporter can call up and scan the full text of about seventy dailies offered by various newspaper databases such as the Nexis database, which carries more than 140 international newspapers, magazines, news services, and newsletters.

A further utilization of Comsats that is changing the structure of daily journalism is facsimile production and distribution of national and international newspapers, pioneered by *The Wall Street Journal*. Daily, a fax of each page of the paper is sent from its production plant in Chicopee, Mass., to twelve or thirteen various printing plants around the country. The page-size fax pages are processed onto offset pages. *The Wall Street Journal* has extended this expertise to Asia for its subsidiary, the *Asian Wall Street Journal*. This kind of technological innovation, plus an informative, well-written news product, has moved *The Wall Street Journal* into first place in circulation among U.S. dailies.

Another national daily newspaper, the Gannett Company's *USA Today*, has employed the same facsimile production methods, circulating 1,168,222 copies from thirty U.S. printing sites. In 1985, *USA Today* began beaming facsimile pages of its international edition to Singapore for printing and distribution in the Far East. Other publications routinely utilize facsimile transmission technology, including the *International Herald Tribune* of Paris, *Die Zeit* of Hamburg, *China Daily*, the *Economist*, *Time*, and *Newsweek*. The national edition of the *New York Times* is printed in several regions of the United States to facilitate its same-day delivery across the nation.

Personalized Media

Innovations in information media—personal computers with Internet connections, photocopiers, printers, fax capabilities, modems, videocassettes, cordless and mobile telephones, interactive television, databases, cable, and satellite connections—are often considered "personalized media" and are having profound effects on the audience or recipients of international news. In fact, the term *audience* is itself becoming a bit obsolete because it implies a mass of passive receivers of communication. Increasingly, personalized media are supplementing traditional media in the affluent West, but less so in developing countries.

In today's information societies, an individual is no longer a passive recipient of news or entertainment but now is an "information seeker" who can select or choose his or her news or information from a widening variety of sources, many of which governments are unable or unwilling to control. Further, individuals themselves, such as those involved in computer networking, become sources of information, that is, communicators. Autocratic governments find it difficult to control personalized communications.

With a personal computer and a modem connected to a telephone, a Westerner can tap into the fast-growing Internet system providing access to thousands of databases, including news publications and other current information from home and abroad. Further, that receiver can become a sender by freely communicating with other computers through the Internet, e-mail, and various networks and bulletin boards.

Another recent innovation enables a traveler to receive at his or her hotel, for a price, a copy of one's favorite newspaper when far from home. The technology, which allows anyone with an Internet connection and a printer to receive images of participating newspapers around the world, was developed by a Russian company, called IBS. So some hotels can receive copies of some eighty-three newspapers and can print on a laser printer a copy of any of these on request by a hotel guest.

The printed word has changed as well. Fax, the same technology that sends the *International Herald Tribune* from Paris to Hong Kong, sends millions of documents, letters, and messages across continents and oceans. Facsimile transmissions have played a role in challenging or even toppling unpopular regimes from Iran to Panama to China to the collapsing Soviet Union. Not only does fax foster immediate human interaction across great distances, it also facilitates the vital flow of information into and out of repressive regimes.

Cassette recorders, both video and audio, have greatly enhanced the ability of individuals to choose what they will hear or see and, as a result, have expanded rapidly in recent years even to remote corners of the Southern Hemisphere. (Because of their cultural impact on developing nations, VCRs are discussed in Chapter 7, "New Media and the Developing World.")

Much of the talk of a "superhighway of information" involves the idea of a merging of computers, telephones, and televisions (video, text, and sound) to provide new delivery systems and content options. Two models for the so-called "infobahn" are offered: broadcast and the Internet. In the broadcast model, entertainment would be the driving force, leading to the five-hundred–channel future, with features such as video on demand, interactive home shopping, entertainment, and advertising. The latter model is on the lines of the Internet, the vast computer/communications network begun in 1969 that now connects many millions worldwide. The two models exist and compete side by side.

The Internet and International News Flow

The potential of the Internet for international news communication is beginning to be realized but is still very much a work in progress. Daily, the Internet carries more news than 1,600 daily newspapers can provide to a worldwide audience of forty to fifty million Internet users. More and more Internet users are getting their news online and from media in far-off places.

In 1990, twenty newspapers were available online; by 2000, 4,925 were worldwide, with 2,799 of them in the United States. Despite the recent fall of technology stocks and the demise of many dot coms, experts believe these numbers in time will only go up, and Web sites will carry more and more news to ever larger audiences. Here and abroad, the print media as well as cable and network broadcasters are in hot pursuit for these proliferating Internet news seekers.

An Internet user in Pakistan, Paris, or Pretoria can read the online edition of the *New York Times*, the *Times* of London, or *Die Zeit* of Hamburg. Major newspapers and other news media such as magazines, radio and television broadcasters, and cablecasters, from a variety of mostly Western nations—what was formerly called the "foreign press"—are available in ways never before possible for those with the means and inclination to log on. The impact on journalism education is obvious: Instead of going to a university library to peruse back copies of several dozen foreign newspapers, a journalism student today using his or her computer can read, study, and compare hundreds of publications and broadcasting outlets of many countries. Many other related sources are available as well. For example, by calling up www.memri.org, the Web site of the Mideast Media and Research Institute, a student can read translations from Arabic of what the Arab press and broadcasters are reporting and proclaiming about the war on terrorism.

The Associated Press has adopted the World Wide Web to distribute its articles and photographs over the global Internet. In so doing, it has followed other mainline news organizations into uncharted journalistic territory. AP's great rival, Reuters, announced in 2000 similar plans to reposition itself as a high-flying Internet player. Reuters plans to spend $802 million to shift its delivery systems to the Internet.

The Web incorporates many elements of various print and electronic media that have preceded it. Computers can be used to send and receive text, sound, still images, and video clips. Yet for all its versatility, the Web is not expected to replace its predecessors but to take its place alongside them as a social, cultural, and economic force in its own right. No longer a curiosity, the Internet has become another way for to people find out what is happening in the world.

Much news or information on the Internet is of dubious value and may be deliberately wrong or misleading. During the weeks after the September 11 attacks, the Internet was overwhelmed with wild rumors, deliberate misinformation, and conspiracy theories. But the discriminating and critical viewer could still find solid, reliable information because the world's best news organizations—newspapers, newsmagazines, television, and radio services—were reporting the real news daily. (An important role for interactive news media is to act as a check on unreliable and unsubstantiated reports.)

The Internet has certain unique advantages. For example, CNN Interactive, which is one of the world's busiest news Web sites with some 3.5 million "page views" a day, features extensive original coverage of environmental and ecological issues. Although Internet users are still comparatively small in numbers, many interactive news media go into depth on all kinds of stories that receive only a minute or two on television or a few paragraphs in a newspaper story. Cyberspace is not limited by the time restraints of broadcast news or the space limitations of the printed media.

Cybernews so far is complementing the traditional news media but may soon become a new kind of journalism. John V. Pavlik wrote, "Since networked news can be interactive, on-demand, and customizable; since it can incorporate new combinations of text, images, moving images, and sound; since it can build new communities based on shared interests and concerns; since it has the almost unlimited space to offer levels of reportorial depth, texture, and context that are impossible in any other medium—new media can transform journalism."[7]

Perhaps the single most significant characteristic of the Internet is that it is a communication device that lets people share ideas (including news and information) on a global network. This feature suggests that international news communication has made tremendous strides in the last twenty-five years, which is the age of the personal computer. A PC with a modem hooked up to a telephone line means that the world—literally the world—is more available than ever before. Not only individuals but professional news media now can reach and hold not just audiences or readers but also communities of people with shared concerns literally anywhere in the world.

But on the Internet, the individual journalist can make himself or herself heard through small, single-issue or single-person commentary. Former *Newsweek* reporter Mickey Kaus presents his political opinions, his readers' views, and links to others sites—all from his home computer. Another example is Smartertimes.com, a daily critique of the *New York Times* by Ira Stoll, a critic of the paper who carries on a one-man effort to point out the paper's flaws. These single-issue sites, often run as hobbies, illustrate how the Internet, as an open marketplace of ideas, breaks down some of the barriers that enable editors to decide what is news. Now readers can help decide what is important to them. But serious readers, of course, rely on professional news media with seasoned editors to provide the global context of the day's events.

Thoughtful persons in mainstream journalism—the "news business"—are well aware of the potential as well as the many pitfalls for journalism on the Internet. Publishers, broadcasters, and journalists believe that the news media must be involved with the Net, but neither they nor anyone else seems to know where this brave new world of communication is headed. Just a few years ago, no one had foreseen even the technology much less the potential of the Internet.

Internet journalism is still in its infancy and is continuing to expand as readers, especially younger ones, turn to the Internet for a fast take on the news. Further, the beneficiaries of this continued audience growth continues to be the largest and best known national news organizations—those that stress national and international news.

The Web is still an ancillary news source for most people, after broadcasting and newspapers, yet the audience for news and information sites grew 14.7 percent from July 2000 to July 2001. Based on the numbers of Internet users, the top ten sites for news during 2001 were, in the following order: MSNBC.com; CNN.com; NYTimes.com; ABCNews.com; USAToday.com; WashingtonPost.com; Time.com; LATimes.com; FoxNews. com; and WSJ.com. These sites grew faster than the rate of the overall news audiences online.[8]

For the news media, two basic uncertainties cloud the future of online journalism. First, will the public pay for news on a medium which, after a basic fee is paid, has been free? Second, will advertising displayed on the Web make money on a medium that lacks effective ways to track advertising response or ascertain the demographics of users—information that advertisers deem essential? Hit by heavy economic blows, many online businesses, the dot.coms, have lost much of their appeal, and numerous online magazines not connected to traditional media organizations have failed. Nonetheless, most media managers are betting that news on the Internet will in time attract great audiences and become profitable.

International Concerns about Cybernews

The rapid spread of interactive journalism has raised some nagging issues. For example, who will benefit and who will not? Globally, the information revolution has been flourishing mainly in America, Japan, Western Europe, and other industrialized countries. The poor nations want the new media but lack the economic and social infrastructure to utilize and sustain them. Only twelve of Africa's fifty-four countries are linked to the Internet, and experts warn that unless Africa gets online quickly, what is already the world's poorest continent risks ever-greater marginalization. Without network connectivity, large areas of Africa will be prevented from participating in many evolving aspects of life on this planet. As in all nations, the younger, better educated, and more affluent are using the Internet; the poor, undereducated, and outcast have no way to access the information highway. But some gains have been made in India and China. (See Chapter 7, "New Media and the Developing World.")

Among Western democracies, there are unresolved questions about how much freedom of expression (including press freedom) can be legally permitted on what is being recognized as the most participatory marketplace of ideas the world has yet seen. The U.S. Supreme Court in 1997 resoundingly supported free expression when it declared as unconstitutional the Communications Decency Act, which made it a crime to send or display "indecent" material online in a way available to minors. The court held that speech on the Internet is entitled to the highest level of First Amendment protection, similar to that given to newspapers and books. The decision was not the final word—new challenges are still ahead—but the decision bodes well for the Internet as a purveyor of serious news and information.

Other democracies are not as tolerant. In Germany, for example, a prosecutor threatened legal action after deciding that certain material carried on CompuServe was offensive. As a result, CompuServe voluntarily denied its four million subscribers access to more than two hundred newsgroups. More such legal challenges may be ahead.

The Internet faces more draconian censorship from authoritarian regimes or despotic rulers. The small, affluent, and authoritarian nation of Singapore thinks it can control the technologies of freedom that threaten its one-party rule. To control television, satellite dishes have been banned, and the country has been wired for cable television, thus enabling the government to screen out objectionable material. Controlling cyberspace is more difficult, but Singapore is trying. Schools are equipped with computers, and Singaporeans are urged to link up with the Internet by dialing a local telephone number. Thus, the government can monitor Internet usage through the local servers. Local officials concede that some users can bypass this system by dialing into the Internet through foreign phone systems. Singapore is not expected to be able to sustain such controls over the flow of electronic information so essential for the global economy.

For now in the West, electronic newspapers and the Internet do not pose any serious threat as yet to the newspapers dropped on millions of front porches daily. Most people apparently would rather browse through a newspaper over a cup of coffee at breakfast than call up information on a computer. But in the long run, the electronic delivery of news and information will only increase and proliferate.

Implications of Rapid Change

To summarize, innovations in communication technology suggest certain broad trends for transnational journalism:

1. The unit cost of international communication of news will continue to drop as usage of the world news systems increases and as the efficiency, speed, and reach of the hardware become greater.
2. Technology is making it possible to send and receive news and other essential information from almost anywhere in the world and with increasing speed. The continuing integration of computers with telecommunication means much more interactive, or two-way, communication.
3. The two-way capability of cablevision, tied in with Comsats and personal computers on the Internet, means that information users can seek out or request specific kinds of information or news and not remain a passive mass audience. The two-way capability of telecommunications means that there will be more two-way flows of information, with consumers having more choice about what they receive. The trend toward such interactive communications systems is clear.
4. Because of continuing technical improvements, the potential numbers of channels and sources of information are virtually unlimited, and the possible varieties and kinds of future "content" stagger the imagination.
5. A gradual merger of the science and technology of computers and electronic communications has been taking place. In fact, a new term, *compunications*, has been coined to reflect this reality. In 1998, five leading high-tech companies introduced a technology that promises to accelerate the convergence of mobile communications and computing by enabling the wireless transfer of voice and data among mobile phones, laptop computers, and other portable devices.
6. These personalized communications, typified by the Internet, e-mail, fax, videocassettes, and cablevision, present a challenge to authoritarian governments, which traditionally control their newspapers and broadcasting. How does Big Brother stop someone from watching a pirated videocassette, or from calling up distant information on the Internet, or picking up Dan Rather off a satellite, or receiving e-mail from a dissident group overseas?

7. So far, this communication revolution is taking place principally in the United States, Japan, and Western Europe. These and other information societies, mostly in the rich, industrialized North, are widening the already broad information gap between themselves and less-developed nations. A highly industrialized nation such as Japan can utilize any new technology much faster than, say, Kenya or Pakistan and, as a result, the resentments of the former Third World over information inequities are exacerbated (even though individuals with computers and modems can participate). The poorer nations want the new communications technology but lack the social and economic bases needed to utilize it. For many of the poor, debt-ridden, and failed nations of the Southern Hemisphere, sophisticated and expensive electronic systems are still out of reach. Such factors only add to the deep rift between the haves and have-nots of the world, a condition many consider the greatest of global problems. (The animosity of many in the Muslim world toward the United States was certainly evident after the September 11 attacks on New York and Washington, D.C.)

8. In the brave new world of international communication, the main players—corporate media giants such as Murdoch, AOL Time Warner, NBC, Vivendi, Bertelsmann in Germany, Fininvest in Italy, Disney, and others—are getting richer, more powerful, and fewer in number because of recent mergers (see Chapter 6, "Globalization of Media"). In the United States, the ownership of major media corporations has consolidated into fewer and fewer hands. However, technological innovation is moving so fast that some of these media powerhouses may fall by the wayside in the global scramble to dominate world markets for the by-products of mass communication.

9. Finally, concern is growing about the effects of all this greatly expanded communication flow on its global audiences. Most people spend no more than an hour a day reading newspapers or getting the news from television or radio, but the news volume cascades on. David Shenk wrote that in the middle of the last century, "We began to produce information much faster than we could process it. We have moved from a state of information scarcity to a state of information surplus—from drought to flood in the geological blink of an eye." In his recent book, *Data Smog: Surviving the Information Glut*, Shenk argues that information overload is bad for your health, promoting stress, memory overload, compulsive behavior, and attention-deficit disorder. Shenk argues that the well-known

global village, created by mass communication, is at the same time growing increasingly fragmented and fractionalized as people, despairing of being able to master a grand overview, retreat into their own special interests. He argues that cyberspace, including the Internet, promotes a highly decentralized, deregulated society with little common discourse and minimal public infrastructure.[9]

Concerned persons here and abroad are pondering the implications of all this. Society, in short, faces the danger of computer/communications technologies advancing faster than our ability to develop methods of controlling and using them for the general welfare of humankind. This has always been true of technologies, but today that gap is becoming ominously wide. Nonetheless, innovations in media technology will continue to shape international news. Julius Barnathan of ABC News sees the development of multilanguage broadcasts as an impending and important innovation. One video will be accompanied by as many as eight narrations.

Finally, Pelton of INTELSAT saw much more to come. "The evolution of new and perhaps totally different architectures for space communications are likely to evolve in the 21st century and the long-term growth and development of space communication seem relatively well-assured. In short, the 21st century should see the beginning of the true long-term road to space communications, making it truly the beginning of the 'golden age' of space communications."[10]

Notes

1. Stuart Loory, "News from the Global Village," *Gannett Center Journal*, Fall 1989, 167.
2. Ibid.
3. Joseph Pelton, "Heading for Information Overload," *Inter-Media*, Autumn 1988, 19.
4. Ibid.
5. Arthur C. Clarke, "Beyond Babel: The Century of the Communication Satellite," in *Process and Effects of Mass Communication*, W. Schramm and D. Roberts, eds. (Urbana: University of Illinois Press, 1971), 952.
6. Pelton, "Heading for Information Overload," 20.
7. John V. Pavlik, "The Future of On-Line Journalism: Bonanza or Black Hole?" *Columbia Journalism Review*, July/August 997, 30–36.

8. Felicity Barringer, "Growing Audience is Turning to Established News Media Online," *New York Times*, August 27, 2001, sec. C, 1.

9. Michiko Kakutani, "Data, Data, Everywhere, and All the World Did Shrink," *New York Times*, July 8, 1997, sec. B, 6.

10. Pelton, "Heading for Information Overload," 21.

CHAPTER 5

The Impact of Great News Events

> The tumultuous throng that poured westward through the rents in the
> Berlin Wall last November [1989] emptied the supermarkets and the
> video shops. Within hours there was neither fast food nor deodorant left.
> West Berlin emporiums were stripped of their ample supplies of soft and
> sometimes hard-core video cassettes. T-shirts and jeans, a currency across
> the Wall in the days of the two Germanies, flew off the shelves. Wide-
> eyed and knowing, moving to the beat of heavy metal and rock, which,
> clandestine or overt, had been the odes to freedom throughout Eastern
> Europe, the young and not so young, enacted the first TV revolution.
> —George Steiner

Great world events of our times have given us insights into the role that
global news communication plays in assisting and accelerating political
change. Intensive television coverage of such an event as the air war over
Kosovo and Serbia does not determine the political outcome of such crises,
but such reporting (or nonreporting) has a clear impact on public opinion,
which in turn may well influence decisions made by diplomats and political leaders of great nations.

Today, fast-moving political and social changes are being shaped and
accelerated by transnational communication. Not only have speed and volume increased along with greater geographical dispersal of international
news flow, but the nature and effects of the content have changed and
diversified as well. Instead of the mere words and numbers of yesteryear's
news, vivid color television coverage of great events is now delivered to the
world's news publics, greatly increasing the impact of the message. As a
result, a new and significant kind of audience involvement in world events
has emerged. The propaganda maxim that the report of the event is as
important as the event itself has greater impact than ever in the age of
media events.

In this chapter, we look at the journalistic aspects of four great political and social upheavals: (1) the collapse of Soviet Communism and the

ending of the Cold War; (2) the 1991 failed coup in Moscow; (3) riots at
Tiananmen Square and China's confrontation with Western media; and (4)
the interactions between terrorist events and global television coverage of
those acts as illustrated by September 11.

Electronic Execution of Soviet Communism

The collapse of communism in Central and Eastern Europe in 1989, along
with the end of the Cold War, were two of the most significant political
events since World War II (some said since 1848) and all the more dramatic
because they were so unexpected. Certainly Western mass communication—
going over, under, and around the Iron Curtain—played a role in raising
expectations and in breaking the communists' monopoly on information
and popular culture.

Critic George Steiner added these words to his remarks quoted at the
start of this chapter:

> Once "Dallas" had come their way [it could be picked up several hun-
> dred kilometers east of Checkpoint Charlie], once tapes of Western soap
> operas and rock jamborees could be multiplied and sold beyond the
> "Dallas line," the cataclysm and saturnalia were inevitable. Television
> sparked the great wild surge toward a consumer economy, and television
> packaged (brilliantly) the actual rush. Why live by bread alone when
> there is peanut butter? Why endure as a Soviet satellite when the word
> "satellite" means cable television?[1]

The dramatic and sudden collapse of communism in Eastern Europe
came after a generation of communication interactions between the Western nations and the socialist nations of Eastern Europe, the USSR, and the
Third World—all set in the context of the Cold War. Recent economic
successes of the West along with the failures of socialist political economies
helped explain the media changes. Further, the sheer pervasiveness of
Western communications accelerated modifications of and, in time, the
abandonment of communism and its press theory.

Western journalism rode the crest of the technotronic revolution
that reshaped global mass communication during the past generation and created the information societies of the West. (One Russian
general said that the USSR lost the Cold War because it was hopelessly
behind the West in computer technology.) Communication satellites,

computerization, global television, high-speed data transfers, and especially new media products such as videocassette and audiocassette players, all spurred by profit-making opportunities, have led to a vast flood of Western television programs, movies, videocassettes, and CD (compact disk) and taped music recordings, moving inexorably from West to East Europe.

Grist for this vast mill has consisted of not only Western pop culture (movies, TV shows, music videos, and rock and other popular music) but also newspapers, magazines, and books. Western versions of the news, along with Western methods of news reporting and presentation, became widely accepted and emulated. AP, Reuters, CNN, BBC and Radio Free Europe, Radio Liberty, and the *International Herald Tribune*, among other media, added diversity to the monolithic news structure of the communist regimes. Whatever their shortcomings, Western media had a crucial advantage over communist media: They were not government controlled and hence achieved a wide credibility. Consequently, centralized communist governments lost their monopoly over their own information.

Western news media acted as catalysts for political change in communist nations in several ways: People in Eastern Europe did listen to Western broadcasts, which carried both world news and news about the satellite nations themselves.

Much of this news went by shortwave radio, some by AM and FM broadcasting and, for East Germany, via television from West Berlin and the Federal Republic. German-language television was received all over the GDR (German Democratic Republic) except in low-lying Dresden, which was locally dubbed the "Valley of the Ignorant" because of the poor TV reception there.

Some observers believe the beginnings of the breakup of the communist empire in East Europe began with the successes of the Solidarity trade union in Poland. The Polish communist regime's monopoly on news was broken in two ways: by the rise of alternative newspapers that challenged the government and supported Solidarity goals; and, second, by a triangular communication flow between the alternative papers, foreign reporters, and international broadcasters. It worked this way: Foreign journalists reported news of Solidarity to their Western media; these stories were beamed back to Poland via international shortwave radio, particularly by BBC, Deutsche Welle, and Radio Free Europe; then the stories were also picked up by the alternative papers in Poland.

This communication model was followed again and again. Michael T. Kaufman, who covered Poland for the *New York Times*, wrote:

It turned out that a few dissidents using non-violent means, and exploiting the freedom of the press and airwaves beyond their borders, could in this increasingly interconnected world bring down autocrat after autocrat. Foreign correspondents wrote for their own papers, but their reports were translated and beamed back to countries where such information as they were writing was banned. The spread of portable radios and videos made such information much more accessible. The official press was forced to offer more information, more truth, as it was forced to compete for credibility with the outsiders. ... Once informed, the people were mobilized. In most places, they marched and chanted and drew placards and with the world press watching such means proved sufficient to expose previous forbidden truths and to make revolutionary changes that had so recently seemed impossible.[2]

In the revolutionary events of 1989, the media played a variety of roles. One was to report that such things happen and that times are changing. Another was to show that the world was indeed watching and that the Berlin Wall could be turned into a sieve. A third purpose was to show potential demonstrators in other countries that the unthinkable was perfectly possible. So, uprisings in East Berlin, Budapest, Prague, and Bucharest all reinforced one another.

For William E. Henry of *Time*, the triumphs owed something to journalism but little to journalists:

The function of news people was not sage or analyst but conduit, carrying the raw facts of an amazing reality to the startled citizenry in each revolutionary nation and to a waiting world beyond. ... The thrills of 1989 and early 1990 came as useful reminders that the most interesting part of the news business is, in fact, the news. For broadcast journalists, events proved anew that the chief element of their much discussed power is the simple capacity to reach many people quickly—and in cases of true turmoil, with a verisimilitude no other medium offers. TV's basic function was as the great legitimizer.[3]

Failed Coup in Moscow

Communications was one of the major reasons the right-wing coup d'etat failed to topple the Soviet government in August 1991. The nine coup leaders arrested Mikhail Gorbachev, closed down all but a handful of Communist Party media, and held a television press conference proclaiming the new government. They assumed that the nation would passively accept the changeover. However, the coup masterminds failed to understand how much the Soviet Union had changed in six years of *glasnost*. With a more open communication system and a new taste for free expression, the resistance in Moscow rallied around Boris Yeltsin. They used fax, photocopying machines, and cellular phones to let fellow citizens know it was not too late to resist the coup. Inexplicably, the plotters shut down neither international telephone calls nor the satellite relay station, and they did not jam shortwave radio. No actions were taken against the large foreign press in Moscow, which sent out a flood of words and pictures to a disapproving world. CNN was even received in some Soviet republics. It was as if the coup leaders became immobilized like deer before car headlights by television camera lights recording and transmitting the events within the parliament and the street barricades outside. Soviet journalists, emboldened by *glasnost*, refused to accept the coup restrictions. Blocked at the printing plants, dozens of independent publications ran off photocopies and passed them out on street corners. Moscow's subway was quickly papered with handbills. Interfax, the independent news agency, distributed underground reports along with its own stories.

The impact of Western radio was even more impressive. The BBC doubled its Russian-language program to eighteen hours, its largest increase ever. It also relayed the banned broadcasts of a Moscow station. Radio Liberty's twenty-four–hour broadcasts in Russian and eleven other Soviet languages reached an estimated audience of fifty million. Gorbachev later said he gratefully listened to BBC, RL, and Voice of America while under house arrest at his dacha in the Crimea.

As *Newsweek* commented, "The coup leaders apparently relied on popular indifference and fear of authority. But those are not the attributes of people in the know. And last week Russians proved that they have entered the information age."[4]

Ironically, the new communications openness that propelled Boris Yeltsin to political power after the failed coup also caused him severe political damage in the winter of 1994–1995 when he sent the Russian army into Chechnya to put down a rebellion. In Moscow and throughout the nation, millions of Russians watched television pictures of the brutal suppression of the revolt and the killing of thousands of civilians. And many Russians did not like what they saw.

China Confronts World Media

Another great anti-Communist uprising occurred in mid-May of 1989 when thousands of Chinese students and others marched in Tiananmen Square in Beijing in support of the pro-democracy movement. After a brief flowering, the movement failed, and protesters were crushed by Chinese soldiers. For one brief week, however, the Chinese people had a glimpse of what a free press would be like. Chinese newspapers and broadcasters themselves suddenly began to give colorful and candid coverage of the sit-in protests at the Square; students were shown as equals asking Premier Li Peng pointed questions and pressing demands.

All the while, Western television networks—CNN, ABC, NBC, CBS, and BBC—were transmitting words and pictures around the world while many thousands of sympathetic Chinese outside of China demonstrated in Hong Kong, Taiwan, Australia, and across America. Many signs carried by protesters in Beijing were in English, intended for foreign television viewers. News photos of the papier-mâché Goddess of Liberty, modeled on the Statue of Liberty, and of the lone Chinese youth standing before a line of tanks became instant and lasting icons of the failed revolt.

Still, the Tiananmen uprising was more than a television event. Before and especially after the Chinese government shut down the foreign television cameras, Chinese students at home and abroad used personal computers, long-distance telephone, and fax machines to communicate back and forth with sympathizers. At Harvard, a Chinese student set up a Beijing-to-Boston hot line, which was a round-the-clock open telephone line that carried news from Tiananmen Square to his Cambridge home. From there, news went by fax, telephone, and computer to Chinese students all over the United States. Chinese students at Berkeley and Stanford created a "news lift" by using fax machines to send back to striking students the latest news from the U.S. media.

Perhaps the major role was played by shortwave radio. Voice of America (VOA) and BBC World Service reached many millions through their Mandarin services. One study found that the VOA was the most important of all international media involved in the event; its Mandarin broadcasts made it the most widely used alternative news medium in China, informing millions in the countryside who could not otherwise obtain the information VOA provided. Conservatively, VOA reached 100 million Chinese people, possibly 200 to 300 million.[5] (See Chapter 8, "Public Diplomacy and Political Warfare," for more on the continued importance of an "old" communication medium, shortwave radio, in international communication.)

The authoritarian Chinese government may have won the battle of Tiananmen Square. However, recently China, while trying to modernize, has been facing a variety of challenges to its state monopoly over information from the fast-multiplying channels of information: newspapers, telephones, television, and the Internet. In fifteen years, the number of telephone users has gone from a privileged few to many millions. Today anyone can buy a cell phone number without showing identification—meaning that the nation is becoming wired in diverse and anonymous ways. Torrents of information are overwhelming the government's control methods.

In 2001, journalist Graham Earnshaw estimated that about seventeen million people in China used the Internet, up from nine million at the end of 1999. These are the intellectuals, academics, students, and white-collar workers who are important for China's involvement with the global economy. The Chinese would like to separate the economically useful aspects of the Internet from the political aspects, but doing so appears impossible given the vast complexity of the Web. Nonetheless, the Chinese still block Internet news sites such as Reuters, CNN, and BBC. The government rationale is that the Internet has "negative influences" that have to be restrained.

Another formidable challenge comes from the "hundreds of thousands of satellite dishes that are sprouting, as the Chinese say, like bamboo shoots after a spring rain. Already, millions of Chinese can hook in via satellite to the 'global village' bypassing the Communist Party commissars and leaving them feuding over how to respond."[6] Nicholas Kristof reported that the information revolution threatens to supplant the Communist Revolution, which long has been sustained by the Party's monopoly on news and propaganda that is now crumbling. The information revolution that began in the 1980s with shortwave radio has spread rapidly. Fax machines are widely available in private homes, and direct-dial international phones and computers are multiplying as well, with many Chinese able to use the Internet, including e-mail and electronic bulletin boards.

The media proliferation in China is fueled by the reality that the country is rapidly modernizing and growing economically. One of the great dramas of modern history is taking place in China: Several hundred million people have risen out of abject poverty and are enjoying unprecedented higher standards of living, including access through telecommunications to the world outside their remote villages. Politically, China is still rigidly communist, but economically it has opted for free enterprise and trade in emulation of its prosperous Asian neighbors. But the resulting "market Leninism" has created severe tensions that may lead to either continued prosperity or, to avoid chaos, an abrupt return to rigid autocracy. Recent evidence is that the Chinese authorities are trying hard to adapt to the onrushing changes.

Ten years ago, China banned the purchase or possession of satellite dishes by ordinary Chinese, but so far Chinese authorities have been unable to enforce the order effectively. Some feel it is too late—the information genie has been out of the bottle for too long. Satellite dishes had sprouted on an estimated five hundred thousand roofs in the country, but because of cable hookups on apartment buildings, the government estimates there are fifteen million subscribers to multichannel systems. In a village near Beijing, even the apartment buildings housing the dreaded public security bureau are wired for satellite programming from the United States, Great Britain, and Hong Kong.

For years, some Comsat-delivered television programming has been coming into China, including Star TV from Hong Kong, CNN International, ESPN, MTV Asia, and BBC World. Most of this the government did not welcome. However, an important change came in October 2001, when AOL Time Warner was given approval to transmit limited programming into a small area of Guongdong province in southern China. In return, AOL will carry Chinese programming on its cable systems in New York, Los Angeles, and Houston. How did the world's biggest media company gain access to the world's most populous country and potentially largest market? The answer is by steering a cautious course through China's political shoals by avoiding sex, violence, and most of all, news coverage. Just when the rest of China will open to foreign broadcasters is not known. AOL's negotiations had extended over two years and eighteen rounds of talks.

Another sign of change is the increased diversity of China's newspapers. When it comes to news about communist leaders or major foreign policy issues, the central propaganda department still directs the media nationwide like a well-rehearsed orchestra. But in some cases of local scandals or disasters, dogged Chinese journalists, often using the reach of the Internet, have produced surprising exposés.[7]

Some Asian countries welcome satellite television, but others see it as a threat to their cultural identity and political stability. The power of satellite television was shown again in Thailand when street riots in Bangkok between Thai soldiers and pro-democracy crowds helped overthrow a military government. Although local television was barred from showing scenes of unarmed civilians being killed in the street, satellite-dish owners taped the scenes of violence shown on BBC and CNN. Within hours the tapes were shown around Thailand, angering the public and speeding the downfall of the military rulers.[8] Singapore and Malaysia restrict the public from owning satellite dishes. Viewers can see satellite channel programs only when rebroadcast over local television, which is government controlled. Singapore cable service carries CNN and HBO Asia but not Star TV, which is owned by Rupert Murdoch.

In 1994, in an effort to curry favor with the Deng regime in China, Murdoch summarily dropped the BBC's World Service Television from his Star TV offerings. Chinese authorities had objected to the BBC's coverage of allegations of human rights violations in China. Then, in February 1998, Murdoch's HarperCollins, the book publisher, abruptly canceled its contract to publish a book by Chris Patten, the last British governor of Hong Kong, because Murdoch thought the Patten book took too negative a view of China. Murdoch has extensive holdings in China and ambitious plans to expand them. Further, Patten had criticized Murdoch's 1994 move against the BBC, calling it "the most seedy of betrayals" for those who champion freedom of speech in one country "to curtail it elsewhere for reasons of inevitably short-term commercial expediency."[9]

However, governments are finding it nearly impossible to stop people from grabbing their entertainment and news from the skies. In 1994, Saudi Arabia banned satellite dishes as "un-Islamic" and ordered more than 150,000 dishes to be taken down; Kuwait was planning to do the same. In India, Hindu fundamentalists, outraged at the racy videos on MTV Asia, demanded that the dishes be banned. In Iran, where people are bored by official television, Iranian-made satellite dishes, costing $700, dot the apartment roofs of Tehran, beaming in BBC news and soft-porn movies from Turkey. But governments that try to shut down satellite TV find themselves outwitted by stubborn viewers. Dishes are easily put together from imported kits, and they are growing smaller, cheaper, and more powerful. Bowing to what seems to be the inevitable, some repressive governments are allowing the dishes to stay. Myanmar places few restrictions on them, and Indonesia seems to welcome satellites as a more efficient way to beam its own programs to its thirteen thousand far-flung islands.

Terrorism and Television

The very nature of global television and telecommunications that can bring people closer together while sharing the mutual grief of tragic events, such as the assassination of John F. Kennedy or the slaughter at Tiananmen Square, also can be manipulated to capture the world's attention. Unquestionably, certain acts of international terrorism, such as jet hijackings, political kidnappings, and civilian bombings as in Oklahoma City, are perpetrated primarily to capture time and space in the world's media. Terrorism has been called "propaganda of the deed"—violent criminal acts, usually directed at innocent civilians, performed by desperate people seeking a worldwide forum for their grievances. Experts disagree over terrorists' motives.

Terrorism, of course, is not new. But the flare-ups of the phenomenon since the 1960s—especially in the Middle East, Northern Ireland, Latin America, Turkey, Italy, West Germany, Spain, and now the United States—have been facilitated in part, some say, by global television coverage that beams images of terrorist violence into millions of television sets around the world. Many terrorist groups have mastered a basic lesson of this media age: Television news organizations can be manipulated into becoming the final link between the terrorists and their audiences, and as with all sensational crimes, the more outrageous and heinous the terrorist act, the greater attention it will receive in the world's news media. Walter Laqueur said, "The media are a terrorist's best friend. ... Terrorists are the super-entertainers of our time."[10]

But the terror attacks of September 11 on the World Trade Center and Pentagon were more horrendous and audacious than most, and have had many far-reaching repercussions. The spectacular nature of the attacks—using hijacked airliners loaded with jet fuel as guided missiles to destroy highly visible landmarks—were well-planned, ingenious, and completely unexpected. Global television was an essential component because it greatly magnified and extended the impact of the terror. Terror and television are linked. What if 9/11 had been reported only by print media? The emotional impact would have been greatly lessened and the nation's reaction would have been slower and perhaps less traumatized.

In this age of global television, the effects of 9/11 were deeply felt in many lands. Whether in London, Jerusalem, Shanghai, or Jakarta, the news and video were filtered through the prisms of differing cultures, ethnicities, politics, and religion. But the most important reaction was in Washington, D.C., where the Bush administration, fully supported by U.S. public opinion, vowed to strike back hard at terrorism.

On September 11, international terrorism became a major concern at the top of the foreign news agenda as well as the global political agenda. After being downplayed by news media for years, terrorism was major news again; the "acts of war" on September 11 immediately triggered a new kind of war with Islamic terrorists and any states supporting them. The possibility of future attacks of such a devastating nature were raised from "possible" and "unlikely" to "probable" and "likely" in the minds of editors and security officials alike.

A positive result was that the American public woke up to the importance of foreign news; the nation was reminded that we live inseparably in one world—a world that can be threatening and dangerous. The news media were reminded of the perils of neglecting foreign news since the 1989 fall of communism. Historians may be critical of American presidential leadership for failing to respond sharply to terrorist acts against America during the 1990s. And much of the news media, particularly local media and broadcast and cable television, can be faulted for not informing the public (and government) adequately about the growing dangers coming out of the Middle East conflicts: the bombing of Marine barracks in Lebanon; the bombing of Air Force living quarters in Saudi Arabia; the blowing up of U.S. embassies in Nairobi and Dar es Salaam; and the attack on the USS Cole in Yemen—all precursors to September 11.

For the first time since 1812, when the British burned down the White House, Americans realized that their two-ocean defensive shield could be penetrated. (In 1941, Hawaii was still a territory.) We realized we were now vulnerable to bioterrorism and even nuclear attacks as well as suicide bombings. In addition, airliner hijackings returned to the news as major threats to the security of commercial aviation. The possibility of being hijacked by suicidal terrorists who used the airliner as a deadly missile attack killing all aboard had hardly been imagined.

No doubt the vivid television pictures multiplied the psychological impact of the terror to the depression, sense of loss, and insecurity felt by so many people. This, apparently, is what the terrorists intended, but did global television assist the terrorists in achieving their aims? Perhaps, but there was no choice. The September 11 terrorism was major news and, of course, had to be reported. Television news might be faulted, however, for repeating again and again the horrific pictures of an airliner crashing into the World Trade Center. For many young children watching, each replaying of the crash video was perceived as a subsequent event.

Television can be faulted, as well, on how it handled early stories of the anthrax scare. Twenty-four–hour cable television, with its built-in tendency to hype and exaggerate a story and jump to conclusions before the facts are fully in, was the worst culprit. Many in the public were unduly disturbed by the ways that the anthrax stories in Washington, D.C. and New Jersey were reported. At the same time there was a lack of incisive and reliable information from public officials.

Be that as it may, terrorism and all its facets are news, and as such it poses worrisome questions for broadcast journalists: Does television coverage really encourage and aid the terrorists' cause? Is censorship of such dramatic events ever desirable? Raymond Tanter wrote, "Since terror is aimed at the media and not at the victim, success is defined in terms of media coverage. And there is no way in the West that you could not have media coverage, because you're dealing in a free society."[11]

Terrorism coverage is a journalistic problem of international scope, just as international terrorism itself is a transnational problem that individual nations cannot solve without international cooperation. Broadcast journalists argue about whether the violence would recede if television ignored or downplayed an act of terrorism. Most journalists doubt that self-censorship by news organizations is a good idea or even possible in such a highly competitive field. However, television organizations have established guidelines for reporting terrorism incidents in a more restrained and rational way.

Two other terrorist episodes involving the U.S. news media, one in Iran and the other in Lebanon, are instructive about the role of media in such crises.

Hostages in Iran

The seizure of the U.S. embassy in Iran in November 1979, with more than fifty American citizens (virtually all diplomatic personnel) held hostage, added a new and deepening dimension to the history of terrorism and the media's increasingly blurred role as both reporter and participant.

For the first time, a sovereign government became an overt party to the terrorism by supporting, instead of ousting, the young militants who took over an embassy compound and imprisoned its personnel. The militants' stated purpose was to dramatize the grievances of Iranians against the deposed Shah Mohammad Reza Pahlavi and force the U.S. government to return him to Iran for trial. Most observers agreed that the militants and Iran's rulers expected that heavy media coverage of the outpouring of support for the terrorists by the huge demonstrating crowds around the embassy gates in Tehran would convince American and world public opinion of the justice of their cause.

The saturation coverage of that year's biggest story quickly engulfed the U.S. news media, especially television, in controversy and brought charges that they were being used and controlled by Iranian militants. Particularly controversial was an interview by NBC News with an American hostage under conditions dictated by the Iranian captors, conditions that both CBS and ABC had found unacceptable.

For the more than three hundred foreign journalists working in Tehran in the first months of the crisis, there was indeed a thin line between being manipulated by the Iranian militants and responding to legitimate demands for the latest information from their own highly competitive news organizations and their publics at home. Indisputably, the Western journalists in Tehran were part of the story and, inevitably, part of the controversy.

Replay in Beirut

In June 1985, TWA Flight 847 out of Athens was hijacked and its crews and passengers held captive in Beirut, Lebanon. For more than two weeks, the three U.S. networks devoted more than half of their evening news shows to the crisis. One study found CBS, NBC, and ABC broadcast a total of 491 hostage stories over the seventeen-day crisis period, comprising about twelve hours of news time. In most newspapers, the story was page one from June 15 to July 7. Indeed the event looked like a replay of the Iranian story and one that the news business could not ignore. As before, television was accused of aiding and abetting the terrorists by sympathetically publicizing their cause. Prime Minister Margaret Thatcher of Britain proposed a voluntary media code of self-censorship during terrorist incidents. The idea was seconded by U.S. Attorney General Edwin Meese. Fred Friendly, a former president of CBS News, said the worst errors in coverage had been caused by a "haphazard frenzy of competition" and the compulsion to obtain "exclusives": "We have to learn that they (the terrorists) watch TV. We need to get across that you can't shoot your way onto our air," Friendly said.[12]

This time, however, a measure of restraint and responsibility by television news was evident in some quarters. Despite the many specific criticisms of television's coverage of this highly emotional story, there was general agreement that such stories must be covered but with restraint and good judgment. After it was over, the Columbia Journalism Review commented, "One of the tasks of journalism is to provide an assessment independent of that of the government and to stand apart from, rather than incite, the jingoism and xenophobia that spread so rapidly in situations involving the seizure of American citizens. In the Beirut hostage-taking, as in Iran, such detachment was hard to find."[13]

Tom Wicker of the *New York Times* summed it up well:

> But the real reason that television was properly present in Beirut, even at those bizarre "press conferences," is just that television exists; it has become a condition of being. It may on occasion be inconvenient, intrusive, and even harmful; but if because of government censorship or network self-censorship the hostage crisis had not been visible, real, on American screens, the outrage and outcry would have been a thousand times louder than what's now being heard, and rightly so; for we depend on television for perception as we depend on air for breath. And that's the way it is.[14]

As with much else in foreign news, a big story in one nation is not necessarily a big story somewhere else. And further, actors in the same violent story can be called "terrorists" in one nation and "freedom fighters" in another. Yet, for the U.S. news media, after September 11, any terrorist attack on Americans will be a major news story.

Notes

1. George Steiner, "B.B.," *New Yorker*, September 10, 1990, 113.
2. Bernard Gwertzman and Michael T. Kaufman, eds., *The Collapse of Communism* (New York: St. Martin's Press, 1990), 352–53.
3. William A. Henry III, "The Television Screen is Mightier Than the Sword," *Time*, May 10, 1990, 51.
4. "How Resistance Spread the Word," *Newsweek*, September 2, 1991, 39.
5. He Zhou and Jian Hua Zhu, "The 'Voice of America' and China," *Journalism Monographs*, no. 143, February 1994, 1, 35.
6. Nicholas D. Kristof, "Via Satellite, Information Revolution Stirs China," *New York Times*, April 11, 1993, 1.
7. Eric Eckholm, "Mine Disaster Shows More About China's News Media Than About Mine Safety," *New York Times*, August 4, 2001, sec. A, 5.

8. Philip Shenon, "A Race to Satisfy TV Appetites in China," *New York Times,* May 23, 1993, sec. A, 12.

9. Warren Hoge, "Murdoch Halts a Book Critical of China," *New York Times,* February 28, 1993, sec. A, 5.

10. Neil Hickey, "Terrorism and Television," *TV Guide,* August 7, 1986, 2.

11. Ibid.

12. "Terror Coverage is Criticized," *New York Times,* July 31, 1985, sec. A, 3.

13. Ibid.

14. Tom Wicker, "Not a Pseudo Event," *New York Times,* July 9, 1985, sec. A, 27.

CHAPTER 6

Globalization of Media

> Mankind has become one, but not steadfastly one as communities or
> even as nations used to be, nor united through years of mutual experi-
> ence ... nor yet through a common native language, but surpassing all
> barriers, through international broadcasting and printing.
>
> —Alexander Solzhenitsyn

If Jules Verne's adventurous Phineas Fogg traveled around the world in
eighty days again today, he would find that as an Englishman abroad he
would have little trouble keeping up with the news and entertainment. At
almost every stopover, he would be able to buy a copy of the *International
Herald Tribune* or possibly the *Financial Times*, and at his hotel's newsstand
he would have a choice of the *Economist, Time,* or *Newsweek,* among other
English-language publications. In his hotel room, he would be able to
watch the day's televised news either from CNN via cable and Comsat
from Atlanta or BBC World Service Television. On the local television station, he could see a world news package of stories put together by Reuters
Television outside London. And if he had a small shortwave radio, he
would be reassured by listening to the BBC World Service from Bush
House in London or the Voice of America. Also, on local television, he
would likely find reruns of his favorite British programs, and if he sought
out a local movie theater, he likely would have a choice of current Hollywood productions. Chances are that a local bookstore or airport newsstand
would have a wide selection of English-language magazines and paperback
books. Finally, if he has a laptop computer and modem, he could send and
receive e-mail messages.

The increasing availability of such Western publications and electronic media fare (most of it in English, the *lingua franca* of international
communication) are examples of the way the major institutions of news
communication—world news services, satellite services, broadcast systems,
great newspapers and magazines—have become increasingly internationalized or globalized in recent years. This change is due in part to innovations

73

in media technology (facsimile printing and satellite distribution in particular) and a growing elite cosmopolitan audience, as well as other social and political realities. Whatever the cause, the fact is that more and more of the activities of the major news media now transcend parochial or national concerns and serve broader transnational purposes.

Out of the capitalistic West have been arising various media conglomerates that some critics feel may dominate, if not unduly influence, much of international communication and entertainment in the near future. Frequently mentioned among these "media baronies" are those of Rupert Murdoch of Australia, Britain, and America; Silvio Berlusconi of Italy; AOL Time Warner, Disney Company (ABC), and Viacom (CBS) of the United States; the Bertelsmann group of Germany; Vivendi/Universal of France; and Sony and Fujisankei of Japan—all multimedia and multinational. The competitive gambits of these media entrepreneurs are being keenly felt in Western Europe as well as the United States.

Whether this trend toward fewer, bigger, and more like-minded media of global communication is good or bad usually depends on the critic's personal tastes and ideology. But the globalization of mass communication is proceeding in response to the needs and economic opportunities of a shrinking world. The transnational media are doing more than seizing the chance for greater profits from new markets, albeit those factors are obviously important. Whether viewed as another example of Western "media imperialism" or as a significant contribution to global understanding and integration, the international media are becoming increasingly cosmopolitan, speaking English, and catering to an internationally minded audience concerned about world affairs.

An American in Paris

The daily, ink-on-newsprint newspaper is still a major prop of journalism, and there are more than eight thousand dailies worldwide and many thousands more weekly journals. A few of the more serious "prestige" papers attract readers far beyond their national borders. Not many Americans read foreign publications, so they are unaware of the extent to which people abroad depend on newspapers and magazines published in other countries. The intellectually demanding *Le Monde* of Paris, famous for its analyses of world affairs, is widely read in the Arab world and francophone Africa. The London-based *Financial Times* uses a plant in Frankfurt to print nearly fifty-three thousand copies daily of an edition described as "Europe's business paper" and has a U.S. edition printed in New York City for American readers. Gannett distributes in Europe copies of *USA Today* printed in Switzerland; the only difference is that the weather maps are of Europe and Asia. Britain's *Guardian, Independent,* and *Daily Telegraph* are found on many foreign newsstands, as are Germany's *Frankfurter Allegemeine* and Switzerland's *Neue Zürcher Zeitung.*

But the newspaper that has evolved furthest toward becoming a truly global daily is the *International Herald Tribune* of Paris. The IHT is the sole survivor of several English-language papers, including the *Chicago Tribune, Daily Mail* (of London), *New York Herald,* and the *New York Times,* that earlier published Paris or European editions for English-speaking travelers. Started by James Gordon Bennett in 1887 as the Paris edition of the *New York Herald,* the IHT has outlived its parents and today is jointly owned by Whitney Communications, the *Washington Post,* and the *New York Times.* The IHT is produced by an editorial staff of forty, including copyboys and clerks. Much of its copy comes from the *New York Times, Los Angeles Times, Washington Post,* and news services. As of recently, much more of the paper is staff written. Averaging about sixteen pages a day, the *Herald Tribune* sold about two hundred thousand copies six days a week in 181 countries (in Europe alone, sales were about 135,000), and no single country accounted for more than 15 percent of the total. This marvel of distribution appears daily on some 8,500 newsstands all over Europe, supplied by editions printed in Paris, London, the Hague, Marseilles, Rome, and Zurich; and more recently in Hong Kong and Singapore. African and Middle Eastern subscribers are served by mail; distribution in North America, Latin America, and the Caribbean comes from a Miami printing plant. The IHT thus became the first newspaper in history to publish the same edition simultaneously on all continents.

Although it remains an American newspaper in outlook and perspective, it has gradually acquired an important non-American readership. Nearly half its readers are an elite group of European internationalists— businesspeople, diplomats, and journalists fluent in English. These non-American readers are part of an "international information elite" who, regardless of geographic location, share a similar rich fund of common experience, ideas, ways of thinking, and approaches to dealing with international problems.

Numerous other publications, particularly magazines, have reached and helped shape this international information elite. Hearst Magazines International has successfully published magazines abroad with sixty-four foreign language editions of eight magazines. In 1995, its leaders,

Cosmopolitan, Esquire, Good Housekeeping, and *Popular Mechanics,* were distributed in fourteen languages to sixty countries.[1]

Another success, *Reader's Digest,* established its first foreign edition in Britain in 1938. By 1995, there were forty-seven international editions printed in eighteen languages. Almost thirteen million copies a month are sold abroad. In some countries, including nearly all Spanish-speaking countries, the *Reader's Digest* is the most popular magazine. So successful has been its adaptation to foreign soil that many readers are unaware that the *Digest* is not an indigenous publication. Although studies show that *Digest* readers abroad belong to a "quality audience" of the affluent, the well-educated, and the well-informed, it is not that same audience of decision makers who read *Time* and *Newsweek,* which are primarily news media.

Time and *Newsweek,* besides spawning such notable imitations as *Der Spiegel* in West Germany and *L'Express* in France, have been successful as transnational publications, and both can claim strong appeal to that internationally minded readership. *Time* has, over the years, evolved into a multinational news medium for a multinational audience. *Time's* total circulation was 5.5 million in 1998. Of that, *Time* Canada's share was about 350,000; *Time* Europe's (including Africa and the Middle East) about 500,000; the edition for the Pacific region about 350,000; and for Latin America 90,744.[2]

Newsweek, with a foreign readership of about one-third of its total 1998 circulation of 3.25 million and with a European circulation of three hundred thousand, has done much the same thing overseas. *Newsweek International* has carried hundreds of exclusive stories and featured numerous covers, all different from the domestic edition. Whereas *Time* tailored its overseas editions to regional interests, *Newsweek* tried to be more global in its approach. Only about 15 percent of its readers abroad are Americans; the rest are from 150 countries.

An American competitor of the newsmagazines abroad is *The Wall Street Journal.* With a satellite-assisted leap across the Pacific, the highly successful *Journal* launched, in 1976, an Asian edition in Hong Kong that covers a sixteen-country business beat from Manila to Karachi. Smaller than the domestic edition, *The Asian Wall Street Journal* tries for the same mix of authoritative business and political news, a risky experiment for a region with so little press freedom. And pressures have been applied, mostly by Singapore's authoritarian ruler, Lee Kuan Yew. In November 1985, the editor of *The Asian Wall Street Journal* apologized to a Singapore court for any possibility of contempt of court raised by a *Journal* editorial commenting on Singapore politics. The incident prompted questions about the appropriate responses when a foreign court challenges the editorial freedom of an American newspaper published abroad. By mid-1990, after three years of harassment and a lengthy legal dispute with Lee, the *Journal* announced that it was ending circulation in the island republic.

The Wall Street Journal also has a European edition, printed in the Netherlands and written and edited in Brussels, Belgium. The paper, which can be purchased on the day of publication throughout Europe and Britain, is edited for the international business executive doing business in Europe.

In Latin America, following the invasion of cable television, American newspapers and magazines have been gaining many new readers in the region. Magazine publishers have launched Spanish-language editions of *Newsweek, Glamour, Discover, People, National Geographic,* and *Rolling Stone.* The *Miami Herald* has become the international English newspaper of Latin America, with ten regional printing plants and an overseas circulation of about 35,000 to 40,000. Brazilian sales of *Reader's Digest* in Portuguese jumped from 35,000 to 600,000 in two years.

Changes in World News Services

The subtle changes in the world news services as they have expanded abroad are further evidence of this growing globalization of transnational media. Although they claim to "cover the world," the agencies historically have tended to serve primarily their own national clients and those in their spheres of influence; that is, Reuters serviced British media and the British Commonwealth, AFP worked mainly for the French press and overseas French territories, and UPI (in its prime) in addition to its U.S. clients long had strong connections in Latin America. But these world agencies have become more international in scope, selling their services to whoever will buy, wherever they may be.

In addition, the personnel of world agencies have become significantly internationalized. Formerly, the AP, for example, boasted that its news from abroad was reported by American AP correspondents who had experience in running an AP bureau in the United States. The agency would not depend on foreign nationals to provide news from their own countries for AP use in the United States. That has changed. With the increased professionalism of journalists abroad, news agencies not only find it more economic to use qualified local journalists but also may get better reporting from staffers who know their own country, its language, and its social and political traditions. Today among its ninety-five international bureaus with about four hundred AP staffers abroad, only one hundred are Americans.

Another facet of internationalization is foreign syndication of news by major daily papers. The New York Times News Service sends more than fifty thousand words daily to 550 clients, of which 130 are newspapers abroad. Its close competitor is the Los Angeles Times/Washington Post News Service, which transmits about 60,000 words daily to fifty nations or about six hundred newspapers, half of which are outside the United States. This total includes papers in West Germany and elsewhere that receive the dpa (Deutsche Presse Agentur) with which the service is affiliated.

As noted previously, there is syndication as well of television news film and videotapes, especially those of America's NBC, CNN, CBS, and ABC, and Britain's BBC and ITN, most of it distributed by two Anglo-American firms—Reuters Television and World Television News—via videotape and satellite (and sometimes by airmail) to almost every television service in the world. There is probably more international cooperation than competition in the transnational video news business, in part because most nations have only one government-controlled television service. Unlike the print media, which usually carry a credit line on agency reports or syndicated material, syndicated television news is usually presented anonymously. Whether watching news from Cairo or Shanghai, the viewer is rarely told who supplied foreign video.

Advertising Goes Worldwide

Advertising, too, has followed the global trend. Recent "megamergers" among advertising and marketing services companies point up how internationalized Madison Avenue, the symbolic home of American advertising, has become. The biggest merger in advertising history took place when Saatchi & Saatchi of London agreed to buy Ted Bates Worldwide for $450 million. Saatchi & Saatchi thus became the world's biggest agency, with U.S. billings of $4.6 billion and world billings of $7.6 billion. (Saatchi changed its name in 1995 to Cordiant after founders Maurice and Charles Saatchi left the firm in a bitter departure.) The second largest advertising empire was created with the amalgamation of three other major concerns—Doyle Dane Bernbach Group, BBDO International, and Needham Harper Worldwide—which combined had world billings of $5 billion and U.S. billings of $3.7 billion.[3] Later, England's WPP agency bought out two American giants: J. Walter Thompson and Olgilvy and Mather.

Agency executives involved in these mergers cited the industry's understanding of the need to offer clients worldwide service as a primary motivation. As an executive of Young & Rubicam pointed out, "There is a trend toward global assignment of agencies. If you don't have a complete set of worldwide resources, you're in danger of being left out in terms of getting the best clients."[4]

Implied is the view that transnational advertising agencies would be in a position to channel standardized advertising from transnational corporations into transnational media with minimum effort. The same commercial—whether for Coke or McDonald's—could just be translated into many languages and placed in media anywhere in the world. However, this "global sell" theory has not worked out, according to Alvin Toffler, who wrote, "What's wrong with the global sell theory is that it makes little distinction between the world's regions and markets. Some are still in a pre-mass–market condition; others are still at the mass-market stage; and some are already experiencing the de-massification characteristic of an advanced economy."[5] Due to cultural preferences, widespread consumer differences about products persist, as do attitudes toward food, beauty, work, play, love, and politics. Toffler concluded that "globalization is not the same as homogeneity. Instead of a single global village, as forecast by Marshall McLuhan, we are likely to see a multiplicity of quite different global villages—all wired into the new media system, but all straining to retain or enhance their cultural, ethnic, national, and political individuality."[6]

Media Changes in Europe

The increasing economic integration of the European Community plus the demassification and deregulation of broadcast media are rapidly internationalizing much of mass communication in Western Europe. Although Europeans, like people everywhere, prefer to read, view, and listen to news and entertainment in their home or native languages, the push toward transnational communication is still strong. This is due to the rapid expansion of cable and satellite options for viewers as well as increased numbers of private or commercial television and radio channels and the increasing popularity of VCRs and the Internet.

As noted previously, major American and British print and broadcasting organizations are each trying to increase their readers and audiences in European nations. And other media conglomerates in France, Germany, Italy, and Japan are buying up media properties abroad. Deregulation and privatization of radio and television and the expansion of cable and pay television, assisted by satellite distribution, also have added potentially important new daily news outlets in English as well as many more entertainment options for Europeans. Europe's broadcasting systems, formerly run by governments or by public corporations (paid for by special taxes or fees), have heretofore generally offered high-quality programming but with limited choices. But Western Europe is now following the deregulated American models, with greatly increased choices. As a result, there has been a rush for the huge profits to be made. Adherents of Europe's tradition of public service broadcasting feel that programming quality will be sacrificed by deregulation and commercialization. The money to be made from advertising, viewer fees, and revenues from movies and video programs is expected to run into the billions.

Western Europe nations, particularly France, concerned about the influence and popularity of American movies and television shows with European audiences, have established quotas on imports and subsidized their own productions. However, another quieter invasion has taken place: American companies have infiltrated nearly every corner of the European television business. AOL Time Warner, Viacom, Disney/ABC, Cox Cable, NBC, and others are getting involved in European-based television programming, in broadcast stations, in cable and satellite networks, and in the coming convergence of telecommunications and entertainment. And they see a huge market: 350 million people in twelve major Western European nations and 650 million overall west of Russia, many of them hungry for televised news and entertainment.

Expanding Media Baronies

Many of the innovative changes in European media, as elsewhere, are being made by the transnational media conglomerates, themselves a by-product of rapid changes in international communication. There is growing concern as well about the economic, and potentially political, influence wielded by these powerful forces in global communication. The prototype of the media barons is Rupert Murdoch and his News Corporation. With 150 media properties in Australia, America, and Britain, Murdoch has been carefully assembling a vertically integrated global media empire. In the United States, he owns the Fox television network, the *New York Post*, and *TV Guide*. In addition, he has a significant share of 20ᵗʰ Century Fox Broadcasting, which produces TV shows and owns thousands of hours of films and television programs. In Europe, he has pioneered in satellite broadcasting and owns 90 percent of Sky Channel (a satellite television system), a new sports network, and a twenty-four–hour news channel that draws from his two London papers, the *Times* and the *Sunday Times*. He owns direct broadcast satellite services in Britain, Italy, Hong Kong, Japan, and Mexico; he owns two-thirds of daily newspaper circulation in Australia; and he owns HarperCollins Publishers, *New York* and *Seventeen* magazines, and other British papers, including the *Sun* and *News of the World*. Constantly juggling his properties (and his considerable debts), his News Corporation, which had revenues of less than $1 billion in 1980, had expanded its revenues to $14 billion in 2000.

Murdoch's current strategy apparently is to own every major form of programming-news, sports, films, and children's shows—and beam them via satellites or television stations he owns or controls to homes in America, Europe, Asia, and South America. He recently said, "We want to put our programming everywhere and distribute everybody's product around the world."[7] Most recently, he seems to be concentrating his efforts on global interactive satellites systems.

Murdoch's media acquisitions apparently influenced several major U.S. media mergers, all of which had implications for the future of international communications. In August 1995, the Walt Disney Company announced its purchase of Capital Cities/ABC in a deal valued at $19 billion. The merger brought together ABC—then the most profitable television network, including its highly regarded news organization (Peter Jennings as anchor)—and its ESPN sports cable service with an entertainment giant: Disney's Hollywood film and television studios, cartoon characters, theme parks, and so on, and the merchandise they generate. (In one recent year, the Disney Company sold more than $15 billion worth of Disney merchandise worldwide, a total more than seven times the global box-office receipts for Disney movies.) Disney is more interested in content, especially game parks, movies, and consumer goods, than in conduits (cable or satellites). For 2000, Disney's total revenue was $25.8 billion, putting it in second place among media giants.

The real giant among the mega-media companies was AOL Time Warner, whose 2000 total revenues hit $36 billion, well ahead of Disney. Viacom (CBS) stood in third place at $20 billion, followed by Vivendi/ Universal at $18 billion, Bertelsmann at $16 billion, and Murdoch's News

Corporation at $14 billion. AOL Time Warner's dominance was well sum-
marized by Ken Auletta:

> No communication company touches as many consumers or controls so
> many interlocking pieces. AOL delivers twice as much mail as the U.S.
> Post Service. Time Inc. is the world's largest magazine publisher, selling
> a quarter of all consumer-magazine advertising. Time Warner Cable is
> the nation's second largest cable system, and its Roadrunner provides
> more high-speed access to the Internet than any competitor. Warner
> Bros. is one of the seven major movie studios, and has a library of 7,000
> major films, 32,000 television programs, and 13,000 animated features.
> Turner Broadcasting generates more revenue than any other cable net-
> work, and CNN reaches about a billion viewers around the world. HBO
> pioneered pay television and now ranks No.1. The company is also one
> of five music giants, owning more than a million music copyrights.[7]

Some critics are concerned about AOL Time Warner's ability to favor
and promote its own content (that is, synergy) and to control access to the
Internet. One critic said he was not concerned about the company's size
but about its opposition to the next important innovation to come along
because that would threaten the company's earnings.

Several similar mergers began with Westinghouse's takeover of CBS
Inc., creating the nation's largest broadcast station group, with thirty-
nine radio and sixteen television stations reaching 32 percent of the
nation. About the same time, Viacom, a hot cable company, bought a
legendary Hollywood studio, Paramount Communications, for $8.2
billion. Several years later, Viacom bought the CBS Corporation for
$37.3 billion, creating the world's second-largest media company. In
May 2000, the FCC approved the Viacom/CBS merger and for its
money CBS brought to the merger $1.9 billion in radio properties,
including 190 radio stations; $4.4 billion in television holdings, includ-
ing the CBS network, CBS Entertainment, CBS sports, and seventeen
television stations; and $546 million in cable properties.

These megamergers positioned the resulting giants—AOL Time
Warner, Disney/ABC, Viacom (CBS), and Murdoch—to better penetrate
and dominate the growing international markets for television, movies,
news, sports, records, and other media programs. At the time of its merger
with ABC, Disney president Michael Eisner spoke glowingly of India's
huge middle class of 250 million as a great potential audience for Disney
movies, cartoons, news, and sports programs. NBA and NFL games have

been gaining large audiences overseas; hence the importance of the ESPN networks. Critics noted that news organizations (and journalists), such as *Time* magazine and CNN, or ABC News or CBS News, were just small players within these entertainment giants.

The keen competition among CNN, MSNBC, and Fox News Channel (FNC) to dominate a twenty-four–hour cable news channel in America (see Chapter 3, "International News System") has strong international potential as well. Broadcast networks have been looking to international markets as a way of gaining hundreds of millions of new viewers. NBC's international holdings currently are about 20 percent of the network's worth of $10 to $20 billion; in the next ten years, half of the network's value is expected to come from international holdings. Asia is predicted to be the main area of global audience growth because about 25 percent of the continent's vast population is expected to receive cable before long. By contrast, the U.S. market, with cable in sixty-five million of its ninety-seven million households, is nearing saturation. Numbers of cable viewers are expected to rise abroad in time for the startup of NBC Europe as well as related NBC services in Latin America. Since September 11, the war on terrorism has given a great impetus to twenty-four–hour global news, and competition has become much more intense because the cable channels were discussing life and death issues instead of the fate of Congressman Gary Condit.

Other European Baronies

Among European media groups with far-reaching holdings is Bertelsmann A.G. of Germany. From a Bible-publishing house, Bertelsmann grew into a media giant with book and record clubs in Germany, Spain, Brazil, the United States, and eighteen other countries. Bertelsmann owns Bantam, Doubleday, Dell publishing in the United States, and Plaza y Janes book publishers in Spain, in addition to thirty-seven magazines in five countries, record labels such as RCA/Ariola, and a number of radio and television properties. In 1998, Bertelsmann shocked U.S. book publishers by buying Random House for an estimated $1.4 billion, consolidating its claim as the world's largest English-language publisher of trade books. Considered the crown jewel of American book publishers, Random House had $1.1 billion in sales in 1996. With the sale, half of the top twenty U.S. publishing firms, with a 28 percent share of the total U.S. market, were in foreign hands. With $15.5 billion total revenue in 2000, Bertelsmann ranked as the world's fifth largest media conglomerate.

Possibly the most swashbuckling of the media barons has been Italy's Silvio Berlusconi, who has built a multibillion-dollar media television and newspaper empire, Fininvest, of unusual power and influence. With 42 percent of Italy's advertising market and 16 percent of daily newspaper circulation, he has concentrated his power more into a single market than any of the aforementioned barons. He owns Italy's three main private television channels, Rete 4, Canale 4, and Italia 1, as well as *Il Giornale*, a leading Milan paper, two leading news weeklies, thirteen regional dailies, and a large book publisher plus television holdings in France and Germany. Using his extensive media power, Berlusconi became prime minister of Italy in April 1994. The media-baron-turned-politician promised a revolution of prosperity and clean dealing. However, he was soon in trouble and in November 1994, the fifty-eight-year-old billionaire was forced to resign when charged with corruption. In 1998, he was convicted on corruption charges. However, by May 2001, although still under a cloud, Berlusconi was voted back into power as Italy's prime minister.

Some observers are concerned that Hollywood's assets have been sold off to foreigners. In November 1990, MCA/Universal, one of the nation's largest entertainment companies, was acquired by Matsushita Electric Industrial Company of Japan for $6.13 billion. MCA/Universal owned, among other entities, Universal Studios, Universal Pictures, MCA Records, theme parks, and the Putnam publishing firm. MCA/Universal was then sold to Seagram, who in turn sold it to Vivendi, a French company. Vivendi/Universal in 2000 ranked fourth among media giants with revenues of about $18 billion, most of it coming from music sales, amusement parks, movies, computer games, and educational publishing including Houghton Mifflin. Vivendi has risen so quickly that few Americans are aware of the French conglomerate's importance and standing among media giants. In December 2001, Vivendi Universal announced a $10.3 billion deal to expand and solidify the company's American movie, television, and theme park assets by setting up a new division called Vivendi Universal Entertainment with mogul Barry Diller in charge of it. Another Japanese giant, Sony, Matsushita's arch-rival and owner of CBS Records, Columbia Pictures, and Tristar Pictures, had total revenues of $10 billion in 2000.

Diffusion of Mass Culture

A major impact of these global media giants is their diffusion of the popular culture of the West to all—literally all—corners of the world, with profound influences that can only be described as revolutionary. The world is beginning to share a common popular culture. Much of the diversity of the world's cultures and languages is being lost forever. This trend is part of a long-term historical process that predates modern media, but the pace in recent years has accelerated.

American films regularly acquire more than 50 percent of the French market; about 50 percent of the Italian, Dutch, and Danish markets; 60 percent of the German markets; and 80 percent of the British markets. Recently, among the world's one hundred most attended films, eighty-eight were American. Seventy five percent of all imported television programs come from America. Millions in Europe can now watch "Oprah Winfrey," subtitled or dubbed. American basketball, played in 192 countries, may become the world's most popular sport. The NBA finals have been broadcast in 109 countries in twenty languages. Here are random examples of American mass culture abroad: "Dallas" has been seen in ninety-eight countries; 40 percent of television programming in New Zealand was American; Mickey Mouse and Donald Duck, dubbed in Mandarin, have been seen weekly in China; "Sesame Street" was seen in 184 countries; and the hottest game show on French television was "La Roule de la Fortune." Popular culture also conveys lifestyles. Like their Russian counterparts, young Chinese prefer American jeans and T-shirts as well as rock music. Young people in Germany are using such slang terms as "rap music," "body building," "windsurfing," and "computer hacking" and, what is more, they are doing these activities.

One of the most powerful influences on global youth culture has been Music Television, or MTV, which first appeared on U.S. cable in 1981. Since then it has grown into a global phenomenon reaching into about 250 million homes worldwide and still expanding. Despite criticism and unease from the older generation, the recording business, by hitching would-be music hits to television, found a marketing tool that brought it unprecedented profits. Much of MTV's success is based on adapting the musical programming to the musical tastes of the teenagers of the region receiving it. The West, it has been said, won not only the Cold War but also the battle for the world's leisure time. Popular culture has been one of America's most lucrative exports, but observers say that the worst, instead of the best, of American culture seems to be flooding the world. Critic Michiko Kakutani commented, "Some of America's culture exports are so awful that you suspect that we are using the rest of the world as a vast toxic waste dump and charging for the privilege."[8] Chinese pop singers provide songs so similar to those in the West that you have to listen carefully to find that the lyrics are in Chinese.

English As the Media Language

Effective communication across national borders, regardless of other cultural and political differences, certainly requires that sender and receiver communicate in a mutually understandable language. More and more, that language is English, which is clearly the leading tongue of international communication today.

Among the "Big Ten" of world languages, English ranked third with 322 million native speakers in twelve countries, after Mandarin Chinese, with about 885 million, and Spanish, with 332 million native speakers. English is ahead of Russian with its 282 million speakers, Arabic with 220 million, and German with 118 million. Furthermore, English is the most widely used geographically, and for about 400 million educated persons around the world, English is their second language. Several hundred million more people have some knowledge of English, which has official or semi-official status in some sixty countries. What is more, this number includes most of the world's leaders. (If a leader wants to get on global TV, he had better know English.) In all, there are about one billion English speakers in the world, and the number is rapidly increasing.

Unquestionably, English has become the global language of science and technology. More than 80 percent of all information stored in one hundred million computers around the world is in English, and 80 percent of all scientific papers are published first in English. English is the language of the information age: Computers talk to each other in English. English is the most-taught language in the world; it is not really replacing other languages but rather supplementing them.

In many developing nations, English is the language of education, providing an entrée to knowledge and information. But one unfortunate result is that many native English speakers, especially Americans, have much less incentive than, say, Israelis, Dutch, or Swedes to learn other peoples' languages. Currently, the U.S. government has an acute shortage of Arabic speakers. Few Americans even learn to speak Spanish, although it is widely spoken here. The nation's Hispanics numbered 35.3 million in 2000, and to inform and entertain them were thirty daily newspapers, 265 weeklies, 352 magazines, and 594 radio stations—all in Spanish.

Globally, English has also become the leading media language for international communication. Most of the world's news is carried in English. Most news agencies carry some of their news in English. Six of the world's biggest broadcasters—BBC, CBS, NBC, ABC, CNN, and CBC—

reach a potential audience of about 300 million people through English-language broadcasting.

The imperialism of nineteenth-century Britain was a major reason that so many people from Singapore to India to Kenya to Nigeria to Bermuda converse today in English. Not unrelated is the phenomenon of numerous English-language daily newspapers flourishing today in countries where English is neither the official nor even the most widely used language. Beginning with the *Chronicle of Gibraltar* in 1801, English-language dailies, catering to expatriates, the foreign community, and local educated elites, have long survived, if not always flourished, in such diverse metropolises as Mexico City, Caracas, Paris, Jerusalem, Taipei, Rome, Athens, Cairo, Beirut, Manila, Bangkok, Singapore, and Tokyo, as well as throughout India and Pakistan and the former British territories of Africa, such as Nigeria, Ghana, Sierra Leone, South Africa, Uganda, Kenya, Tanzania, Zimbabwe, and Zambia. In parts of polyglot Africa, English has almost evolved into another African language because of the role it plays in education, commerce, and mass communication.

Most of the "content" of mass culture that moves across national borders is in English. Jeremy Tunstall said that English is the language best suited for "comic strips, headlines, riveting first sentences, photo captions, dubbing, subtitling, pop songs, billboards, disc-jockey banter, news flashes, and sung commercials."[9] A great appeal of English as an international language is that it is easy to speak badly.

This thrust of English as a world media language has become self generating, and any educated person of whatever nationality who wishes to participate in this shrinking and interdependent world finds it useful to know English. In fact, because English is now spoken as a second language by more people around the globe than by the British and the Americans combined, it must now be considered as belonging to the world, as indeed it does. For when two persons of differing linguistic backgrounds are able to converse, the chances are they will be speaking English.

Notes

1. Deidre Carmody, "Magazines Find Green Pastures Abroad," *New York Times*, March 20, 1995, sec. C, 5.
2. 1998 IMS Directory of Publications (Ft. Washington, Pa.: IMS Press, 1998), 727–28.

3. Richard W. Stevenson, "Ad Agency Mergers Changing the Business," *New York Times*, May 13, 1986, 1.
4. Ibid.
5. Alvin Toffler, *PowerShift*, (New York: Bantam Books, 1990), 340.
6. Toffler, *PowerShift*, 341.
7. Ken Auletta, "Leviathan," *New Yorker*, October 29, 2001, 50.
8. Michiko Kakutani, "Taking Out the Trash," *New York Times Magazine*, June 8, 1997, 31.
9. Jeremy Tunstall, *The Media Are American: Anglo-American Media in the World* (London: Constable, 1977), 128.

CHAPTER 7

New Media and the Developing World

There is always something new out of Africa.
—Pliny the Elder (23–79 A.D.)

Broadly speaking, the media of mass communication are unevenly distributed around the world. There are far more newspapers, magazines and journals, broadcast and cable TV, AM and FM radio stations, Internet users, movie theaters, and cell phones, per capita in the affluent industrialized Western nations than in the struggling, developing nations of the "South." In the West, media are plentiful throughout a nation; in poor countries, media are found mainly in the capital or large cities, and rural areas are media starved. That picture, although generally accurate, is an incomplete one, however, for the proliferating "new media," so integral to the Information Age, are today found all over the world. Although they do not yet exist in great numbers, these new media are being utilized in surprising and useful ways to assist poor nations in their long ascent to modernization and democracy.

In this chapter, we look at some of the ways that satellite television, videocassettes and VCRs, mobile phones, cable television, FM radio, and regional news agencies have been successfully adapted and utilized in some developing nations. These quiet media revolutions are changing some societies just as in the 1960s the small, battery-powered transistor radio changed much of Africa by broadcasting news, information, and music to rural peoples in vast areas that had never known mass communication.

Videocassette Revolution

The global dissemination of popular culture, especially movies and music videos, was greatly facilitated by the rapid dissemination of videocassette recordings and the equipment, videocassette recorders (VCRs), to play them on. The terms *explosion* and *revolution* have been used to describe the

VCR phenomenon. In less than a decade, the VCR and videotape penetrated remote areas that the printing press and other information devices had not yet successfully reached after centuries. The spread has been to poor nations as well as to the affluent West, but for different reasons. Depending on culture and political traditions, VCRs can have profound effects not only on viewers but also on broadcasting and other media.

Widespread use of VCRs can challenge the usual system of government control of television by providing diversity of views and variety in entertainment. (Audiocassettes have done much the same thing to radio broadcasting.) VCRs circumvent the utilization of broadcast television for development and political control by bringing about a de facto decentralization of media. People in poor countries, including youth, now often have the freedom to view what they want to see, not what Big Brother or even their parents think is best for them. And apparently much of what they want to view are movies, pop music, and videos from the West.

In Saudi Arabia, the only choice for viewers of over-the-air television has long been the puritanical, heavily controlled, and dull programming of government television. (For example, religious orthodoxy requires that a Saudi woman's face not be shown on television.) As a result, VCRs have proliferated, and much of the viewing includes the forbidden fruit of Western movies, including X-rated films, most of them smuggled into the country.

In India, many people annoyed by the inadequacies of state-run broadcasting have turned to private enterprise "alternative television" news on videocassettes. The producer of "Business Plus," a monthly tape on political and economic issues, said that India has the only private video news magazines in the world. The tapes, made in English and Hindi, rent for about sixty cents a day or sell for about $8. The audience is small but consists of middle class, cosmopolitan Indians dissatisfied with the vacuity of official news and documentaries. The trend to news-oriented videotapes began earlier with "Newstrack," a fast-paced monthly video of investigative reporting with a segmented format like that of "60 Minutes."

Throughout emerging nations, small shops renting or selling videotapes from the West have become commonplace. In the remote nation of Bhutan, on India's northern border, people were watching videos on television sets for years before the nation had over-the-air television service. To an American, the VCR is an easy way to watch a movie or to record a television program for a more convenient time and place, but to many millions in developing nations, VCRs are a means of gaining alternative news sources or enjoying sometimes prohibited Western culture—activities that authoritarian countries have largely failed to censor or control.

Another threat to authoritarian rule or illegal activities is the ubiquitous camcorder, a lightweight, handheld television camera with a built-in VCR. Private ownership of camcorders in Third World nations is increasing by the thousands, and anyone can record a newsworthy or controversial event that later appears on television or for private showing to select audiences. The prevalence of camcorders in authoritarian nations has the effect of undermining the government's monopoly of news and information.

Al-Jazeera: CNN of the Arab World

Throughout the Arab world, television viewers are accustomed to stale, heavily censored, state-controlled television and have had little access to independent and reliable news in Arabic. All that changed in 1996, when Al-Jazeera began broadcasting out of the tiny oil sheikdom of Qatar on the Persian Gulf. The Doha-based satellite channel has become the most free-wheeling station in the Arab world, delighting millions of viewers across the Middle East and annoying many rulers.

Al-Jazeera has become the Arab world's CNN, with round-the-clock, all-news and public affairs programs reaching millions in twenty Arab states, mostly through private satellite dishes, which can be purchased for less than $100. Millions of Arab families now own TV dishes, whether in the slums of Cairo or the mansions of Kuwait. Al-Jazeera is also available in Britain and the United States, where 150,000 viewers pay $30 a month to receive a multichannel Arabic "package." With more than 350 editors, anchors, and technicians and more than thirty-five bureaus around the world, the network has focused on subjects considered subversive in most Arab nations: persecution of political dissidents; absence of democratic institutions; the inequality of women; torture; polygamy; and rival interpretations of Islamic teachings. Its talk shows have infuriated Arab rulers by bringing in to its studio political dissidents from Egypt, Saudi Arabia, Algeria, Syria, Morocco, Jordan, and Iraq. The network has built a reputation for independent, ground-breaking reporting that contrasted markedly with other Arabic-language stations. Broadcast by satellite, Al-Jazeera is difficult to censor, although Arab nations have tried. Algeria's regime reportedly shut off electricity in parts of the country rather than allow television sets to pick up a debate on the country's bloody civil war.

Al-Jazeera has even scooped governments that control their own media. In 1999, it broadcast in advance of the Iraqi media Saddam Hussein's Army

Day speech, in which he called on Arabs to overthrow their leaders if they were allied with the United States. Al-Jazeera has relentlessly reported strife in the occupied territories of Israel and has kept the Palestinian cause very much alive in living rooms of the Muslim world. After September 11, Al-Jazeera became a central player in the emerging propaganda war. The network gained access to news sources in Afghanistan and during the first weeks of the war had the only television footage from inside Afghanistan. Britain's prime minister, Tony Blair, has been interviewed, as has Secretary of State Colin Powell. But as the war went on, American policy makers grew troubled by the frequent broadcasts of Al-Jazeera's exclusive December 1998 interview with Osama bin Laden, in which he urged Muslims to "target all Americans," and by the anti-American oratory of many of its analysts, guests, and callers on its popular talk shows.

Fouad Ajami, a U.S. Middle East expert, was highly critical and said Al-Jazeera was more inflammatory than other Arab media outlets. He wrote, "For the dark side of the pan-Arab worldview is an aggressive mix of anti-Americanism and anti-Zionism, and these hostilities drive the station's coverage, whether it is reporting on the upheaval in the West Bank or on the American raids on Kandahar. Although Al-Jazeera has sometimes been hailed in the West for being an autonomous Arabic news outlet, it would be a mistake to call it a responsible one. Day in and day out, Al-Jazeera deliberately fans the flames of Muslim outrage."[1]

Nonetheless, the station's Arab viewers are able to see things they are not supposed to see. For the first time, Arabs with a satellite dish can have access to uncensored news. The station offered silent footage of Bright Star, a joint Egyptian-American military exercise off the coast of Egypt — a potent commentary on the cooperation of the Egyptian military with the Pentagon. The station also gets credit for being one of the few Arab television stations to interview Israelis. But Ajami concluded, "Al-Jazeera's virulent anti-American bias undercuts all its virtues. It is, in the final analysis, a dangerous force. And it should be treated as such by Washington."[2] In more peaceful times in the Middle East, if they ever come, Al-Jazeera may play a more useful journalistic role.

Mobile Phones for Rural Workers

Mobile or cell phones have proliferated throughout the Western world in recent years and have proved to be exceedingly useful tools for peripatetic journalists who need to file stories from remote places or just want to keep in touch with their editors or colleagues. But their use has grown even faster in developing nations.

Currently, sales of cell phones have been increasing rapidly in rural India, where unexpected uses have been found for them. For example, in the seas off Kerala state, crowded with fishing boats, fishermen use cell phones to keep in touch with the dozen-odd seafood markets, checking prices at different ports. Since acquiring the mobile service, fishermen have markedly increased their profits and efficiency. The five thousand fishermen who work off the coast are not alone in embracing wireless technology. From garment workers in the south to farmers in the Punjab, rural India has discovered the convenience of doing business on mobile phones. Many people in rural areas have no alternative. Half of India's 660,000 villages have never been wired for fixed-line service, and those connected have had outdated equipment and long waits for service.

Increased economic activity and cultural change have been accelerated by increased communication capabilities from both mobile phones and better transportation. Some parts of the Indian countryside have more mobile phones per capita than some of India's biggest cities. India has only a tiny fraction of the mobile phones that China has, but research has shown that the growth rate for mobile phone subscribers in India will soar from a mere 3.1 million at the end of 2000 to surpass anywhere else in Asia, reaching thirty million by 2005. India will still lag behind China, which is expected to have more than three hundred million mobile connections by 2005.

For many of the same reasons as in India, demand for mobile phones is growing even faster in poor nations such as Haiti and elsewhere in the Southern Hemisphere. For those who can afford them, the wireless phone is considered a necessity—not just a popular convenience as in America and other prosperous nations. With financially strapped governments often unable to provide adequate public services, people are turning to privately built wireless networks for telephones. In beleaguered Haiti with its deep economic and political problems, one of the few systems that works reliably is the cellular phone network built by the local unit of an American company. Fewer than one percent of Haitians have conventional phone service, compared with 95 percent in the United States. Some four hundred thousand Haitians are on the waiting list for a conventional phone line, and the wait can last as long as five years. That explains why the number of mobile subscribers in Haiti climbed 150 percent in 2000 compared with 1998, to about twenty-five thousand users, enabling mobile users to account for one third of the nation's telephone customers.

Haiti is not alone. In some Latin American nations, wireless customers outnumber customers of fixed-line companies. In Paraguay, wireless users account for 60 percent of all phone users and have increased by 88 percent in 2000 to 436,000 users. In Venezuela, some 57 percent of phone subscribers use mobile phones. Poor countries, where perhaps four-fifths of the world's people live, had about 40 percent of mobile phone lines in 1999, up from 20 percent in 1995. But these countries had only about 5 percent of the hub computers of the Internet, according to the World Bank. Apparently, wireless technology has so far had a far greater impact on people's lives in developing countries than the Internet.

FM Radio and Political Change

In sub-Saharan Africa, radio has long been the most potent mass medium, reaching far more people than newspapers or television. But in most African countries, AM radio has been a heavy-handed government monopoly. However, in Ghana, a West African nation of twenty-six million, a significant change took place in 1995 when the previous government, led by President Jerry Rawlings, gave up its monopoly on the airwaves and permitted the establishment of private FM radio stations. After that, more than forty FM stations cropped up around Ghana, broadcasting in English and Ghanaian languages. The stations offered local music and their own news, and most important, they broadcast hours and hours of live talk radio, during which Ghanaians could tell government and anyone else what was on their minds.

The resulting national dialog that took place over FM radio enabled challenger J.A. Kufuor to win an election over Rawlings, whose tired and corrupt party had controlled the country for twenty years. This was the first ever peaceful transition from one elected civilian government to another in Ghana. Observers said that when people saw something that concerned them, they called in to their FM station, which gave the public a voice. Politicians could hear ordinary people talk about many problems—unemployment, corruption, food prices. People were fed up and they told each other about it. Of Ghana's ten provinces, eight had these flourishing FM stations, and in all these provinces, Kufuor won. In the two provinces without FM stations, the incumbent Rawlings won. Since the election, the FM stations, all run by young Ghanaians who had worked or been educated in the West, have been trying to force more transparency on the new government.

One official said, "The minute people were able to talk freely—and anonymously—on the radio and ask what officials were up to was the beginning of accountability for government in Ghana."[3] Finally, the four most democratic nations in West Africa today—Ghana, Mali, Senegal, and Benin—all have flourishing FM radio stations.

Burgeoning Cable Television: India versus China

The rapid and dizzying onrush of cable television among developing nations can be analyzed by looking at the two countries that each have a billion people. China has the most households hooked up to cable—eighty million—whereas India has forty million. But India is far more open to a variety of domestic and foreign programming, creating one of the most vibrant television markets in the world. India has been referred to as the "Wild West" of global media. The cable television market has been likened to the teeming streets of Bombay: India has 30,000 to 50,000 cable operators, mostly mom-and-pop operators, stringing cables from trees to houses. With advertising slowing and new channels squeezing in every month, competition has become intense. India has been compared to the United States in the early 1980s, when cable television, then unregulated, was growing at a rapid pace. Ever since satellite-delivered cable arrived in India in 1991 (after the Persian Gulf war had turned CNN into a global phenomenon), the government has permitted cable growth.[4]

Yet television is far from commonplace in that sea of Indian humanity. About seventy million homes have television sets; of those, about thirty million have cable, making India the third largest cable market after the United States and China. Although the Chinese receive only a handful of channels because of restrictions on foreign broadcasters, Indians can get up to eighty-five channels for a monthly fee of 150 rupees, about $3.26. The pell-mell growth of Indian cable stands in marked contrast to China. Despite more foreign investment and efforts by Rupert Murdoch and AOL Time Warner to penetrate the Chinese market, China remains a place where CNN is seen mainly in hotel rooms and diplomatic quarters.

Indian cable viewers are faced with bewildering choices. Indian MTV, a branch of the American MTV, is only one of six music-video channels. Movies, sports, news, general entertainment, children's, and regional programs can all be found on cable. Often, two or three channels compete in the same category. However, the big foreign satellite cable companies, Murdoch's Star TV and Sony, will probably survive a shakedown of the wild cable market. In Bombay, India's media capital and home of its large and lively movie industry, cable is edging out the movies for the mass market. Cable, too, carries many Indian movies.

In July 2000, the Indian version of the popular British and American television game show "Who Wants to Be a Millionaire?" went on the air and riveted the public for weeks. Known in Hindi as "Kaun Banega Crorepati" or literally "Who Wants to Be a Ten Millionaire?," the show shattered ratings records and spawned several copycat game shows. The game show was a homegrown hit and shot Star TV from an also-ran to the No. 1 cable service in India. Ratings are still an inexact science in India, but by some counts "Crorepati" was being watched by one hundred million people nightly. The hit show was a wake-up call of sorts for American broadcasters in India: a non-Indian programming concept tailored to Indian tastes. Sony and another cable channel, Zee, have produced similar game shows and are trying to exploit other American genres, such as reality-based shows. Sony, which also has an entertainment and movie channel, as well as distributing CNB India, has produced a series for cable that will feature a princess trapped on an island. Fifteen contestants will try to surmount a series of hurdles to free the princess and claim a prize. Because of its relative freedom to compete and innovate in cable television and movies, as well as its rapid growth in high-technology industry based in Bangalore, India is emerging as a future powerhouse in the Information Age.

Another significant development has been the expansion of alternative and regional news agencies that, using new technology, can supplement and add variety to news coming from Western news organizations. The oldest alternative agency is the Non-Aligned News Agencies Pool (NANAP), which dates from the Fourth Non-Aligned Summit in Algiers in 1973. Although about eighty nations were involved, it has had little impact even in the media of its strongest supporters.

A more important example was the Inter Press Service Third World News Agency (IPS).[5] IPS is a nonprofit cooperative based in Rome and specializing in non-Western news, which it distributes to media in Europe and North America. With bureaus or correspondents in sixty countries, two-thirds of them in the former Third World, IPS maintains exchanges with thirty national news agencies. The focus is on news relating to development news rather than spot news. Other alternative agencies that have been adding diversity to global news flow include Depthnews, Gemini, and South-North News Service.

Africa In and Out of the News Spotlight

For twelve days in March 1998, American newspapers and television news were full of stories and vivid video about Ghana, Uganda, Rwanda, South Africa, Botswana, and Senegal—all stops on President Bill Clinton's tour of Africa, with an entourage of eight hundred, including more than two hundred journalists. For that brief time, the public was deluged with considerable information about that complex and troubled region. But after the President returned to Washington, D.C., the news spigot from Africa was abruptly shut off. This reaffirmed a journalistic truism about Africa: The continent usually makes news when a famous personage comes calling, such as President Carter did in 1978 or Pope John Paul II did in 1982 and 1998. Africa gets our attention as well when American soldiers' lives are at risk, as in 1992 when U.S. Marines landed in Somalia. (See Chapter 10, "Covering the World's Hot Spots.")

Yet most of the time, sub-Saharan Africa, except for South Africa, continues to be the least reported region of the world. One reason is that Africa's own news media, weak and usually government controlled, have not been effective in reporting reliable news to Africans, much less to the outside world, and generally are not much help either to foreign journalists trying to report from Africa.

During the 1960s and 1970s, independent black Africa received special attention in the Western press as some forty new nations with promising futures stepped onto the world's stage. But as many of these countries foundered and regressed, and as the Cold War waned, the global media's interest in Africa dropped sharply. Today, there is a grudging consensus among journalists that Africa is badly neglected in the news. Jim Hoagland of the *Washington Post* said Africa has gotten short shrift in the media for a long time, and David Gergen of *U.S. News* commented, "The history of American media has been one of general inattention to Africa, except when there's been a major famine or conflict."[6]

Africa's Media Image, a book edited by Beverly Hawk, with contributions by Africanists and journalists with African experience, gives detailed analyses of shortcomings of Western reporting of major African news stories over the past generation, confirming a near-unanimous view of African specialists that U.S. news media need to do better. News flows out of Africa to Europe and America in much the same ways that it does from other developing nations in Latin America, Asia, and the Middle East, with many of the same traits.

Parachute Journalism

A story breaks that captures the world's attention: widespread famine in
Somalia or Ethiopia, genocidal warfare in Rwanda, civil war in Congo
(Zaire). The foreign press arrives in large numbers, covers the story, shoots
pictures and video, and then abruptly leaves. This kind of reporting, typically seen on television, fails to provide needed context and follow-up that
such stories require for public understanding.

Declining Coverage

Since the end of the Cold War, much less news has been coming out of
Africa as many civil wars and upheavals ended. Many small nations, among
them Benin, Botswana, Burkina Faso, Mali, Burundi, Guinea, Niger,
Lesotho, and Togo, not only have rarely had resident correspondents but
also are seldom visited by Western reporters passing through the region. A
few years ago, armed conflicts were going on at the same time in Angola,
Chad, Djibouti, Ethiopia, Liberia, Rwanda, Somalia, Sudan, and Western
Sahara, but little reporting about them appeared in the U.S. news media.
On June 8, 1998, Nigeria's military dictator, Sani Abacha, died suddenly.
This major story from Africa's most populous nation received only brief
mention on the evening television news. The next day, the *New York Times*
and *Washington Post* both gave the story several pages of coverage.

Barriers to Reporting

Journalists in Africa face barriers not found elsewhere. Few correspondents
know the many local languages, although knowledge of English and French
is usually sufficient for dealing with news sources. Distances are greater, communications less reliable, and air travel inconvenient and often haphazard.
Reporters sometimes have to fly through London or Paris to get from one
African capital to another. African governments often treat reporters badly;
some at times just bar all foreign reporters. Often, reporters may be permitted in, but access to news sources or officials is severely limited.

Failures to Report Bad News

By gathering news that authorities do not want reported, correspondents
face the threat of expulsion. Over the years, many Western reporters have

been forced out of Africa and refused visas when they sought reentry. Because of this possibility, some journalists believe that sometimes the bad news does not get reported. A British journalist, Ian Smiley, suggested that such self-censorship was a standard feature of reporting throughout the Third World and was nowhere more rigorously observed than in Africa.

Because of this reluctance to report fully, a darker side of Africa may be ignored. True, the coverage has been thin and violence prone, but the need may not be just to provide more positive, cheerful, and sympathetic coverage. The need may be for more realistic coverage of the Continent's deepening crisis. Not much of this gloomy scenario gets into daily news reports.

Two respected journalists have sounded warnings. Robert Kaplan painted a disturbing picture of West Africa which, he said, is "becoming the symbol of worldwide demographic, environmental, and societal stress, in which criminal anarchy emerges as the real 'strategic' danger. Disease, overpopulation, unprovoked crime, scarcity of resources, refugee migrations, the increasing erosion of nation-states and international borders, and the empowerment of private armies, security firms, and international drug cartels are now most tellingly demonstrated through a West African prism."[7]

Columnist William Pfaff voiced similar concerns: "The destitution of Africa has been an all but forbidden topic in political discourse. The time has arrived, however, for honest and dispassionate discussion of this immense human tragedy, for which the Western countries bear a grave, if partial, responsibility and which will worsen if not addressed. Much of Africa needs, to put it plainly, what one could call a disinterested neocolonialism."[8]

These are controversial views, and some argue that they show a lack of belief in the survival skills of ordinary people and may convince the concerned and sympathetic outsiders to give up on Africa. The plight of Africa reflects a central quandary about reporting Africa. Despite the steady decline in news about Africa, the U.S. media's selective, violence-ridden reports have painted a negative and discouraging picture of Africa. Yet, if Kaplan and Pfaff are correct, the reality may be bleaker than we believed, and there indeed may be a need for Western nations to intervene. That is not something the American public wants to hear.

Finally, considering the erratic and sparse coverage of Africa on television and in the news magazines, it is imperative that the handful of prestigious newspapers not dilute their African coverage. Three papers, the *New York Times*, the *Washington Post*, and the *Los Angeles Times*, continue to produce superior daily reporting out of Africa.

Perhaps as the United States becames reengaged with the world as the result of the events of September 11, the news media will provide more news out of Africa and the developing world.

Notes

1. Fouad Ajami, "What the Muslim World is Watching," *New York Times Magazine*, November 18, 2001, 50.
2. Ibid.
3. Thomas Friedman, "Low Tech Democracy," *New York Times*, May 1, 2001, sec. A, 27.
4. Mark Landler, "A Glut of Cable TV in India," *New York Times*, March 23, 2001, sec. C, 1.
5. C. Anthony Giffard, "The Inter Press Service," *Journalism Quarterly*, 62, no. 1, Spring 1985, 17.
6. Beverly Hawk, ed., *Africa's Media Image* (New York: Praeger, 1992), 224.
7. Robert Kaplan, "The Coming Anarchy," *Atlantic Monthly*, February 1994, 44–76.
8. William Pfaff, "A New Colonialism," *Foreign Affairs*, January/February 1995, 2–6.

CHAPTER 8
Public Diplomacy and Political Warfare

When it came to radio waves the iron curtain was helpless. Nothing could stop the news from coming through—neither sputniks nor minefields, high walls, nor barbed wire. The frontiers could be closed, words could not.

—Lech Walesa

In wartime, truth is so precious that she should always be guarded by a bodyguard of lies.

—Winston Churchill

Public diplomacy and political warfare have much in common with the armed forces: in peacetime, somewhat ignored and diminished, but during time of war they are mobilized by government to join the fray and to win the "hearts and minds" of followers and adversaries.

In modern times, shortwave radio, which reaches many millions almost anywhere on the globe, has been a preferred medium in political warfare—in World War II, the Cold War (including the Korean and Vietnam Wars), and other international crises—and now since September 11, it has come to the fore in the war on terrorism. In the United States, the tools, strategies, and messages of political warfare had been neglected but were quickly being sharpened for the conflict in Central Asia. (See Chapter 2, "War on Terrorism Challenges News Media.") Commentators have seen the current struggle in large part as an effort to convince world public opinion of the rightness of the antiterrorism cause.

Since the end of the Cold War and before September 11, global broadcasting over shortwave radio had not, however, receded in volume. On any given evening, an Arab in a café in Algiers, a Peruvian llama herder in a shelter in the Andes, or a Chinese dissident in Beijing can share a common communication experience. By merely flicking on a shortwave radio receiver and twisting the dials, each will hear the same polyglot cacophony of sounds detailing the news, unfolding diverse feature programs, and playing all sorts of music. The variety of languages spoken is immense, but each listener can, with little difficulty, find a program he or she understands. Nowhere is the prism of international communication more apparent. In shortwave radio broadcasting, one person's "truth" or news is another person's "propaganda," and vice versa. And again, one person's music is another's "noise." Transnational radio (now supplemented by global television, the Internet, and AM radio) is also a major conveyor of what is sometimes called public diplomacy.

For more than forty years, public diplomacy (a government's overt efforts to influence other governments and their publics) and shortwave radio were dominated by the great East-West struggle called the Cold War, which in effect ended in 1990 with the reunification of Germany and the withdrawal of Soviet troops from Central Europe. But public diplomacy and propaganda wars continued on other polemical battlefields: in the Persian Gulf after Iraq invaded Kuwait; in the tragic and protracted struggle among Serbs, Croats, and Bosnian Muslims in the former Yugoslavia; and in clashes over human rights in China.

With the globalization of the economy, international frictions were for a time more concerned with economic competition and business contentions between nations rather than political and ideological differences. Concerns about incipient war on, say, the Korean peninsula, in Kashmir, or in the Middle East were partially replaced by worries about the flagging economies in Indonesia, Japan, or Argentina and how these trends might undermine more stable economies of the West. For a time, political espionage was replaced by economic espionage and concerns about the global pirating of videos, movies, CDs, and computer software. For example, 90 percent of software used on China's computers is reported to have been pirated. The privacy issue has been pushed aside by national security concerns raised by international terrorism.

Much of the torrent of messages constantly washing over the globe is not neutral or "disinterested" information (that is, news) but "purposive" communication—words, sounds, and images intended to influence people's perceptions and opinions. A great deal of what refracts through the prism of international radio is purposive and is often called "propaganda," that is, the systematic use of words or symbols to influence the attitudes or behaviors of others. *Propaganda* is a loaded term, a pejorative epithet subjectively defined as a "persuasive statement I don't like." No one—journalist, broadcaster, writer, or educator—wants to be called a propagandist. Transnational communicators put on their ideological blinkers when they insist, "We deal in information or truth. They deal in propaganda."

International political communication (IPC), cumbersome term though it is, is a useful and neutral expression encompassing such terms as public diplomacy, overseas information programs, cultural exchanges, and even propaganda activities and political warfare. A useful definition for IPC is as follows: the political effects that newspapers, broadcasting, film, exchanges of persons, cultural exchanges, and other means of international communication can achieve.

However, a distinction should be made between official and private communications and between international communications designed to have a political effect and those that are not. Here, then, are four broad categories of IPC:

1. Official communications intended to influence foreign audiences (that is, public diplomacy), such as those by the (former) U.S. Information Agency, Voice of America, Radio Moscow, British Information Service, Deutsche Welle, Radio Havana, and BBC's World Service. Most international shortwave broadcasting falls into this category, and almost every nation with the capability will sponsor some broadcasting efforts across its borders.

2. Official communications not intended to influence foreign audiences, a small category indeed. One example has been the U.S. Armed Forces Radio and Television Network. At its peak, AFN operated some two hundred radio and thirty television transmitters serving American forces overseas and had large eavesdropping audiences.

3. Private communications intended to influence foreign audiences politically. This is another small category, including various organizations and groups working to promote international understanding—for example, peace groups advocating a freeze on nuclear weapons.

4. Private communications without a political purpose. Among these would be Western news agencies, media enterprises overseas such as advertising agencies, and distributors of motion pictures, television programs, videos, and so forth. Activities of relief organizations, important in poor countries, belong in this classification as well. The vast flood of American mass culture (much of it movies, music videos, pop recordings, and television programs, most of it produced within a five-square-mile area of Hollywood), has both negative and positive effects (but not intentional effects) on international political communication.

Without doubt, the overseas impact of private U.S. communications is far greater than that of U.S. public diplomacy, but the actual influence is difficult to assess. As we have seen, Western pop culture certainly contributed to political change in Eastern Europe in recent years. Unintended effects sometimes can be more profound than those caused intentionally.

Lines between these four categories often become blurred. Years ago, we were puzzled to find U.S. paperback books selling far below U.S. prices in African bookstores. Later, I learned that the U.S. government covertly subsidized the sale of these paperbacks. Whether they are "propaganda," even if the books are of clear educational value, is an arguable point. Often, newsreels and short features were shown in African movie theaters without being identified as a free service of the French or British governments. Much of the popular music heard on private radio stations in Latin America was provided by the Voice of America. Official IPC efforts are usually a supplement to diplomacy—serving as ways by which governments try to extend their influence abroad and pursue their foreign-policy objectives.

The international news media of all nations play a significant role in international political communication. The privately owned media organizations of the West serve their own commercial purposes by distributing and selling news and entertainment around the globe without intentional political aims. Yet at the same time, the news media transmit a good deal of purposive official information, that is, propaganda, because all governments work hard at getting their versions of news and events into the world's news media. Much of the news from official sources in national capitals is intended to serve foreign-policy goals. News and propaganda are not mutually exclusive categories. The media serve the purposes of public diplomacy when they carry a story of President Bush's views of Osama bin Laden, yet what the U.S. President says is always "news." A continuing problem for professional journalists is that of separating legitimate news from self-serving official "interpretations" of the news, whatever the source. Nevertheless, the two are often identical.

Authoritarian as well as communist news media, which are much less independent of official controls, often serve as unquestioning conduits of political communication from their own governments. Editors in Beijing or Baghdad usually face no professional dilemmas over whether to carry stories supporting their governments' foreign policies. Less-developed nations are mostly on the receiving end of public diplomacy because most lack the communication capability to compete effectively on a global basis. A partial exception at times has been the extensive radio broadcasting by a few developing nations; Egypt and North Korea send out more hours of foreign broadcasting than France, India, or Japan.[1] On the other hand, many poor nations and their elites have benefited from the development aid, cultural exchanges, famine relief, and educational assistance—all of which are aspects of international political communication—that they have received from developed nations.

International Radio Broadcasting

In this day of direct-broadcast satellites, global television, and the Internet, the powerful and pervasive medium of international radio broadcasting, long capable of carrying messages around the world almost instantaneously, is easily underestimated or ignored. According to audience surveys, listening on shortwave radio continues to increase. A BBC study found that two hundred million people daily tune in and, according to sales figures, there are about six hundred million shortwave radios around the globe—half in Asia and Africa.[2] That is indeed mass communication, beamed mainly at the most populous and poorest nations.

In the 1930s, political leaders such as Nazi Germany's Josef Goebbels talked of international radio as a "limitless medium" and saw it as a powerful instrument of international diplomacy, persuasion, and even coercion. For more than half a century, transnational radio has been just that—a key instrument of international political communication as well as many other things. The medium enjoyed a rapid and diverse expansion and by the late 1930s was being used by national governments, religious organizations, commercial advertisers, domestic broadcasters, and educators to carry their messages across national borders.

As the twentieth century was closing, the total number of national broadcasters rose to more than 150, and the number of hours broadcast almost doubled that of the 1960s.[3] Shortwave radio messages are sent from transmitters directly throughout the world to receiving sets, but international radio's growth and diversity continue today with the utilization by national broadcasters of local AM and FM with signals sent down by satellites. BBC does this with eight hundred stations around the world, two hundred of them in the United States. But most Americans, unlike many other nationalities, do not listen much to international radio and so are unaware of how pervasive it is: 1,600 shortwave stations emanating from 160 countries. These stations offer a choice of some sixty or more language services broadcasting for ten to one hundred hours a day or more. The formats are equally diverse: newscasts, talks, interviews, editorial comments, press reviews, documentaries, and a good deal of music. News on the hour, every hour about domestic and foreign events is a common feature, but other informational programs try to reflect the broader cultural, social, and economic aspects of particular nations through dramas, music, sports events, and religious services. Today, international broadcasters often have Web sites as well to transmit their messages over the Internet.

Here we are concerned with the largest international broadcasting operators. Currently, in order of total hours of weekly broadcasting abroad, they are the United States, the People's Republic of China, Russia, Great Britain, Germany, Egypt, North Korea, France, India, and Japan. The loudest voices in world broadcasting—Radio Moscow, Radio Beijing, Voice of America, Deutsche Welle and Deutschland Funk, BBC World Service, Radio France Internationale, and Radio Cairo—rely mainly on the following languages, in descending order of usage: English, Russian, Mandarin Chinese, Arabic, Spanish, French, Japanese, Indonesian, Portuguese, German, Italian, Persian (Farsi), Swahili, Hindi, Hausa, and Korean.

A significant portion of international political rivalries and frictions are refracted through the prism of international broadcasting: the nationalistic and ethnic animosities in the post-Cold War world; the Arab-versus-Israeli tensions as well as those between moderate and radical Arab regimes; the North-South disputes between rich and poor nations; plus dozens of smaller regional controversies and disagreements between neighboring nations. And since September 11, concerns about terrorism have dominated. Any major global crisis will be widely reported, analyzed, and commented upon on shortwave radio.

As the Cold War was winding down, Radio Moscow and its related Soviet broadcasters were on the air 2,257 hours weekly during 1988.[4] The United States countered with sixteen hours daily of Russian-language VOA broadcasts into the Soviet Union, while U.S.-backed Radio Free Europe broadcast into Eastern Europe, and Radio Liberty broadcast in non-Russian languages to various parts of the Soviet Union. In 1988, the United States was broadcasting globally 2,360 hours weekly; China, 1,517 hours weekly; United Kingdom, 756 hours; and India, 444 hours.[5] By June 1994, after the demise of the Cold War, the United States had dropped to 2,000 hours weekly and Russia to 1,400 hours; China was steady at 1,600 hours, Britain was up to about 1,800 hours, and India was steady at 500 hours.[6]

Amid the cacophony of sometimes strident and pejorative voices clashing over the international airwaves, it is important to remember that international radio also is a substantial news source for many millions, but nowhere is the truism that one person's news is another person's propaganda more apparent. Listeners can twist the dials to find a version of world events that suits their own needs and world views; this is especially true for people living under dictatorships that lack popular support. News on international radio may often be acrimonious and self-serving, but without question it provides a diversity of news and views for untold millions. The importance of shortwave news is demonstrated, for example, when a political crisis or attempted coup occurs in an African nation. At such times, local broadcasters usually go off the air, and local residents habitiually tune to BBC or VOA to learn what is really happening in their own country.

With so much of what fills the night air (when reception is best) perceived by many as propaganda, the credibility of an international station's news and commentaries is crucial for its reputation among foreign listeners. The international broadcaster that has long enjoyed the best reputation for believability and objectivity is the World Service of the BBC. As a public corporation, the domestic BBC radio is financed by license fees paid by each British household with a radio or television set. The BBC World Service is not funded by license fees; instead, it receives about $160 million annually in parliamentary grants-in-aid. The government, in consultation with the service, has the final decision over which languages are broadcast, but editorial control of the programs rests entirely with the BBC. The World Service broadcasts in English and forty-four other languages and, according to its research, reaches 143 million regular listeners in a week. Of those, 122 million listen directly, whereas about twenty-seven million, with some overlap, listen to rebroadcasts on local stations. Of the total audience, thirty-five million listen in English. The World Service receives about half a million letters a year; the total in 1996 was 671,002. Languages used in most letters were English, with 119,897, followed by Hindi, 107,602; Burmese, 103,602; Tamil, 86,102; and Arabic, 38,303.

During Britain's war with Argentina over the Falkland Islands, Prime Minister Margaret Thatcher bitterly criticized the BBC for not sufficiently supporting the British war effort. Some saw this as evidence of BBC's independence—the independence that draws so many listeners to BBC during times of crisis.

Shortly after the BBC World Service announced the start of the Gulf War in January 1991, it expanded its Arabic-language broadcasts to fourteen hours a day, five hours longer than before the crisis. An estimated ten million Arabs from North Africa to the Persian Gulf listened in, a far larger number than listened to either Voice of America or Radio Moscow.

Two other separate organizations—the British Information Services and the British Council, which deals with cultural affairs and exchanges—supplement the broadcasting service in Britain's efforts at public diplomacy overseas.[7]

U.S. Activities in Public Diplomacy

In the past, U.S. activities in public diplomacy shared many similarities with those of Britain, but with some important differences. The United States Information Agency (USIA) was one of the key organizations, working closely with but separately from the Department of State. The Voice of America began broadcasting in 1942 and was largely under the aegis of the USIA. During the Cold War, VOA's efforts were supplemented by Radio Free Europe, which broadcast 555 hours weekly in European languages to Eastern Europe, and by Radio Liberty, which broadcast 462 hours weekly in Russian and fourteen other languages (but not English) to the Soviet Union.[7]

The USIA, usually operating with a budget of about $900 million, employed about twelve thousand people between Washington and some 275 U.S. Information Service (USIS) posts in 110 countries. Typically, a USIS post worked under a U.S. ambassador and included a public library. USIS personnel cooperated with local media by providing news and related material, holding exhibits, running language courses, giving seminars of various kinds, and arranging visits and cultural exchanges of both Americans and local people. (However, on October 1, 1999, the USIA was abolished.)

The USIA and VOA have long had an identity crisis: Are they objective news and cultural organizations reflecting the diversity of American life and culture, or are they arms of the State Department, vigorously advocating U.S. foreign policy objectives? (This dispute has risen again during the war against terrorism.) Past managerial participation by such well-known journalists as Edward R. Murrow, Carl Rowan, and John Chancellor suggested the former. At other times, as during the Vietnam War and Reagan administration, the latter role has been stressed. Under Reagan, the VOA was accused of repeatedly compromising its news integrity by broadcasting misleading and biased reports.[8]

Another policy issue debated within the USIA is audience targeting, revolving around the question of who are we trying to influence? If it is the ruling elites of the world's nations, then the person-to-person efforts of

USIS posts and various cultural and educational exchanges seem called for. If the target is the mass public, then expanded and more aggressive radio broadcasting seems appropriate.

Policy matters aside, there is no question that under President Reagan's USIA Director, Charles Wick, the agency reflected a tougher anticommunist approach, especially in commentaries following VOA newscasts. After 1981 the agency underwent a transformation as thorough as any in its history. The agency undertook the development of a government television network called Worldnet, with the potential of linking sixty overseas television systems to USIA headquarters in Washington. In addition to producing cultural and public affairs programs for local overseas networks, Worldnet employed satellite links for two-way televised news conferences between foreign journalists and American public figures. Part of the programming in its first years included a two-hour program of news and features to Europe five days a week. During the Gulf War crisis, President Bush used Worldnet to address foreign publics.

Another Reagan project was Radio Marti, a VOA-linked facility patterned after Radio Free Europe to broadcast news and commentary specifically to Cuba. Named for a Cuban independence hero, the radio station went on the air in May 1985 broadcasting news, entertainment, and sports in Spanish for fourteen hours daily from studios in Washington and a 50,000-watt AM transmitter in the Florida Keys. A Television Marti service was later added and has since been more controversial. Opponents had argued that since Cubans regularly listen to non-jammed U.S. radio and television stations from Miami, the new service was unnecessary. At a cost of $60,000 a day, this Spanish-language TV station broadcast news and entertainment to Cuba—from 3:30 a.m. to 6 a.m. to avoid violating global signal agreements. Although controversial, it was a project popular with Cuban émigrés in Miami. By 2001, Radio/TV Marti was still on the air, even though legislators, diplomats, and technical experts of various political stripes had called the service a major boondoggle, counterproductive, and almost wholly ineffective. And yet Presidents Reagan, Bush 1, Clinton, and Bush 2 have all backed the $22-million-a-year operation.

Public Diplomacy after the Cold War

The dramatic and unexpected ending of the Cold War during 1989–1990 and the accompanying demise of communist regimes in Eastern Europe profoundly altered public diplomacy because East-West rivalries had so long dominated the propaganda wars. Most agreed that the West had "won" the Cold War. However, there was not the same certitude about many aspects of the victory. Foreign radio broadcasting by VOA and Radio Free Europe and Radio Liberty as well as BBC and the other Western broadcasters had proved far more effective than most Western experts had supposed. In 1990, journalist Morton Kondracke commented, "If ever there was an American foreign policy success story, it's in international broadcasting. By the testimony of everyone from Václav Havel (of Czechoslovakia) to Lech Walesa (of Poland) to ordinary people in the streets of Bucharest and Beijing, democracy would not be what (and where) it is today without the two U.S. foreign broadcast networks, the Voice of America and Radio Free Europe/Radio Liberty."[9]

A recent book by Michael Nelson, *War of the Black Heavens: The Battles of Western Broadcasting in the Cold War* (Syracuse, 1997), argues that the Western radio programs presented a compelling message of the good life that undermined communist regimes and connected listeners with the cultures of Europe and North America. Nelson believes that radio, not diplomacy or the global economy, raised the iron curtain.

Despite their Cold War successes, U.S. planners talked of consolidating the U.S. radio services as well as cutting back on their budgets because they no longer seemed needed. But due to the uncertainty of economic reforms and political instability in Russia, unrest in the former Soviet Republics, and unresolved crises in the Balkans, the survival of both Radio Liberty and Radio Free Europe seemed necessary. President Václav Havel of the Czech Republic and the new democratically elected leaders of Poland and Hungary all pleaded that the stations be saved because they considered those broadcasts irreplaceable. The administration and Congress agreed to continue funding the stations. So, with pared-down budgets, RFE and RL moved to Prague in 1995 from Munich, where they had been since the CIA established them in 1951.

The unchallenged success of RFE and RL during the Cold War led to proposals in Congress for a similar broadcaster to beam news and persuasive communications into China, still ruled by a Communist government and beset with human-rights problems. As pointed out in Chapter 5, "The Impact of Great News Events," VOA and BBC had played a key role during the Tiananmen Square events in 1989 by providing the only Mandarin-language news reports not controlled by China's government that were received throughout the Chinese hinterland, where most Chinese live.

Congress agreed in early 1994 to establish a new radio service, Radio Free Asia, to beam news and other programming to mainland China,

Burma, Cambodia, Laos, North Korea, and Vietnam—all authoritarian nations with serious human-rights problems. The station was modeled after RFE and RL, with grants to the new station set at $30 million a year. Radio Free Asia got off to a shaky start in September 1996. Neighboring countries loudly opposed it and it was resented by other international broadcasters. Most Chinese who listen to radio broadcasts are devoted to the BBC, VOA, and Radio France International, all of which had bolstered their Asian broadcasting in the two previous years.

By early 2001, Tibet and China's western deserts were the scene of a radio battle for the hearts and minds of restive minorities in the region. VOA was transmitting in two Tibetan dialects, and Radio Free Asia had eight hours daily of Tibetan broadcasting. Other foreign broadcasters represented Muslim separatists and Saudi religious programming. Beijing was fighting back by expanding programming in local languages and extending Chinese radio into remote corners of Tibet and the Muslim region of Xinjiang. Further, the Chinese were building facilities to jam foreign broadcasts. The jamming was called China's new Great Wall and part of the effort to rein the restive western province with its threat of Muslim fundamentalism and terrorism.

On April 30, 1993, President Clinton signed the International Broadcasting Act establishing the International Broadcasting Bureau, which for the first time combined all U.S. government international broadcasting services under a Broadcasting Board of Governors. The board oversees the operation of VOA, Worldnet television service, and Radio and TV Marti to Cuba, as well as Radio Free Europe/Radio Liberty and Radio Free Asia. These services transmitted nearly two thousand hours a week in sixty languages. No one knows how much money is wasted due to duplication. No one knows how many people are listening. VOA says surveys show sixty-five million, but that figure could be eighty-six million. RFE/RL may have twenty million "listeners," which are defined as any person who tunes in one or more times a week.[10]

U.S. global broadcasting employed about 3,500 people. Millions more listen to VOA programs placed on local AM and FM stations around the world. VOA's original programming, all of it produced in studios in Washington, D.C., totals almost seven hundred hours a week. Most programs concern news and news-related topics. Music programs from jazz to rock, classical to country, are popular.

Radio Free Europe/Radio Liberty broadcasts from Prague more than five hundred hours weekly in twenty-three languages, including its Czech and Polish affiliates, to Central Europe, Russia, and the various republics of the former USSR, several of them near Afghanistan. In December 2001, RFE said it would resume broadcasts to Afghanistan soon if Congress approved.

In 1994, VOA began distributing via the Internet its newswire and selected newscasts and program audio files in nineteen languages, along with VOA frequency and satellite information. VOA launched a Web page on the Internet in May 1996. (BBC World Service offers similar information on the Internet.) Using a network of fourteen relay stations worldwide, VOA transmits its programs to its global audience via satellite, shortwave, and medium wave. The connection is instantaneous, so listeners may never realize that the signal passes through several different channels before it reaches their receivers.

Since September 11, there has been concern that since the abolition of the United States Information Agency in 1997, the nation's ability to conduct public diplomacy has been diminished. On a per capita basis, France and many other countries, including Spain, spend more money on public diplomacy than does the United States. Yet public diplomacy is needed by a nation at war.

After the Soviets withdrew from Afghanistan in 1989, the United States began losing interest in Pakistan. After budget cuts, five American cultural centers there were either closed or greatly reduced in scope. Pakistan was only one of many countries where the United States cut its public diplomacy programs in the early and mid-1990s. Across the Arab world, where anti-Western propaganda is a staple, Voice of America broadcasts are barely audible and reach less than 2 percent of the population in the twenty-two countries targeted. The budget in 2001, which allotted $370 billion for the military, gave $22 billion for all nonmilitary spending abroad, including foreign aid grants, VOA and radio projects, and budgets of the State Department, which has absorbed the USIA functions. Funding for foreign exchanges such as the Fulbright grants, measured in constant dollars, fell by nearly a third from 1993 to 2000. But now policy makers in Washington are listening again to advocates of increased cultural exchange and public diplomacy.[11]

In 1994 when public diplomacy was being dismantled, Historian Walter Laqueur warned:

> No specialized expertise is needed to realize that, far from being on the verge of a new order, the world has entered a period of great disorder. This refers to all kinds of regional conflicts as well as to the proliferation of the means of mass destruction, all of which makes nuclear war in the

not-too-distant future a distinct possibility. It also refers to a potential second coming of fascism and communism and anti-Western onslaughts by other forces. … Cultural diplomacy, in the widest sense, has increased in importance, whereas traditional diplomacy and military power (especially of the high technology variety) are of limited use in coping with most of these dangers.[12]

The "long thin war" against terrorism, the first of its kind, has no end in sight. Without question, public diplomacy and propaganda have important roles to play; and very likely Congress will substantially strengthen various facets of our public efforts—VOA and more targeted broadcasting, cultural exchanges, and more person-to-person contacts with foreign nationals overseas.

A key question for policy makers at war is whether the Voice of America should be a propaganda tool, pushing hard for American policy objectives or whether the Voice should be a reliable source of accurate, unbiased news. A former VOA director, Sanford Ungar, commented recently that before September 11, VOA had evolved into a

"…highly effective and credible player in the worldwide flow of information across borders. In many hot spots around the world, its correspondents are among the best and most courageous. Its two-source rule prevents it from making mistakes common to some other internationl news services. It reflects the daily experience of American democracy, warts and all. … Now more than ever, the Voice of America has important work to do. It must be able to interview anyone anywhere at any time, without fear of rebuke or reprisal, in order to provide honest and full coverage of momentous events. The State Department should keep its hands—and editing pencils—off the news."[13]

Notes

1. David Binder, "Shortwave Radio: More Preachers, Less Propaganda," *New York Times*, August 28, 1994, sec. 5, E.
2. Ibid.
3. "Candor Becoming a Staple of Shortwave," *New York Times*, March 13, 1989, 18.
4. Ibid.

5. Ibid.
6. Binder, "Shortwave Radio," 6.
7. Deborah Stead, "BBC is Expanding Its Arabic Radio Broadcasts," *New York Times*, February 18, 1991, 27.
8. Carolyn Weaver, "When the Voice of America Ignores Its Charter," *Columbia Journalism Review*, November/December 1988, 36–43.
9. Morton Kondracke, "Fine Tuning," *New Republic*, May 28, 1990, 8.
10. Mark Hopkins, "A Babel of Broadcasts," *Columbia Journalism Review*, July/August 1999, 44.
11. Stephen Kinzer, "Why They Don't Know Us," *New York Times*, November 11, 2001, sec. A, 5.
12. Walter Laqueur, "Save Public Diplomacy," *Foreign Affairs*, September/October 1994, 19.
13. Sanford J. Ungar, "Afghanistan's Fans of American Radio," *New York Times*, October 5, 2001, sec. A, 23.

CHAPTER 9

New Ways to Report the World—or Not

> The cause of the decline and fall of the Roman Empire lay in the fact that there were no newspapers of the day. Because there were no newspapers, there was no way by which the dwellers in the far-flung nation and the empire could find out was going on at the center.
>
> —H.G. Wells

> The press should be free to go where it wants, when it wants, to see, hear and photograph what it believes is in the public interest.
>
> —Walter Cronkite

The craft of gathering foreign news by journalists stationed overseas has been undergoing substantial changes in recent years. Because of financial cost cutting and new technologies, less news is reported from abroad and by very different methods. The foreign correspondent—that widely traveled and glamorous specialist of American journalism—is becoming a different breed of reporter from the old days of the Cold War. The public today seems less interested in foreign news, and editors and broadcasters are giving them a lot less of it.

The preceding paragraph describes foreign affairs journalism *before* the momentous events of September 11. Now foreign news extensively reported dominates the media and the public cannot seem to get enough of it. The question is, how long will this situation last? Covering the multifaceted war on terrorism and maintaining reporters overseas is very expensive. Television broadcasters lost nearly $100 million a day in local and national advertising because of extended coverage in the first few days that often ran without commercial breaks. Expenses of reopening bureaus, staffing them, and using the latest technologies to send words and images cost news organizations about $25 million in the first week as journalists arrived in Pakistan, Afghanistan, Tajikistan, Yemen, and Bahrain. Set-up costs for satellite communications equipment can be as much as $70,000 for each uplink and about that much a week to maintain it. As the crisis seems to ease, audience ratings for war news are starting to drop and television executives hint that cutbacks may be coming. Yet most news media seem determined to report the story wherever it goes as long as they can afford to.

September 11 triggered one significant shift: Most Americans were turning to cable news for daily reports about terrorism and the war, and the number has increased since mid-September 2001. A Pew Center survey found that fully 53 percent of respondents cited cable as their primary source for news on the crisis, versus 17 percent for network television and 18 percent for local television. The number relying mostly on newspapers for war news since September 11 has increased from 11 percent to 34 percent. All types of media could take comfort in the fact that 66 percent of respondents say they are more interested in news now that before September 11.

No one knows how long this unprecedented foreign news glut with high public interest will last. During the decade before 9/11, the news media were indifferent to foreign news at a time when ethnic conflicts killed millions and globalization touched most American communities. A Harvard study found that during the 1970s, network television devoted 45 percent of its total coverage to international news. By 1995, foreign news represented only 13.5 percent of total coverage. Budgets and staff were cut, bureaus closed, and the media emphasized shifts to economic and entertainment/trivia concerns.

Yet serious journalists have long held that foreign news is important and should be reported thoroughly and well. Many of the best and brightest journalists have spent part of their careers in what must be among the most demanding jobs in journalism. Transnational news gathering is an exacting occupation for the professional newsmen and newswomen who put together the various stories, reports, rumors, and educated guesses that make up the daily international news file. To them, theirs is a difficult, dangerous, and badly misunderstood enterprise. They understand its shortcomings and difficulties far better, they believe, than politically motivated critics or cost-conscious media owners.

In a real sense, the world's ability to learn the news about itself depends on what gets into the news flow in the fifteen or twenty open societies with highly developed media systems. After an important story appears, for example, in New York, London, Paris, Rome, or Tokyo, it immediately starts flowing through the arteries of the world's news system and will be widely reported elsewhere—but not everywhere, and certainly not every story; the majority of non-Western governments act as gatekeepers, screening news in and out of their nations. These political controls, as well as poverty and illiteracy, deprive the great majority of the world's peoples from learning even the barest outline of major current events. But any major story that "breaks" in the West has at least the possibility of being reported throughout the world.

To the few thousand foreign correspondents, the world's nations are strung out on a continuum from "free" or open at one end to "not free" or closed at the other and with many variations in between. To illustrate, the Associated Press has little difficulty gathering news in open Sweden, because several newspapers there take AP services and share their own news and photos with the agency. In addition, AP correspondents can use other Swedish media as sources and can develop their own stories or easily gain access to public officials.

Sudan, like other developing nations, offers a different kind of challenge. AP has no clients in Sudan, largely because the Sudan News Agency lacks the hard currency to buy the Comsat-beamed AP world service. The local media are subject to official controls, and the AP cannot justify the expense of maintaining a full-time correspondent in Khartoum. Therefore, AP "covers" Sudan by using a local stringer (a part-timer who is paid for what news is used). Periodically, the AP may send a staff correspondent to Sudan to do background or round up stories. At other times, AP may try to report on events in Sudan from Nairobi, in neighboring Kenya. Yet the world knows too little about Sudan, which has been accused of harboring terrorists in past years.

At the "not free" end of the continuum are a few countries that for years barred all foreign journalists and news agencies. In the Cold War days, when something important happened in Tirana, Albania, for instance, AP and the world usually found out about it belatedly from a government-controlled Albanian radio broadcast monitored abroad or from travelers or diplomats leaving the country. Albania has since opened, and Western analysts were surprised that Albanian refugees knew about the collapse of communism, which they learned about by listening carefully to English broadcasts on BBC and VOA.

A foreign correspondent often defines a country as free or not free according to how much difficulty he or she has in reporting events there. This may sound narrow and self-serving, but it has validity: the freedom of access that a foreign reporter enjoys is usually directly related to the amount of independence and access enjoyed by local journalists themselves. If local journalists are harassed or controlled by a particular government, so very likely will be the foreign journalists.

With the availability of impressive gadgets used by today's foreign correspondents—satellite telephones, videophones, laptop computers, reliable phone lines, and faxes—the reporter abroad is better able to do his or her job. The latest new gadget is the video telephone so widely used in Afghanistan. Even so, collecting news throughout the world is still an erratic and imperfect process. Some significant events are either not reported or reported long after the fact. Certain areas of the world, such as central Africa, rarely get into the world news flow.

In the dangerous and confusing post-Cold War world, foreign reporters and news organizations went through an identity crisis over what is news. As John Walcott of *Newsweek* said, "The Cold War provided us with a coherent global road map, in terms of what to cover and how to cover it."[1] The press is not used to reacting to a world full of conflicts and violent encounters that, as George Kennan put it, offer no "great and all absorbing focal points for American policy."[2] Now the war on terrorism has provided a focus for global news comparable to the Cold War.

A key challenge are disagreements between journalists and government officials over the very nature of news. To journalists, news is the first, fragmentary, and incomplete report of a significant event or happening that editors think will be of interest or importance to their readers or listeners. To many government officials, news is "positive" information that reflects favorably on their nation (and hence themselves) and serves their country's general interests and goals. Yet those same leaders want to know all that is happening elsewhere that affects their own interests and country. An AP man said that news is what a government official wants to read about somewhere else, whereas propaganda is what the official wants the world to read about his or her country. Politicians and government leaders in every nation attempt to manage or manipulate the news so that it favors their causes, their programs, their image.

Certainly before September 11 the news media, especially television and news magazines, paid less attention to foreign news. Always expensive to cover, the consensus in the news business has been that you can expect international news to turn a profit only when it is really domestic news in a foreign setting, such as a U.S. military intervention when it is "our boys" who are "over there," as in Afghanistan.

CBS News, long famed for its international coverage, once maintained twenty-four foreign bureaus. By 1995, it had reporters in only four capitals: London, Moscow, Tel Aviv, and Tokyo. Dan Rather told a group of Harvard students, "Don't kid yourself. The trend line in American journalism is away from, not toward, increased foreign coverage. Foreign coverage requires the most space and the most air time because you are dealing with complicated situations, in which you have to explain a lot. And then there's always somebody around who says people don't give a damn about this stuff anyway ... 'If you have to do something foreign, Dan, for heaven's sake, keep it short.'"³ But currently, the situation has changed.

The three major news magazines, each of which has long emphasized foreign news gathered by its own overseas correspondents, reflected the declining interest in international news. Throughout 1995, *Time* devoted 385 pages to international news, or about 14 percent of the magazine, yet ten years earlier, in 1985, *Time* published 670 pages of foreign news, or 24 percent of its news content. Circulation for *Time, Newsweek,* and *U.S. News* is sharply up with war news but, ominously, advertising revenue was lagging during 2001.

Changing Correspondents

"What is commonly referred to as the world flow of information," AP correspondent Mort Rosenblum wrote, "is more a series of trickles and spurts. News is moved across borders by a surprisingly thin network of correspondents.... The smaller countries are squeezed into rapid trips during lulls between major stories in the larger countries." Rosenblum quoted a comment from a Latin American academic that "news breaks in South America along the direct line of the international airline route."⁴

In some places it may seem that way, and yet the total flood of daily news reports from abroad is immense. One study estimated that the big four agencies send out about thirty-three million words a day, with seventeen million from AP, eleven million from UPI, 3.4 million for AFP, and 1.5 million from Reuters. Among the smaller agencies, dpa of Germany was set at 115,000, ANSA of Italy at 300,000, and efe of Spain at 500,000.

Considering the demand for foreign news and the difficulties of reporting from far-flung places, there are probably too few correspondents stationed overseas. Rising costs and inflation have made maintenance of a staffer overseas quite expensive. Estimates range from $150,000 to $250,000 for maintaining a newspaper bureau overseas (that is, at least one reporter) for one year, and the costs keep going up. A television bureau can cost more than $1 million a year. It is not surprising, therefore, that many news media rely on the news agencies for their foreign news. In America, that means the Associated Press.

AP and other news agencies are using more and more "locals"—nationals of countries they cover. Western journalism is increasingly relying on foreign nationals to help report the news. Foreign journalists are not only less expensive but often have a grasp of local languages and knowledge of their own countries that American journalists cannot match. Journalist Scott Schuster attributed the trend to a global acceptance of English as a media language and the global influence of American journalistic methods: "American influence is most profound among broadcasters, and foreign broadcast journalists need only to turn on their TV sets to receive lessons on how to do the news American-style," he said. Schuster goes on:

> American methods of news production are being adopted all across Western Europe and in many Third World countries. ... During the coming decade journalistic styles in both print and broadcast media are likely to experience continuing international homogenization. The nationality of the reporter will no longer be an issue. Brits will cover Britain. Ghanaians will cover Ghana, and a large number of American journalists will become "foreign correspondents"—covering America for foreign media.[5]

Increasingly, to deal with rising costs and tighter budgets, news media are relying on stringers or freelancers. A recent study by Stephen Hess of the Brookings Institution of 404 foreign correspondents working for U.S. news media found that 26 percent are freelancers. Moreover, more of these are underemployed, with 40 percent saying they do other work as well. All suffer the usual fate of freelancers: low pay, no benefits, and a precarious relationship with their employers.[6] Hess found six types of stringers: "spouses" of other correspondents; "experts," who know languages and the area; "adventurers," like Oriana Fallaci; "flingers," a person on a fling who might start a serious career; "ideologues" or "sympathizers," who are often British; and the "residents," who are often longtime residents and write occasional stories.

Although stringers and freelancers remain marginal, many prominent journalists started their careers that way, including Stanley Karnow, Elie Abel, Robert Kaiser, Elizabeth Pond, Caryle Murphy, and Daniel Shorr.

A significant change has been the increased number of women among foreign correspondents, especially as war reporters. Before 1970, their numbers were small, although there had been a few famous names: Dorothy Thompson, Martha Gellhorn, Marguerite Higgins, and Gloria

Emerson. Hess found that, by the 1970s, about 16 percent of new foreign reporters were women; this doubled during the 1980s to about 33 percent. This ratio of two men for every woman was also found in Washington media as well as in U.S. journalism generally.

Some women correspondents have earned outstanding reputations, including Caryle Murphy of the *Washington Post*, Robin Wright of the *Los Angeles Times*, syndicated columnist Georgie Ann Geyer, and Elaine Sciolino and Barbara Crossette, both of the *New York Times*. Christiane Amanpour of CNN has become a kind of celebrity because of her aggressive and frankly partisan reporting of such stories as the Gulf War, civil upheaval in Africa, civil war in Bosnia and in Afghanistan. A significant number of women have been covering the war in Afghanistan for western media.

Foreign correspondents today are better educated, know more foreign languages, and have higher-status backgrounds than their predecessors. Current salaries range from about $50,000 to $90,000, with more experienced reporters earning even more.

American reporters working abroad have been steadily increasing in number. A 1969 study found 929 Americans working abroad, including broadcasting. In 1972, the number dropped to 797; by 1975, there were only 676. But in 1990, there were 1,734 and, in 1993, the total neared 2,000.[7] A big part of the increase was due to more staffing abroad by business and economic publications and news services such as Reuters, Bloomberg, and Dow Jones.

Bureaus located in key capitals are a good indicator of a news medium's commitment to foreign coverage. And some papers, such as the *New York Times*, have more than one reporter per bureau, such as in Moscow. Among U.S. dailies maintaining overseas bureaus in 1994 were the *New York Times*, twenty-four bureaus; *Los Angeles Times*, twenty-two; *Washington Post*, nineteen; *The Wall Street Journal*, thirteen; *Christian Science Monitor*, thirteen; *Chicago Tribune*, eleven; *Baltimore Sun*, eight; and *Boston Globe*, five.

Among U.S. television broadcasters, CNN led the pack with nineteen bureaus, NBC had eleven, ABC had five, and CBS had four. In radio broadcasting, ABC Radio had nine bureaus, CBS had four, National Public Radio had three, and Mutual Radio/NBC had but one bureau.[8]

When not reporting a war, the networks increasingly seem to be relying on news film supplied by the syndicates, Reuters Television, APTV news and WTN, and other foreign broadcasters for international coverage. These less costly ways of collecting news have undermined the credibility of some foreign news. A few years ago if you saw a foreign news story on NBC News, chances are that it was reported by an NBC reporter at the scene with film shot by an NBC crew. Now the networks are relying more on less expensive, and often less experienced, free-lancers and independent contractors whose products are rarely identi-fied on the air, leaving the impression that the story was reported by network staffers. This practice gives rise to a growing concern about quality control. "By the time the tape gets on the air, nobody has the foggiest idea who made it and whether the pictures were staged," con-tended Tom Wolzien, a former NBC news executive.[9] More loss of authenticity results when U.S. network correspondents, based in Lon-don, add voice-overs to stories they did not cover. Bert Quint, former CBS correspondent said, "There's no reason to believe the person [doing the voice-over] because odds are he or she was not within 3,000 miles of where the story occurred."[10]

Not only are foreign correspondents comparatively few, they are unevenly distributed as well. One study found that more than half of all American reporters abroad were stationed in nineteen European countries. During the Persian Gulf crisis more than eight hundred Western reporters descended on the region, but few were experts on Middle Eastern affairs. Many of the hundreds covering the terrorism war in Afghanistan and Cen-tral Asia have had no previous overseas experience. Such "parachute jour-nalism" does not always provide informed coverage because so many of these reporters lack previous experience or understanding of the area about which they are reporting.

For American readers and listeners, serious questions have been raised about the quantity and quality of foreign news they receive. The debate tends to be circular. AP and other agencies have long maintained that their services gather ample amounts of foreign news but that their newspaper and broadcast clients do not use very much of it. The media clients in turn argue that their readers and viewers are not very much interested in foreign news. Yet critics say that Americans are uninformed about the world because their news media report so little about it. The widespread shock and fear felt by many Americans after the September 11 terror attacks was partially related to their lack of knowledge about terrorism and the Mid-dle East.

Certainly the generalization that the majority of Americans, with access to the world's most-pervasive media, are ill-informed about world affairs has substance. A panel at Columbia's School of Journalism criticized the audience:

There is a crisis in international news reporting in the United States—
and not one that should simply be blamed on the reporters, the gatekeepers, or the owners. We know there is stagnation, and even shrinkage,
in the number of international stories in the media and the number of
correspondents in the field for most U.S. media outlets. But the primary
reason for this decline is an audience that expresses less and less interest
in the international stories that do appear. What we're increasingly miss-
ing, as a culture, is connective tissue to bind us to the rest of the
world.[11]

Foreigners traveling in the American heartland are uniformly
impressed by the lack of world news in local media and the ignorance
shown by most Americans about the outside world. By contrast, the average German, Dane, or Israeli knows more global news because his or her
media carry more. Part of the problem is that Americans, like Russians and
Chinese, have a continental outlook, living as they do in the midst of a vast
land mass that encourages a self-centered, isolationist view of the world.
With two friendly neighbors and protected by two oceans, Americans are
slow to recognize their interdependence with others. It's too early to tell,
but September 11 may have modified that mindset.

Americans' interest in foreign news has its ups and downs, depending
on the perceived impact of any current crisis on their lives. During the
Vietnam War, much concern was focused on happenings in Southeast
Asia, but not in Latin America or Africa, where news coverage dropped off.
After Vietnam, foreign concerns receded as the nation became enthralled
by Watergate and its aftermath. But after the rapid increases and then
decreases in the price of foreign oil, the Soviet incursion into Afghanistan,
continuing Arab/Israeli conflict, and a rising level of terrorism directed
against Americans, the average American's interest (if not knowledge) in
foreign news, especially that of the Middle East, clearly increased. Then,
during the summer of 1990 after Iraq invaded Kuwait and American forces
were moved into Saudi Arabia before war began in January 1991, American interest in and anxiety about the Persian Gulf soared. At that same
time, U.S. concern about the economic and political turmoil of the Soviet
Union and Eastern Europe seemed low considering the severity of the
crises in the Gulf region. (Americans, and their media, seem to be able to
concentrate on only one crisis at a time.)

In late 1994 and early 1995, interest in foreign news plummeted as
the U.S. news media became mesmerized with the murder trial of O.J.
Simpson and the domestic politics of the Republicans' legislative zeal in

Washington, D.C., after winning control of Congress in the November 1994 elections.

In 1998, the nation's prosperity and the continuing story about President Clinton's personal problems seemed to push foreign news off the nation's news agenda, at least for a while. The continuing crises in the former Yugoslavia, Iraq, and Israel and the teetering Asian and Russian economies did not go away; they just seemed less urgent and less visible. By mid-1998, nuclear tests by India and Pakistan and the possibility of war in South Asia brought a heightened interest in foreign news. The aerial war over Kosovo and Serbia led by America and NATO held the spotlight while it lasted. But terror attacks of 9/11 have brought a sea change in Americans' attitude toward the outside world. Many were clearly frightened and saw themselves as vulnerable to perils faced by Israelis and many Europeans.

Before the 9/11 moment of truth, some believed that television had profoundly affected Americans' news perceptions. Neil Postman believes television projects a "peek-a-boo" world, "where now this event, now that, pops into view for a moment, then vanishes again. It is a world without much sense or coherence. ... Americans know of a lot of things but about almost nothing. Someone is considered well informed who simply knows that a plane was hijacked or that there was an earthquake in Mexico City."[12]

Despite ignorance of the world, there is a growing recognition that perhaps the term "foreign news" is a misnomer and that in our interdependent world we are potentially affected by any event almost anywhere. Failing overseas economies threaten the U.S. stock market and prosperity. American workers who lose jobs in manufacturing due to cheap foreign imports or farmers unable to sell wheat abroad due to the overvalued dollar are becoming more knowledgeable about world economic trends. And the Iraq war and later bombings reminded Americans again of their dependence on Middle Eastern oil and the lack of a conservation policy to deal with that dependence. Since September 11, many Americans for the first time now believe they could die in a terrorist attack.

The reporting of foreign news has been criticized as being too crisis oriented. An ABC News poll found that among viewers polled, 55 percent said, "Television news only does stories about foreign countries when there's a war or some other violent crisis going on."[13] Media critic Hodding Carter said the networks "concentrate on showing kids throwing rocks at troops or guns going off or planes bombing or rubble falling. These are the repetitive images that block out the complexities." In addition, he cited the "extraordinary lack of continuity and perspective, which is the shadow of all television news."[14] Inevitably, much of what happens in the world will go unnoted. Wherever he or she may be, the average person obviously does not have the time or interest to follow all the news from everywhere. As one editor asked, "Who wants to read about Zaire if there is nothing going on there?" Gerald Long of Reuters explained more fully: "The prevalent school of journalism throughout the world is a 'journalism of exception.' In other words, you don't report that everything is fine in Pakistan. You report that there has been an air crash."[15] This approach contributes to an inevitable imbalance and distortion of reality.

The journalism of exception—reporting civil unrest, the coup d'etat, the train wreck, the drought—is at the root of much hostility and antagonism toward Western reporting. Journalists who work abroad say it is difficult to gain access to many parts of the world, particularly Africa, the Middle East, and Asia.

Journalists have had particular difficulty in reporting the eight-year conflict between Iran and Iraq and the prolonged civil war involving Serbia, Bosnia, Croatia, and Kosovo. In its early stages, the war in Afghanistan was dangerous and challenging to report. Before 9/11, in India, the foreign cable networks, CNN and BBC's World Service Television, became a target for Indian politicians looking for scapegoats to blame for secessionist movements, religious strife, and natural disasters. India's own television network, Doordarshan, owned and controlled by the government, is well known for delaying and sanitizing news broadcasts. CNN and BBC came to India in 1991 while reporting the Gulf War and later aggressively reported the razing of the Babri Mosque in late 1993 by Hindu fundamentalists, which led to national riots in which 1,800 died. In response, Indian political leaders of both left and right demanded strong action against the networks. However, when things go in favor of the politicians, they praise foreign coverage.[16]

A major point of contention, as mentioned, is that most governments believe the press, including foreign reporters, should serve the host country's national aims, whereas the Western press believes it must decide for itself what news to report.

Physical Dangers

Foreign correspondents often risk their lives to cover wars, civil unrest, and other forms of violence. Within unstable nations, journalists, both foreign and domestic, are often singled out as targets for arrest, beatings, or assassination. Sometimes they are just in the wrong place at the wrong time.

Algeria, beset by a long struggle between an authoritarian government and a militant Islamic opposition, has proved a deadly place to report the news: As of January 1998, 70,000 to 80,000 people have been massacred. Since 1993, some sixty Algerian journalists have been murdered because of their profession. In 2001, two more Algerians were slain. Many Algerian journalists have gone underground, fled into exile, or left the profession.

The admirable Committee to Protect Journalists keeps track of such violence and reported that during 2001, thirty-seven journalists were killed because of their work. The toll by country was as follows: Afghanistan, nine; Algeria, two; Bangladesh, one; Bolivia, one; China, one; Colombia, three; Costa Rica, one; Georgia, one; Guatemala, one; Haiti, one; India, one; Latvia, one; Mexico, one; the Palestinian territories, one; Paraguay, one; the Philippines, two; Russia, one; Thailand, two; Ukraine, one; U.S., two; the United Kingdom, one; and Yugoslavia, two. One of the U.S. cases was a freelancer who had rushed to the World Trade Center to report the story; the other died of inhalation anthrax during the anthrax attacks. (In 2000, twenty-four journalists were killed worldwide.)

In Afghanistan, the eight journalists and cameramen were slain in about a week's time, one of the highest tolls in the shortest time span for journalists. In contrast, during the same period, no U.S. military fatalities had been reported in that country since U.S. Special Forces began operating about a month earlier. That all fatalities were non-American journalists was a reminder of how committed many news organizations around the world were to the pursuit of the story.

In February 2002, Daniel Pearl of *The Wall Street Journal* became the tenth journalist and among the first several American newsmen to die covering September 11 and its aftermath. While investigating a terrorist in Pakistan, Pearl was kidnapped by terrorists, held hostage for several weeks, and then executed.

Governments and warring armies are not the only foes of press freedom; sometimes terrorists and thugs attack the press. Louis Boccardi, president of AP, said, "On the international scene, the world continues to grow more difficult to cover. The physical dangers abound. Dozens of journalists have been killed in the last few years and many more injured in the pursuit of a story, their story, wherever it was."[17]

Finally, it should be said that the Western practice of "journalism of exception" continues to rankle critics of the press everywhere. In America, many feel that the media report far too much negative news. But as Daniel

Patrick Moynihan said, "It is the mark of a democracy that its press is filled with bad news. When one comes to a country where the press is filled with good news, one can be pretty sure that the jails are filled with good men."

The reporting of modern wars—their own wars—have presented special challenges to American and British news media in recent years. That problem is discussed in the next chapter.

Notes

1. Leon Hadar, "Covering the New World Disorder," *Columbia Journalism Review*, July/August 1994, 27.
2. Ibid.
3. Stephen Hess, *International News & Foreign Correspondents* (Washington, D.C.: Brookings Institution, 1996), 61.
4. Mort Rosenblum, *Who Stole the News?* (New York: John Wiley & Sons, 1993), 20.
5. Scott Schuster, "Foreign Competition Hits the News," *Columbia Journalism Review*, May/June 1988, 45.
6. Stephen Hess, "The Cheaper Solution," *American Journalism Review*, April 1994, 27.
7. Rosenblum, *Who Stole the News?*, 18.
8. Hess, "The Cheaper Solution," 29.
9. Hess, *International News & Foreign Correspondents*, 100.
10. Ibid.
11. "World News: Truth or Consequences," *Columbia Journalism Review*, January/February 1995, 4.
12. Sally Bedell Smith, "How New Technologies are Starting to Change the Nation's Viewing Habits," *New York Times*, October 9, 1985, sec. A, 10.
13. Sally Bedell Smith, "Why TV News Can't Be A Complete View of the World," *New York Times*, August 8, 1982, entertainment section, 1.
14. Ibid.
15. Rosemary Righter, *Whose News: Politics, the Press and the Third World* (New York: Times Books, 1978), p. 70.
16. Arthur J. Pais, "Anger in India," *Columbia Journalism Review*, May/June 1993, 17.
17. Mark Fitzgerald, "A Dangerous Affair," *Editor & Publisher*, November 2, 1985, 18.

CHAPTER 10
Covering the World's Hot Spots

The first casualty when war comes is truth.
—Senator Hiram Johnson, 1917

Three recent wars—the 1991 Persian Gulf War, the aerial war over Serbia and Kosovo, and the war against terrorism—have dramatically altered the ways that armed conflicts are reported to America and the world. Although long-standing frictions and suspicions persist between the press and military officials, the use of new communication techologies has altered journalism for better or worse.

In the forty-two–day Gulf War, television and especially CNN turned much of the world into a global community witnessing a televised real-time war as the brief conflict evolved from armed confrontation to spectacular aerial bombardment and finally to lightning ground warfare. The war became the biggest global news story in years and telling it utilized the full resources of the U.S. news media and much of the international news system as well. More than 1,600 print and broadcast journalists were on hand to report it.

The 1999 NATO bombing campaign against Serbia as its ground forces were mauling Kosovo civilians was a new kind of war: an effort, mainly by U.S. air power, to bomb a nation into submission without deploying ground troops or even incurring casualities. As in the Gulf War, the U.S. press accused the military of withholding news and of "spinning" combat reports for political and strategic reasons. The seventy-eight days of NATO bombing finally forced Yugoslavian dictator Slobodan Milosevic to yield and permit 16,000 NATO soldiers to chase the fleeing Serbian forces out of Kosovo and thus bring relief to the battered ethnic Albanians. In this last war of the twentieth century, global news coverage was greatly facilitated by the satellite telephone, twenty-four–hour cable TV coverage, and, for the first time, the Internet.

During the opening months of the September 11 war on terrorism, press and military relationships were still evolving in this latest war that

President Bush said could last for many years and never reach a clear-cut conclusion. The Bush administration made it clear that the press would receive less access to combat-related information than in previous conflicts. Yet the news media, here and abroad, poured out a steady torrent of news, speculation, commentary, and pictures about this many-faceted conflict. The world of 2001 was more completely "wired" for 24/7 coverage. The U.S. government found that by controlling information so tightly, it was failing to make clear to Americans and to the world what its war aims and goals were. Yet one of the reasons that modern democracies are usually successful in warfare is that through public debate and even protest, ineffective policies and goals can be modified and improved.

Background of Press Controls

How did the abrasive relations between American journalists and the U.S. military come to this point? In World War I, some five hundred American correspondents covered the conflict for newspapers, magazines, and press associations in France and, unlike British and French reporters, they were free to go to the front lines without military escorts. Still, everything written by such star reporters as Richard Harding Davis, Will Irwin, or Floyd Gibbons was passed through the censorship of the press section of the Military Intelligence Service. Details about specific battles, numbers of casualties, and names of units could be released only after being mentioned in official communiques.

U.S. miltary censorship followed the same general pattern in World War II with the added feature of controlling radio broadcasts. The Office of Censorship was headed by Byron Price, a former AP editor, who handled with distinction the most difficult part of his job: the direction of voluntary press censorship that applied to print media outside the combat zones. In far-flung combat "theaters," reporters were generally free to move about and join military units but were always subject to possible censorship. About five hundred full-time American reporters were abroad at any one time and provided coverage that many considered the best and fullest ever seen. With mobile units and tape recordings, radio coverage greatly increased. Relations between the military and reporters were mutually trusting and supportive. Despite occasional conflicts over withheld information, everyone seemed to be on the same team. During the Korean war, the press-government relations were pretty much the same.

The change began in the 1960s Vietnam War when relations soured and reached their lowest ebb. Reporters and camera crews, working within military guidelines, were given free access without field censorship to roam Vietnam; some called it the best-reported war in history. Yet many in the U.S. military believed critical press reporting contributed to the American defeat by over-stressing negative aspects, including graphic pictures of dead and wounded, highlighting scandals such as the My Lai massacre, and misinterpreting key events, such as the Tet offensive, which the military pronounced a defeat for North Vietnam and not a Vietcong victory as the press reported. Such reports, the military argued, aided the antiwar movement at home.

The war reporters felt that the U.S. military had misled and lied to them in Vietnam and that officials consistently painted a much rosier picture of the war than the facts justified. Given the record of deception, the press, it was argued, was correct in being skeptical of the military. A view prevailed within the military that the free rein given reporters in Vietnam led to reporting that seriously damaged morale and turned American public opinion against its own troops. If news or information is a weapon, then, the generals argued, it should be controlled as part of the war effort.

The brief war in 1982 between Britain and Argentina over the Falkland Islands in the South Atlantic provided a model for the Pentagon on how to manage the press during wartime. Only British reporters were permitted to accompany the task force, and reporters were carefully selected. The seventeen journalists chosen had to accept censorship at the source and were given a government handbook telling them they would be "expected to help in leading and steadying public opinion in times of national stress or crisis." The Ministry of Defence effectively imposed censorship at the source, and most war information followed a policy of suppression or subtle control of emphasis. After the war was over, the British press gave a very different picture of the conflict, detailing losses, mishaps, and failures previously unreported.

For America, the war news issue surfaced again on October 25, 1983 when U.S. forces invaded the tiny island of Grenada. The Defense Department barred all reporters from covering the initial invasion. After two days of rigorous protests from the press, a pool of twelve reporters was finally flown in with a military escort. By the end of one week, with the fighting winding down, 150 reporters were ferried to the island and allowed to stay overnight. The press, however, was not mollified. Walter Cronkite said the Reagan Administration had seriously erred, arguing, "This is our foreign policy and we have a right to know what is happening and there can be no excuse in denying the people that right."[1] But as in the later Gulf War, opinion polls showed that the public supported the ban on press coverage. As a result of the furor, the Defense Department appointed a commission that recommended that a select pool of reporters be allowed to cover the early stages of any surprise military operation and share its information with other press organizations. This seems a fair compromise between the military's need for surprise and the public's need for information. The new guidelines were first tested in December 1989 when U.S. forces invaded Panama. The press arrangements failed miserably. The Pentagon did not get the sixteen-reporter pool into Panama until four hours after fighting began, and reporters were not allowed to file stories until six hours later. Most critics blamed the White House for the mix-up and for insisting that only the military facilitate press coverage. When the Persian Gulf war loomed, the American generals, Colin Powell and Norman Schwarzkopf, and other Vietnam veterans were ready to deal with the press.

War with Saddam Hussein

Global television came into its own as CNN and other broadcasters reported a war as it was happening, or as it appeared to be happening—a "real time" war. After hostilities began early on January 17, 1991, reporters described antiaircraft tracers in the night sky of Baghdad and flashes of bomb explosions on the horizon. On succeeding nights, viewers were provided with live video reports from Tel Aviv and Riyadh of Scud missiles, some apparently intercepted by Patriot missiles, exploding against the night sky, and of television reporters donning gas masks on camera. The press talked of the "CNN effect"— millions anchored hour after hour to their television sets lest they miss the latest dramatic development. Restaurants, movies, hotels, and gaming establishments all suffered business losses. "People are intensely interested in the first real-time war in history and they are just planting themselves in front of their television sets," one expert said. Ratings for CNN soared five to ten times their prewar levels.[2] The Gulf War was a worldwide media event of astonishing proportions. Global television had never had a larger or more interested audience for such a sustained period of time. Television became the first and principal source of news for most people, as well as a major source of military and political intelligence for both sides. CNN telecasts, including military briefings, were viewed in Baghdad as they were being received in Riyadh or Washington, D.C.—as well as in other non-Western countries.

The combatants, particularly the governments of Iraq and the United States, tried to control and manipulate the media with subtle and not-so-subtle propaganda and misinformation messages. Western journalists chafed at the restraints on news coverage of the war itself and complained that there was much news they were not permitted to report. Most coalition news came from military briefings and from carefully controlled and escorted "pools" of reporters. Some official news presented at the briefings was actually disinformation intended to mislead the enemy, not to inform the public. For example, viewers were led to believe that Patriot missiles were invariably successful in neutralizing Scud missiles, but such was not the case.

Information was tightly controlled; one observer called it "the illusion of news." For its own self-defined security reasons, the military often held back or distorted the news it did release. In the opening days of the war, much was made of the "smart bombs" that hit their targets with about 90 percent accuracy. After the war, the U.S. Air Force admitted that smart bombs made up only 7 percent of all U.S. explosives dropped on Iraq and Kuwait. The Air Force later said that 70 percent of the 88,500 tons of bombs dropped on Kuwait and Iraq missed their targets.[3]

Peter Jennings of ABC News reminded viewers that much of what was revealed in the opening days of war was speculation, mixed with some hard facts and some rumors in the rushing river of information. But whether they were getting hard news or not, many millions of viewers stayed by their television sets. Public opinion polls showed that the overwhelming majority of Americans supported both the war and the military's efforts to control news; further, some thought there should be more controls on press reporting. A *Los Angeles Times* Mirror poll found that half of the respondents considered themselves obsessed with war news, but nearly 80 percent felt that the military was "telling as much as it can." About the same proportion thought that military censorship may be a "good idea."

But after the war, many in the press felt that the traditional right of U.S. reporters to accompany their combat forces and report news of war had been severely circumscribed. Michael Getler of the *Washington Post* wrote, "The Pentagon and U.S. Army Central Command conducted what is probably the most thorough and consistent wartime control of American reporters in modern times—a set of restrictions that in its totality and mind-set seemed to go beyond World War II, Korea, and Vietnam."[4]

President George Bush and the Pentagon followed a deliberate policy of blocking negative and unflattering news from the U.S. public lest it weaken support for the war. Long after the conflict, the public learned that some Iraqi soldiers had been buried alive in trenches by U.S. plows and earthmovers and that the military had waited months to tell the families of thirty-three dead soldiers that their loved ones had been killed by friendly fire. Not until a year after the war did the public learn that key weapons such as the stealth bomber and the cruise missile had struck only about half of their targets, compared with the 85 to 90 percent rate claimed by the Pentagon at the time.[5] American casualties were reported, but there were few pictures of dead and wounded. Details of tactical failures and mishaps in the bombing campaign were not released, nor was the information that at least twenty-four female soldiers had been raped or sexually assaulted by American servicemen.

The older generation of military leaders had long believed, despite evidence to the contrary, that critical press coverage in Vietnam had contributed to the U.S. defeat there. They were determined it would not happen again. Some journalists blamed their own top editors and news executives for agreeing ahead of time to the field censorship and pool arrangements instead of vigorously opposing them.

But the shooting war itself was quite a media spectacle, which started just as the evening news programs were beginning at 6:30 Eastern Standard Time (January 16 in the United States; January 17 in the Middle East). The networks and CNN interrupted their prepared news shows to report that aerial bombing had begun in Baghdad. Then followed one of most memorable nights in television history: the opening phases of a major conflict reported in real time by reporters in Iraq, Saudi Arabia, and Washington.

CNN stole the show that night as three CNN correspondents, John Holliman, Peter Arnett, and Bernard Shaw, gave vivid eyewitness descriptions of the U.S. air attack from the windows of their Baghdad hotel room. As in old-time radio, reporters relied on words, not video, that first night. Other networks reported the fireworks, but CNN with its previously arranged leased lines stayed on the longest after the lines were cut for the other networks. The next day, General Colin Powell jokingly said that the Pentagon was relying on CNN for military information. The second night gave prime-time viewers another long, absorbing evening when CNN and NBC reporters in Tel Aviv reported live as Scud missiles landed. Reporters, often wearing gas masks, provided raw and unevaluated information. At one point, NBC reported dramatically that nerve gas had been detected in one Scud attack. Tom Brokaw decried the situation for some minutes, but, after the report proved false, NBC apologized. For the first three days, people everywhere stayed glued to television and radio sets, including shortwave receivers. Networks expanded to near twenty-four–hour coverage for the first thirty-six hours, and even the daytime soap operas were preempted briefly for war coverage. There was not that much to report at that point, and the same facts, theories, and speculations were repeated again and again. Nevertheless, the mesmerized public stayed tuned.

During this early bombing phase of the war, the Pentagon withheld detailed military information, such as the extent of the bombing and destruction within Iraq. Restrictions were placed on interviews with troops and returning pilots. Reporters could cover field combat only in designated pools, with groups of reporters being accompanied by an escort officer. (One reporter likened a press pool to a group of senior citizens on a conducted tour.) All interviews with soldiers were subject to censorship before they could be released.

Most information came from the daily briefings held by military spokespersons in both Riyadh, Saudi Arabia, and at the Pentagon, but much of this was rather general, vague, and lacking in detail. The military had coherent arguments for its restrictive policies. Destroying Iraq's military command and communications capability was a high priority of the bombing strategy, and it was important to withhold useful information, via the media, that would reveal troop movements and intentions of coalition forces. Keeping Iraq's forces off balance and without reliable information was a key part of U.S. strategy. However, some news executives and critics claimed that the press restrictions went well beyond security concerns and appeared aimed at both preventing politically damaging disclosures by soldiers and shielding the American public from seeing the brutal aspects of war. If the war had gone badly, the press would have had difficulty reporting the negative aspects. With more than 1,600 reporters in the theater, only about one hundred could be accommodated by the pools to report on the American force of five hundred thousand. As the ground war neared, the large press corps became increasingly restive and frustrated at this lack of access.

The response of some reporters was to "freelance"—to avoid the pools and go off on their own. Malcolm Browne reported, "Some reporters were hiding out in American Marine or Army field units, given GI uniforms and gear to look inconspicuous, enjoying the affection (and protection) of the units they're trying to cover—concealed by the officers and troops from the handful of press-hating commanders who strive to keep the battlefield free of wandering journalists."[6] Browne noted that nearly all reporters who tried to reach front-line U.S. troops were arrested at one time or another (including reporters for the *New York Times, Washington Post,* Associated

Press, and Cox papers), sometimes held in field jails for up to twelve hours and threatened with revocation of their press credentials. After the ground war began, these freelancers, particularly John Kifner and Chris Hedges of the *New York Times*, produced some outstanding reportage. Forrest Sawyer of "ABC News," who traveled unofficially with Saudi forces, provided some of the earliest and best reports on the freeing of Kuwait City.

Had the ground war been longer, more heavily contested, and taken a higher toll of U.S. casualties, relations between the military and the free-lancing journalists probably could have turned quite acrimonious. But these journalists felt that they were doing what they were supposed to do in time of war: maintain the flow of information that Americans need to know when half a million of them are at risk in a foreign war.

Triumph of Twenty-Four–Hour Global News

During the American Civil War, in 1861–1865, the demand for news was so great that U.S. newspapers for the first time went to seven-day publication. During the 1963 Kennedy assassination, live television emerged as the preeminent medium for reporting breaking news. This story positioned ABC, CBS, and NBC as major news gatherers, but as still reaching essentially U.S. audiences.

During the forty-two–day Gulf War, CNN established the importance of a twenty-four–hour news network with true global reach. The concept has certainly changed the international news system, especially during times of international crisis and conflict. The three major U.S. networks were shaken by CNN's success. After CNN's historic scoop on the first night of the war, a number of independent television stations, radio stations, and even several network affiliates relied on CNN in the crisis. Although the three networks had more talented and experienced reporters, they could not compete with CNN either in time on the air or in the vast audiences CNN reached in about one hundred countries. The success of CNN encouraged similar services, such as BBC's World Service Television.

The Gulf War certainly conditioned viewers everywhere to keep their television sets tuned to CNN (or its later cable imitators) during times of high crisis. Newsrooms from Milwaukee to Cairo to Shanghai routinely keep a television set tuned to CNN or BBC for the first report of any global crisis. Perhaps the news business today places too much emphasis on immediate and fast-breaking news "as it happens." Video shots of F15s roaring off runways, of "smart bombs" scoring direct hits, of Tomahawk missiles flying through Baghdad, and of tank formations rolling through the desert made memorable viewing. But after the fog of war had cleared, the press and the public found that the Gulf War was not quite what they thought it was.

The tragic events in the volatile Middle East also reminded the public that wars and political crises are complex and intricate processes that can still best be reported and explained by the printed word. The best and most complete reporting of the Gulf War came ultimately from print media, which rounded out the picture and provided the context and perspective necessary for full understanding. During the first several weeks after the cease-fire, it was the print reporters, not television, who dug out and filled in the details of what actually happened during the air campaign and the brief ground war—details that the military on both sides had so effectively screened from public view.

Wars between nations are by definition major international news stories and should be reported by the press as completely and thoroughly as conditions permit. The American public may be blasé about much foreign news but it certainly pays close attention when American armed forces go to war. Yet governments at war, even the most democratic, will try to control and manipulate war news to their own strategic and political advantage. The Gulf War provided ample reminders of this generalization. Censorship and propaganda, the twin arms of political warfare, are integral components of modern warfare, so both sides often deny their own press the opportunity to report what has occurred.

From all indications, the U.S. military as well as the first Bush administration were pleased with the results of their media policy and would do the same thing again—as has been happening in Afghanistan. But among American and British journalists, there was a general conclusion that the press had been unduly and even illegally denied access to information about the Gulf War.

After the Gulf War, a report that called military restrictions in the Gulf War "real censorship" that confirmed "the worst fears of reporters in a democracy" was delivered to Defense Secretary Dick Cheney. It was signed by seventeen news executives representing the four networks, the AP and UPI, and major newspapers and news magazines. The report bitterly complained that the restrictions placed on reporters by the Pentagon were intended to promote a sanitized view of the war. The war was called the first in this century to restrict all official coverage to pools. "By controlling what reporters saw and when they saw it, the military exerted great power to shape and manage the news," the report said. Also criticized were the use of military escorts and "unwarranted delays in transmitting copy."[7] After more than eight months of talks with news executives, the Pentagon in May 1992 issued a set of principles intended to guarantee that journalists have greater access to future military operations than they had in the Gulf War. However, news media and the government could not agree on whether there should be any official "security review" of news reports before they are published or broadcast. The statement affirmed that "open and independent reporting will be the principal means of coverage of U.S. military operations. The guidelines limited the role of military escorts and said that 'press pools' are not to serve as the standard means of covering operations."[8]

Other Conflicts

Subsequent military operations in Somalia, Haiti, and Bosnia have not really provided an adequate test of these new principles. But certainly the Gulf War showed that despite all the wonders of rapid or instant communication (and perhaps in part because of them), the Western news media still can be severely restricted by their own democratic governments in wartime.

The incursion of U.S. Marines into Somalia in December 1992 was intended to provide military protection to the relief organizations trying to feed starving Somalis caught in the cross fire of warring clans. Under these conditions, the Pentagon decided to place no restraints on the media. Howard Kurtz called what happened the most embarrassing moment ever in media-military relations: "...the infamous night in December 1992 when Navy SEALS hitting the beach in Somalia were surrounded by a small army of reporters and photographers who blinded them with television lights, clamored for interviews, and generally acted like obnoxious adolescents. That sorry performance, turning a humanitarian mission to aid starving Africans into a Felliniesque photo op, underscored what the Pentagon had been saying for years: that the press simply could not discipline itself, that reporters would blithely endanger the safety of American troops for the sake of journalistic drama."[9] It was not one of the news media's finer days.

David Hackworth of *Newsweek* wrote, "To lurch from thought control to no control is plain stupid. When the press corps beats the Marine Corps to the beach, everyone loses."[10] The Pentagon wanted full coverage of Somalia, so no controls were placed on the press, and what resulted was a confused circus. There are those, however, who suspected that the Pentagon deliberately orchestrated the fiasco to make the media look bad. Somalia raised the question of whether the media, by its heavy barrage of pictures and stories of starving Somalis, had pushed President Bush during his last days in office to send troops on their humanitarian mission. The answer is unclear, but Bush did react by committing U.S. armed forces to a limited and supposedly feasible assignment of famine relief. When the Somalia assignment expanded in the early Clinton administration to include warlord hunting, it provoked a devastating firefight in the streets of Mogadishu. When eighteen U.S. soldiers were killed and the pictures shown on U.S. television, the American public was unprepared to accept casualties when vital U.S. interests were not at stake. The White House soon announced that the United States was getting out of Somalia.

James Hoge, editor of *Foreign Affairs*, commented, "From its understanding of Vietnam came the military's subsequent emphasis on quick solutions, limited media access and selective release of 'smart' weapons imagery. The public, however, will not remain dazzled when interventions become difficult. As in Vietnam, public attitudes ultimately hinge on questions about the rightness, purpose and costs of policy—not television images."[11]

NATO's Air War over Yugoslavia

After NATO bombs started falling on Serbia and Kosovo in 1999, military relations with the press deteriorated abruptly. Critics protested that the lack of detailed after-action reports—routinely provided in earlier conflicts—made it impossible to assess NATO's claims that they were steadily dismantling Milosevic's war-making powers. At both the Pentagon and Brussels NATO headquarters, spokespersons stubbornly refused to provide specific information about bombing sorties. These policies were considered even less forthcoming than in the Gulf War, which the press had considered overly restrictive. Of course, NATO had its reasons: the need to hold the somewhat reluctant alliance together and the need to retain the support of the American public for military action. But most journalists covering the war were highly critical.

Yet the war was reported and, in some basic ways, differently from others. After being forced to watch seventy-eight days of bombing through the lenses of official video cameras, some 2,700 journalists had a chance to see for themselves when NATO troops rolled into Kosovo in June 1999.

Even though military censors blocked specific information, satellite communications enabled reporters from Brussels to Kukes, Albania, and other points to triangulate information more easily than in earlier wars. According to editors, the key device for putting together information into coherent stories was the satellite telephone and more broadly, satellite communications. The satellite uplink was the key information medium for the air war. "Instantaneous communication has changed everything," said Andrew Rosenthal, foreign editor of the *New York Times*. "The ability of a reporter on the Macedonian border to call a reporter on the Albanian border or to call a reporter in Brussels or Washington instantly made a huge difference. Newspapers were able to put together groups of reporters to do joint efforts in a way that was previously impossible," he said.[12]

For television, the same satellite technology allowed a profusion of images to be transmitted at great speed. Whether the vivid video showed the fate of Kosovar refugees or fleeing Serbian troops, the emotional impact of television was great indeed. Some thought such reportage helped to justify the humanitarian aspects of the hostilities and convinced otherwise dubious viewers to support the NATO effort. The expanded role for the Internet and cable television news meant that there were far more outlets for instantaneous reporting and analysis. CNN, MSNBC, and Fox Cable Channel also offered frequent and compelling debates about the conflict, even though much of it was discounted by critics as lacking in depth and context. For the first time, the Internet was a player in war reporting, providing a plethora of Web sites presenting war issues and other information from diverse viewpoints: Serbian, Albanian, Republican, Democratic; and ranging from the in-depth reporting of the BBC to the erratic sensationalism of Belgrade news outlets. As a result, some observers thought that the sum total of these trends amounted to sharper, speedier coverage. David Halberstam wrote: "Despite all the restrictions and just God-awful limitations and dangers, there were enough different people in different places to give you the dimensions you needed."[13]

Even though CNN had more competition this time—BBC World, MSNBC, and Fox—than in the Gulf War, the Atlanta cable network emerged from the Yugoslav conflict in a much-enhanced *international* role for its news dissemination as a global twenty-four–hour cable news channel. During the Gulf War, some ten million households outside the United States had access to CNN. In the Yugoslav war, the number jumped to 150 million households.

The air war in Yugoslavia demonstrated that the democracies of America and NATO were unwilling to be candid and forthcoming with reliable information to their own peoples while engaged in hostile actions against other states. As in the Gulf War, the Pentagon gave misleading and exaggerated accounts of the effectiveness of the bombing campaign. Yet despite such deceptions, the events surrounding the air war also showed that today's news organizations can still get much of the news out if they pursue the events with vigor and imagination and make use of their varied tools of communications technology.

Opening of War against Terrorism

The world's press—mainly Americans and Europeans—geared up to cover the war in Afghanistan with essentially the same technologies as well as the limited access to the battlefields that characterized NATO's air war with Yugoslavia two years earlier. But now, global audiences were larger and the news flow, from many more reporters, was much heavier. Unlike earlier wars, individual reporters can now deliver news from war zones in real time, but often they may have less to tell. Because the military sharply limits access and thus what reporters can know, the war reporter is not in a position to decide what is appropriate and safe to report. Basically, the military today is very uneasy with new media technology. The old battlefield censorship is no longer feasible because reporters carry their means of transmission (that is, satellite phones and video phones) with them. More and more, reporters are kept away from troops and military organizations. As a result, much of what is considered "war coverage" has originated in the Pentagon press briefing room. Today, the global audience is accustomed to getting its news quickly and often. People will check their favorite Web sites four or five times a day, or tune in to twenty-four–hour cable stations for the latest developments.

As mentioned earlier, the Afghanistan war may go down in history as our first "videophone war." From the earliest days of the conflict, the closest views of the fighting were provided in live reports by reporters using videophones, which are literally cameras plugged into satellite phones. The videophone has enabled television news crews to venture out to remote and dangerous areas of Afghanistan untethered to the more cumbersome satellite uplinks that can weigh over a ton. The videophone can fit into two briefcases, one with one or two satellite phones and the other with the videophone. With that and a car battery, they are ready to roll. The videophone is actually a variation on videoconferencing, which businesses have used for years. The video-phones, at about $8,000 each, combine videoconferencing equipment with "store and forward" technology that helps compress very high bandwidth feeds so that they can be transmitted by satellite. The satellite phones also cost about $8,000 each. Early in the war, much of what the public saw and heard on television seemed to come from a correspondent reporting live via a videophone from a remote location in Afghanistan.

The networks have also been using the "traditional" satellite uplinks in places such as Islamabad, Pakistan, to complement the videophones. Videophone reporting has been criticized for being "too sketchy" or almost "undecipherable." Yet the technology will only improve over time, and it does get the television reporter closer to the battlefield.

But what the press has gained in time and convenience, it has lost in access to the military itself. For families of servicemen and women, this was not considered a good precedent. News about casualties caused by "friendly fire" and other battlefield mishaps tend not to be reported if there are no reporters on the ground. The press has been likened to an uncle representing the family. They go to the front line and say, "Well, how is Johnny doing? What's going on here? Who's running this operation? Are there needless frontal assaults?" Walter Cronkite has said that there is another reason people should care about how the military operates: "We must know what they are doing in our name."[14] But so far, the journalists' concerns have not yet aroused similar concern from the public. As noted in a recent survey by the Pew Research Center, half of the respondents said the military should have more control over war news than news media have.

During the opening months of the Afghan war, almost all significant information was released from the Pentagon, far from the battlefields, and much of it was considered dated and vague. The extremely restrictive policy toward release of information was set by Defense Secretary Rumsfeld, who said that the nature of the war against terrorism made the constraints necessary. Rumsfeld several times stated that defense officials who leak information may be in violation of federal criminal law. Because the war reporters could not accompany military units in combat zones, reporters early in the Afghan war had to do what they did decades ago in Cambodia: strike out on their own. The Afghan situation may be the most dangerous of modern times. As noted previously, eight correspondents were killed in the first several weeks. As one critic said, we know less but we are more of a target.

First Amendment Concerns

From Grenada to Panama to the Persian Gulf and, recently, to Afghanistan, the press has been barred from fully covering wars or military incursions that it has historically and traditionally reported. This is important because the U.S. Supreme Court has ruled that the press, in order to inform the public, has a First Amendment right to those places that "historically" and "traditionally" it has had the right to cover, such as trials and town meetings. The Supreme Court has also ruled that the press has a First Amendment right to be present at all "public" events. Certainly an invasion lasting more than several hours or a full-scale war is a public event.

Perhaps the press's Constitutional rationale for war coverage was best expressed by Justice Hugo Black in the Pentagon Papers case:

> The Government's power to censor the press was abolished so that the press would remain forever free to censure the Government. The press was protected so that it could bare the secrets of government and inform the people. Only a free and unrestrained press can effectively expose deception in government. And paramount among the responsibilities of a free press is the duty to prevent any part of the government from deceiving the people and sending them off to distant lands to die of foreign fevers and foreign shot and shell.[15]

The press has no "right" to report sensitive military information that could aid an enemy, nor would it want to do so, but it does have a right to be there, to keep a watchful eye on the military, just as it does on the proceedings of a criminal trial. No modern wars have been fought as quickly and effectively, and with as few allied casualties, as by the U.S.-led forces in the Gulf War and the recent war against the Taliban. But when wars go badly, as they often can, with incompetent leadership, confused tactics, and unnecessary casualties, it is essential that the press, as independent representatives of the public and of the forces themselves, be there to report then or later what occurred. The people of Iraq and Afghanistan had no independent press reporting back to them about the military disasters and political incompetence that led to the battlefield deaths of thousands of their young men—a basic difference between a democracy and a dictatorship.

The Supreme Court of the United States is unlikely to come to the defense of the U.S. press in this matter. Perhaps the best hope of the press is to protest and complain until a significant portion of the public supports their own right to know. In the Gulf War, it was apparent that the American news media and their owners did not complain loudly and vehemently enough about the pool and censorship restrictions before the bombs started dropping.

In the highly charged patriotic atmosphere after September 11, few Americans were willing to second-guess the military policy of harsh controls over war news. A sitting president is not likely to modify such restrictions of free expression in wartime until forced to by political pressures. Yet it is imperative for the press to keep pushing for greater access to news relating to our military.

Ironically, the greatly expanded capability of global television and videophones to report instantly on any new information in a modern war provides perhaps the major rationale for governments to control and censor war news. And when American or British journalists are denied access to war news, the rest of the world is denied access as well.

The war of the United States and its allies against international terrorism is still in its opening stages, and it is too early to know how the legitimate needs for national security can be accommodated with the rights of the press, protected by the First Amendment, to report that war to the American people.

Notes

1. "Media Access to Grenada Stirs Controversy," *AP Log*, October 31, 1991, 1.
2. "Tourism Shaken by CNN Effect," *New York Times*, January 28, 1992, sec. A, 8.
3. Tom Wicker, "An Unknown Casualty," *New York Times*, March 20, 1991, sec. A, 15.
4. Michael Getler, "The Gulf War 'Good News' Policy is a Dangerous Precedent," *Washington Post National Weekly Edition*, March 25–31, 1991, 24.
5. Howard Kurtz, *Media Circus* (New York: Times Books, 1993), 215.
6. Malcom Browne, "The Military vs. The Press," *New York Times Magazine*, March 3, 1991, 45.
7. Jason DeParle, "17 News Executives Criticize U.S. for 'Censorship' of Gulf Coverage," *New York Times*, July 3, 1991, sec. A, 4.
8. Robert Pear, "Military Revises Rules to Assure Reporters Access to Battle Areas," *New York Times*, May 2, 1992, sec. A, 8.

9. Kurtz, *Media Circus*, 214.

10. David Hackworth, "Learning How to Cover a War," *Newsweek*, December 21, 1992, 32.

11. James F. Hoge, Jr., "Media Pervasiveness," *Foreign Affairs*, July/August 1994, 139–40.

12. Felicity Barringer, "A New War Drew on New Methods to Cover It," *New York Times*, June 21, 1999, sec. C, 1.

13. Ibid.

14. Kim Campbell, "Today's War Reporting: It's Digital But Dangerous," *Christian Science Monitor*, December 4, 2001, online edition.

15. *New York Times v. United States*, 403 U.S. 713, 717 (1971).

CHAPTER 11

Changing Ideologies of Press Control

A journalist is a grumbler, a censurer, a giver of advice, a regent of sovereigns, a tutor of nations. Four hostile newspapers are more to be feared than a thousand bayonets.

—Napoleon

Abuses of the freedom of speech ought to be repressed, but to whom dare we commit the power of doing it?

—Benjamin Franklin

The impressive technological improvements in international news exchanges cannot give editors and broadcasters any real control over how news will be perceived as it emerges from the global news prism, whose planes and surfaces have been cut and polished by diverse and frequently antagonistic political and social systems. As the news passes through the prism, what one journalist considers to be truthful, objective reporting can bend into what another journalist elsewhere in the world considers to be distortion or propaganda.

Despite our impressive technological expertise, political differences and cultural conflicts prevent the international news process from working smoothly and harmoniously. More and faster news communication across national borders does not automatically lead to better understanding; often, it results in enmity and distrust, because the profound cultural and social differences that characterize the world community preclude agreement on what is legitimate news. As mentioned, one person's truth is another person's propaganda, and vice versa.

As a result, international journalism has often been the subject of rancor and mutual suspicion. Mass communication's powerful ability to publicize, to expose, to glorify, to criticize, to sensationalize, to denigrate, and to mislead or propagandize is universally recognized and often feared. At one time or another, government leaders in every land become unhappy or dismayed with the press. In the West, a president or prime minister may

147

complain bitterly that his or her programs are unfairly reported by press opponents and try to bring pressure to bear on the offending publication.

In an African country, an offending foreign correspondent may be thrown into jail or expelled from the country. In Iraq, Farzad Bazoft, an Iranian-born journalist with a British newspaper and carrying a British passport, was executed after he investigated an explosion at a secret chemical plant. Under duress and perhaps torture, Bazoft confessed to spying for Israel. The incident illustrated the often narrow line between espionage and journalism in Iraq, as elsewhere. Throughout the world today, journalists have become the victims of violence from those who do not want some particular information reported.

The differing perceptions about the nature and role of journalism and mass communication are rooted in divergent political systems and historical traditions and are broadly reflected in five political concepts of the press found in the world today: (1) Authoritarian, (2) Western, (3) Communist, (4) Revolutionary, and (5) Developmental.[1] These are normative concepts that reflect how the media ideally should perform under certain political conditions and social values. We believe that an understanding of these contrasting approaches to the role and function of transnational journalism can help to clarify some of the issues that divide the world's press.

Authoritarianism is the oldest and most pervasive concept and has spawned two twentieth-century modifications: the Communist and Developmental concepts. The Western concept, under which the press in Western democracies with market economies generally functions, represents a fundamental alternative to the Authoritarian concept and contains elements of both eighteenth-century political liberalism and twentieth-century views of Social Responsibility. The Revolutionary concept has one trait in common with the Western: they both try to operate outside of governmental controls. The Developmental concept is an emerging pattern associated with the developing nations, most of which still lack adequate media resources.

Newspapers, television, and other mass media, always and everywhere, function within some kinds of governmental, societal, and economic constraints. Even the "freest" or most independent press system must deal with varying degrees of regulation by political authority. In the relationship between government and mass communication, the basic question is not whether government controls the press but the nature and extent of those controls. All press systems exist somewhere along a continuum, from complete controls (absolute authoritarianism) at one end to no controls (pure libertarianism) on the other. Absolute freedom of expression is a myth. Beyond that, controls on the press are so varied and complex that it is difficult, if not impossible, to compare press freedom in one nation with that in another. In one country, newspapers may be under harsh, arbitrary political restraints; in another, they may be under more subtle, yet real, economic and corporate restrictions.

A basic tenet of the following analysis is that all press systems reflect the values of the political and economic systems of the nations within which they operate. The trend toward globalization notwithstanding, print and broadcast systems are still controlled and regulated by their own national governments. And in this era of increasing transnational communication, journalists from an open society often must work and collect news abroad in a closed or autocratic society, thereby increasing opportunities for friction between divergent concepts.

Authoritarian Concept

Authoritarian political systems were the norm at the time the printing press was invented by Gutenberg in the mid-fifteenth century and, in the years since, more people have lived under an authoritarian press concept than under any other. The basic principle of authoritarianism is simple: The press is always subject to direct or implied control by the state or sovereign. A printing press (or, later, a broadcasting facility) cannot be used to challenge, criticize, or in any way undermine the sovereign. The press functions from the top down: The king or ruler decides what will be published because truth (and information) is essentially a monopoly of those in authority.

To the authoritarian, diversity of views is wasteful and irresponsible, dissent is an annoying nuisance and often subversive, and consensus and standardization are logical and sensible goals for mass communication. There is a certain compelling logic behind this.

Under traditional authoritarianism, the press operates outside government and is permitted to gather and publish news, but it must function for the "good of the state." The government usually leaves the press alone as long as it does not criticize authority or challenge the leadership in any way. If the press does attack authority, then the political authority intervenes, imposing censorship or even closing down publications and jailing editors. Under the Authoritarian concept, the constraint of potential censorship, if not actual prior restraint itself, always exists. Editors and reporters exercise a good deal of self-censorship but never know for sure just how far they can go without triggering official disfavor and intervention. They must support the status quo and neither advocate change, criticize the nation's leadership, nor give offense to the dominant moral or political values.

So wherever governments arbitrarily intervene and suppress independent newspapers and broadcasters, the Authoritarian concept flourishes. For example, the Suharto government barred from Indonesia a *New York Times* correspondent, Steven Erlanger, for a published story about the business interests of Suharto's children and their success in winning government contracts. The *International Herald Tribune*, which carried the story in Asia, was barred from circulating in Indonesia.[2]

The Authoritarian concept is alive and well today in other South Asian nations, especially Singapore and Malaysia. Singapore, despite its prosperity and economic ties to the West, has been unusually hostile to foreign publications, having restricted or banned distribution of *The Asian Wall Street Journal, Time, Asiaweek,* and *Far Eastern Economic Review* at various times. In July 1995, the Singapore courts ordered the *International Herald Tribune* to pay libel damages of $670,000 to the country's top three leaders for a story that would have amounted to mild political comment in the West.

Authoritarianism is widespread today, especially if, as some scholars aver, the Communist and Developmental concepts are understood to be variations of traditional authoritarianism. Other nations recently under Authoritarian press controls include Algeria, China, Cuba, Pakistan, Belarus, Ethiopia, Syria, Turkey, and Iraq. Many apparently democratic nations, with political parties and elected presidents, are not in fact very democratic because rulers often act arbitrarily, dissidents and minorities lack legal rights, and local journalists operate under strict controls, including harassment, torture, and imprisonment. In 2001, the Committee to Protect Journalists lists these leaders as among the ten worst enemies of the press: Jiang Zemin of China; Fidel Castro of Cuba; Vladimir Putin of Russia; Charles Taylor of Liberia; Robert Mugabe of Zimbabwe; Ayatollah Khamenei of Iran; and Leonid Kuchma of Ukraine.

Moreover, authoritarian practices cannot always be clearly delimited. Democracies in time of war or crisis (Britain during World War II, for example) sometimes adopt authoritarian controls on the press for the duration. Democratic France, under Charles de Gaulle and several of his successors, suffered under heavy-handed authoritarian control of its television system. In many nations, especially in Latin America, the media have moved back and forth between freedom and controls as the governments changed from military to democratic regimes and back again.

Foreign correspondents pose a special challenge to authoritarian regimes, and Western journalists often encounter a variety of difficulties: Entry visas are denied; stories are censored; telephone and Comsat facilities are refused; and sometimes reporters are harassed, mistreated, jailed, or expelled.

Western Concept

The Western concept represents a distinct deviation from the traditional authoritarian controls and evolved during the rise of democracies in Europe and North America. During the long constitutional struggle in England among the crown, the courts, and the Commons and, later, in the United States, a press relatively free of arbitrary government controls slowly evolved. In fact, one definition of freedom of the press is the right of the press to report on, comment on, and criticize its own government without retaliation or threat of retaliation from the government. This has been called "the right to talk politics." Historically, seditious libel meant criticism of government, laws, or officials. The absence of seditious libel as a crime has been considered the true pragmatic test of a country's freedom of expression, because politically relevant speech is what press freedom is mostly about. By this demanding test the Western concept—the right to talk politics—is comparatively rare.

Although many authoritarian governments give it lip service, a free or independent press is usually found in only a dozen or more Western nations that share these characteristics: (1) a system of law that provides meaningful protection to individual civil liberties and property rights (here, common-law nations, such as the United States and Britain, seem to do better than nations, such as France or Italy, with civil law traditions); (2) high average levels of per capita income, education, and literacy; (3) governance by constitutional parliamentary democracy or at least with legitimate political oppositions; (4) sufficient capital or private enterprise to support media of news communication, that is, market economies; and (5) an established tradition of independent journalism.

Any list of nations meeting these criteria for a Western press today would certainly include the United States, United Kingdom, Canada, Sweden, Germany, France, Netherlands, Belgium, Australia, New Zealand, Norway, Denmark, Austria, Iceland, Ireland, Israel, Italy, and Switzerland.

In addition to these Western nations, highly developed and westernized
Japan surely should be added. And India, the world's largest democracy,
has enjoyed a remarkably free press despite its diverse problems.

Journalists in many other nations support and practice the Western
concept but, because of political instability, their media over the years have
swung back and forth between freedom and control. Such nations, among
others, include Spain, Greece, Portugal, Colombia, Brazil, Argentina,
Chile, Turkey, and Venezuela, and happily, most are recently counted
among the democracies.

By and large, the Western nations that meet the criteria include the
handful that do most of the world's news gathering from other nations
and whose correspondents most often come in conflict with authoritarian regimes. This is because the Western concept holds strongly that a
government—any government, here or abroad—should not interfere in
the process of collecting and disseminating news. The press, in theory,
must be independent of authority and, of course, exist outside government and be well protected by law and custom from arbitrary government interference. And so an independent press usually means one
situated in a democratic, market economy and enjoying the same autonomy as other private business enterprises.

The ideals of Western libertarian journalism are, to a large extent, a
by-product of the Enlightenment and the liberal political tradition
reflected in the writings of John Milton, John Locke, Thomas Jefferson,
and John Stuart Mill. Primarily, there must be a diversity of views and
news sources available, a "marketplace of ideas" from which the public can
choose what it wishes to read and believe, for no one person or no authority, spiritual or temporal, has a monopoly on truth. United States Judge
Learned Hand expressed it well:

> That [newspaper] industry serves one of the most vital of all general
> interests: the dissemination of news from as many different sources, and
> with as many different facets as is possible. ... It presupposes that right
> conclusions are more likely to be gathered out of a multitude of tongues
> than through any kind of authoritarian selection. To many this is, and
> always will be, folly; but we have staked upon it our all.[3]

Underlying this diversity of views is the faith that citizens will
somehow make the right choices about what to believe if enough voices
are heard and government keeps its hands off. In American Constitutional theory, this libertarian view is based upon certain values deemed

inherent in a free press: (1) by gathering public information and scrutinizing government, the press makes self-government and democracy possible; (2) an unfettered press ensures that a diversity of views and news will be read and heard; (3) a system of free expression provides autonomy for individuals to lead free and productive lives; and (4) it enables an independent press to serve as a check on abuses of power by government.[4]

Carried over to the international context, the Western concept argues that there must be a free flow of information unimpeded by any intervention by any nation. ("Free flow," it is argued, does not necessarily mean a balanced or two-way flow of news, as desirable as that may be.) No government anywhere should obstruct the gathering and dissemination of legitimate news. Only news media free of official restraints will be credible to readers and viewers here and abroad. Advocates say that the Western concept serves the cause of global news flow in several important ways. It makes possible the gathering and dissemination of reliable and accurate news. In a global economy, the business press plays an essential role of providing fast and reliable news of global business and finance.

A free press provides news and important information to peoples living in authoritarian regimes that censor their own media. International shortwave radio broadcasters—BBC, VOA, and others—relay news from Western news gatherers.

Western news media, of course, are not without their shortcomings. Critics charge that too many news media have become submerged into giant, entertainment-oriented conglomerates all primarily concerned with turning a profit. In so doing, Western media are accused of slighting serious news in favor of sensation, scandal, and celebrity. Furthermore, Western media certainly are not immune to pressures from their own governments. Political freedom does not preclude economic and corporate interference with journalistic practices. A privately owned media system will, in varying degrees, reflect the interests and concerns of its owners. Yet to stay independent of outside controls, including government, the publishers and broadcasters must be financially strong and profitable. Journalistic excellence and profitability are not identical goals, although some of the best news media are also very profitable; for some owners, however, making money is the primary purpose of journalism, and independence and public service mean little. Then, too, diversity at both national and international levels appears to be in decline, and the marked increase of media conglomerates and ownership concentration has reduced the number of independent voices heard in the marketplace.

In some democracies, such as Norway and Sweden, the government maintains diversity of political views by providing subsidies to the newspapers of various political parties, a practice not without potential danger to press independence.

Some modifications of the Western concept fall under the rubric of Social Responsibility. This view holds that the media have clear obligations of public service that transcend moneymaking. Public service implies professional standards for journalists as well as reliable and objective reporting. The media are obligated, in addition, to ensure that all voices and views in the community are heard. Further, government is granted a limited role in intervening in media operations and in regulating conditions if public interests are not being adequately served. Government regulation of broadcasting in its earliest years in the United States, for example, represented an example of the Social Responsibility position.

Two other related modifications are the Democratic Socialist concept and the Democratic Participant concept. Expressing fears concerning the abuses of private ownership, the Democratic Socialist theory says that state action is needed to institute new forms of ownership and management and to intervene in the economics of the media.[5] Similarly, Democratic Participant theory reflects a reaction against commercialization and monopolization of the privately owned media as well as against the centralism and bureaucratization of public broadcasting. Denis McQuail summarized several of its principles: (1) media should exist primarily for their audiences and not for media organizations, professionals, or clients of media; (2) individual citizens and minority groups have rights of access to media (rights to communicate) and rights to be served by media according to the peoples' own determination of need; (3) organization and content of the media should not be subject to centralized political or state bureaucratic control; and, finally, (4) small-scale, interactive, and participative media forms are better than large-scale, professionalized media.[6]

These evolving views, which represent some disillusionment with mass-media performance, are found throughout Western democracies but especially in Northern Europe. Their major disadvantage is that such decentralized, small-scale media are less able to check the abuses of government and corporate power, whether at home or abroad. Yet this debate illustrates a built-in advantage of the Western concept: It enjoys the freedom to criticize and reform its own media system through democratic processes, something that is lacking in the other concepts.

Finally, the Western press concept, with its emphasis on the individual's rights to send and receive information, is well suited as a conceptual framework for the new "personalized media"—computers with modems, faxes, interactive television, and the Internet—that are now playing a growing role in international communication. (See Chapter 4, "Internet, Comsats, and New Media.")

The Rise and Fall of the Communist Concept

For more than seventy years, the Western concept of the press had been under direct challenge by advocates of the Communist press theory just as capitalism itself was under assault by Marxist/Leninist economic doctrines. Lenin had written that "'freedom of the press' of a bourgeois society consists in freedom of the rich systematically, unceasingly, and daily in the millions of copies to deceive, corrupt, and fool the exploited and oppressed mass of the people, the poor."[7]

Many intellectuals and writers were convinced that the Western liberal democracies and their press were outdated and doomed and that the USSR's communism and its party-controlled media were the wave of the future. Even among its critics, the Leninist theory was seen as something new and different—certainly more positive and meaningful than the traditional Authoritarian concept.

Mass media controlled and directed by the Communist Party, Lenin argued, can concentrate on the serious task of nation-building by publishing news relating to the entire society's policies and goals as determined by the top party leadership. To Lenin, the press was an integral part of the Communist Party, which was itself seen as a teacher to instruct the masses and lead the proletariat. The basic postulates of the theory deriving from Marx and Engels with rules of application of Lenin were summarized by McQuail:

> Media should serve the interests of, and be in control of, the working class and should not be privately owned. Media should serve positive functions for society by socialization to desired norms, education, information, motivation, and mobilization. Within their overall task for society, the media should respond to wishes and needs of their audiences. Society has a right to use censorship and other legal measures to prevent, or punish after the event, anti-societal publication. Media should provide a complete and objective view of society and the world according to Marxist-Leninist principles. Media should support progressive movements at home and abroad.[8]

Aside from normative theory, the characteristics of the Soviet press concept that set it apart from Western journalism were these: It was, first, a planned and completely government- and party-controlled system that permitted no competing private media. As Lenin said, there is no freedom for the enemies of socialism; his concept would avoid the abuses of the capitalist press. Second, this one-party press enjoyed a monopoly on news, both coming in and going out. Information was controlled by the state; the Party version of events was all that mattered. This condition lasted through the Stalin years, when foreign broadcasts were jammed and foreign publication barred at the borders. Third, news itself was defined as "positive" information that furthers the goals of the Party, not information of direct interest or relevance to the lives of the Soviet people themselves. A plane crash or a nuclear accident was not news; a government farm report or a new tractor factory was. Finally, the press, in concert with the Communist Party and secret police, was used to control the people as well as to promote government policies and prepare the public for future policy changes.

The Communist media faithfully served the Party's ruling elite, but their fatal flaw was that they did not serve the interests of the people themselves. As the peoples under communist regimes in Central and East Europe, deprived of political freedoms, saw their economies crumble and fall behind the West, they became increasingly disillusioned with their own mass media, which spoke only for authority and failed to criticize or report weaknesses in the ruling communist elites. In the USSR, much of the same disillusionment existed, but it can be argued that some impetus for reform came from above as Gorbachev's *glasnost* policies led to media changes beginning in 1985, well before the upheaval of 1991.

The Communist press theory unraveled over a number of years. First came loss of faith in Leninist ideology: the slogans and buzzwords became increasingly empty. From the 1970s onward, Marxist press advocates no longer extolled the superiority of communist theory and focused instead on criticizing Western media. The practices of communist mass communication, especially as a means of controlling and leading public opinion, continued with some modifications into the 1980s but without the old ideological fervor. In the Soviet Union's final stages, the communist media were reduced to playing a role similar to that of the secret police: another means of controlling the people.

Concurrently, Western mass communication kept intruding on the closed societies of the East and appears to have facilitated the demise of communist regimes. The Soviet media's monopoly on news began to crack early in the Cold War. BBC World Service, Voice of America, Radio Free

Europe, and other Western broadcasters were widely heard. East Germans watched Western television beamed from West Berlin and the Federal Republic of Germany. Alternative and unofficial forms of publication flourished in the USSR, and the West learned a new word, *samizdat* ("self-publishing" in Russian).

Despite efforts to keep them out, Western rock music and videocassettes found their way into communist cultures and became hugely successful.

The nuclear accident at Chernobyl in April 1986 signaled a change in the Soviet media's handling of a major "bad news" story. At first, the Soviet government made an extraordinary effort to deny that any catastrophe had occurred and restricted information even while airborne radiation was detected in Scandinavia and Poland. This reflexive retreat into secrecy illustrated the Kremlin's traditional unwillingness to concede any failings before its people and the world. But abroad, the Kremlin was harshly criticized for failing to provide prompt information about the radioactivity spreading across Europe and for neglecting to warn its own citizens. Gradually, Soviet media were forced, by Western media coverage, to report details even though they were released weeks after the event.

The news void on Chernobyl was filled in part by Radio Free Europe and Radio Liberty, which provided breaking news to communist bloc listeners. In such emergencies, Eastern Europeans were likely to turn to Western radio for information unavailable elsewhere. To obtain information by radio, Voice of America officials reported, people traveled out of the cities to rural areas where jamming was ineffective. Finally, four years later, in April 1990, the Soviet Union finally acknowledged that the medical, environmental, and political consequences of the Chernobyl disaster had been much greater than the Kremlin had ever frankly discussed.

As the Chernobyl disaster showed, the communist media could not deal with foreign competition, something unforeseen in Lenin's closed-system press theory. With Mikhail Gorbachev's proclamation of *glasnost* and *perestroika* in the mid-1980s, changes in media theory and practice accelerated. A Soviet weekly, *Argumenti i Fakti*, with a circulation of more than twenty million, published in 1989 the most detailed account of Stalin's victims yet presented to a Soviet mass audience, indicating that about twenty million Soviet citizens died in labor camps, forced collectivization, famine, and executions. The same year in Warsaw, the first independently published daily newspaper in the Eastern bloc appeared: *Gazeta* supported the newly legalized Solidarity trade union. And, in East Germany, the communist media turned on their former masters and behaved like Western investigative reporters. *Neues Deutschland,* the main communist paper, *Berliner Zeitung,* and *Junge Welt* all published accusations of corruption and profiteering by high Communist officials under Erich Honecker. East German television, a week earlier a subservient tool of the Honecker regime, ran a series of sixteen reports depicting the high living of the top Communists. These revelations scandalized the public and reinforced the outcry that forced the Honecker regime from power. From East Berlin to Warsaw to Prague to Budapest to Moscow, the Communist theory of the press has been left in shambles—in effect tossed into the much-utilized dustbin of history.

Recently, as Roger Cohen has reported, "Journalism has been reinvented in Eastern Europe as a craft involving independence and objectivity, but politicians remain uneasy and sometimes ruthless about the new press freedom. Through satellite dishes, cable systems and a wide range of publications, the people of the former East Bloc have access to a range of information and entertainment unthinkable under Communism."[9] This is not to say that authoritarian or even totalitarian controls will not return from time to time to some of the news media of Central and Eastern Europe. News processing has become faster with computers than with typewriters. In Prague, there are fifteen dailies, not all of which may survive. Although media diversity has been established, various problems remain because of economic collapse, legislative confusion, and nationalist awakening. Much concern exists over the future of television, as always a powerful political instrument. Despite efforts to end state television monopolies and open the way for private networks, governments hesitate to act.

Although still somewhat free, Russia's media have increasingly been endangered since Vladimir Putin became president and began presiding over an alarming assault on press freedom. The Kremlin imposed censorship on news about the lingering civil war in Chechnya, orchestrated legal harassment again private media outlets, and granted sweeping powers of surveillance to security forces. During 2000–2001, numerous violent attacks on journalists were carried out with impunity across Russia. In April 2001, the Kremlin-controlled Gazprom corporation took over NTV, the country's only independent national TV network. Within days, the Gazprom coup had shut down a prominent Moscow daily and ousted leading journalists from the country's most prestigious newsweekly. Despite Gazprom's insistence that these changes were strictly business, the Committee to Protect Journalists reported that the main beneficiary was Putin himself, whose primary critics have now been silenced. Many of NTV's best journalists joined TV-6, which was Moscow's only independent television outlet and had a smaller, but still loyal audience. But then in December 2001, a Russian court also shut down TV-6. The station's managers and most outside analysts called it a Kremlin plot to force it off the air. Authoritarian may be the best adjective to describe Russia's news media today.

Revolutionary Concept

Lenin provided both some of the ideology and rationale for another and more ephemeral view: the Revolutionary. Simply stated, this is a concept of illegal and subversive communication using the press and broadcasting to overthrow a government or wrest control from alien or otherwise rejected rulers.

Lenin in his famous work *What Is to be Done?* (written in exile before the 1917 Revolution) proposed that the revolutionaries establish a nationwide, legal newspaper inside czarist Russia. Such a paper could obviously not advocate revolutionary goals, but its distribution system could be an excellent mechanism for a political machine. The newspaper, Lenin postulated, would be a cover for a far-flung revolutionary organization. The early *Pravda*, although it was not a legal newspaper (and was edited by Stalin at one time), was published outside czarist Russia, and smuggled copies were widely distributed—a fine example of the Revolutionary concept.

The revolutionary press is a press of people who believe strongly that the government they live under does not serve their interests and should be overthrown. They believe they owe such a government no loyalty whatsoever. Pure examples are difficult to find, but one surely was the underground press in Nazi-occupied France during World War II. The editors and journalists of the clandestine press literally risked their lives to put out their papers and pamphlets. Other examples of the Revolutionary concept were the *samizdat*, the secretly typed and mimeographed copies of books, political tracts, and the like that were passed at great risk from hand to hand among dissidents inside the Soviet Union.

The history of anticolonialist movements in the former Third World is replete with examples. Throughout the British Empire, especially in West Africa, political dissidents published small newspapers, often handwritten, that first expressed grievances against the British rulers, then encouraged nationalism, and finally advocated political independence. Aspiring political leaders such as Azikiwe, Awolowo, Nkrumah, Kaunda, and Kenyatta were all editors of these small political newspapers that informed and helped organize the budding political parties and nationalist movements. British authorities were surprisingly tolerant, even though they disapproved of and sometimes acted against the publications and their editors.

Much in the Anglo-American political tradition supported these newspapers, and the editors claimed the rights of British journalists. Had not Thomas Paine used political pamphlets to help run the British out of the American Colonies? Had not Thomas Jefferson said that the people have a right to revolution, including the right to subsequent revolutions if that proved necessary?

In the postindependence years, radio broadcasting has become a valuable tool of revolutionary groups seeking to overthrow the fragile governments of developing nations. Black Africa has been plagued with numerous coups d'etat, and during times of acute political crisis, radio broadcasting has often played a significant role as the primary medium of communication in most nations. So rebels have recognized the importance of controlling information at the political center of power. Hence, insurgents often seized the radio station before heading for the presidential palace. Military struggles during a coup attempt frequently occur outside the broadcast station, because if rebels can announce over the nation's only radio station that a coup has been accomplished (even while the issue is still in doubt), it helps accomplish the desired end.

More recently, two other communication devices—the photocopying machine and the audiocassette—have proved useful in revolutionary efforts. In Iran, the revolution of the Ayatollah Khomeini has been called the first cassette revolution. Thousands of cassette recordings of the Ayatollah's speeches propagating his revolutionary ideas were played in the mosques, which were not kept under surveillance by the Shah's secret police. These small, portable instruments were able to reach millions while circumventing the government-controlled press, radio, and television. At the same time, when revolutionary "night letters" and pamphlets arrived mysteriously at offices in Tehran, sympathetic secretaries made many photocopies, quickly and more secretly than possible with a printing press.

Anthony Sampson said that "the period of television and radio monopolies may prove a passing phase, as we find ourselves in a much more open field of communications, with cassettes and copied documents taking the place of the books and pamphlets that undermined 18th century governments." He suggested an epitaph for the Shah's regime: "He forgot the cassette."[10]

Personalized media, with their interactive capabilities, all present challenges to centralized autocracies trying to control news and information. The continuing struggle of Chinese dissidents for civil rights is an example of the Revolutionary concept. That struggle goes on with dissidents now using the Internet as well as other new media to advocate democratic change in China. (See Chapter 5, "The Impact of Great News Events," for more details.)

Developmental Concept

By its very nature, the Revolutionary concept is a short-term affair: The successful subversive use of mass communication to topple a despised regime is self-limiting. After goals are achieved, the gains must be consolidated and then another concept takes over. In recent decades, a variation on the Authoritarian concept—the Developmental concept—has been emerging in the wake of political independence in impoverished nations throughout the developing world.

The Developmental concept is an amorphous and curious mixture of ideas, rhetoric, influences, and grievances. As yet, the concept is not clearly defined. Some aspects are straight from Lenin and the Communist concept of the press. Perhaps of greater importance are the influences of Western social scientists who have posited a major role for mass communication in the process of nation-building in newly independent countries. American academics such as Wilbur Schramm, Daniel Lerner, and others, all democrats at heart, have argued that the communication process is central to the achievement of national integration and economic development. In so doing, they may have unintentionally provided a rationale for autocratic press controls.

Other more radical academics, mostly Europeans, have echoed Marxist views and added a touch of anti-Americanism to the concept, for the concept is to some extent a critique of and reaction against the West and its transnational media. It also reflects the frustrations and anger of poor and media-deficient nations.

The Developmental concept is an approach to mass communication in nations that are clearly lacking in newspapers, broadcasting, and video facilities—the world's "have-nots" in media resources.

In general, the concept holds that

- All the instruments of mass communication—newspapers, radio, television, motion pictures, national news services—must be mobilized by the central government to aid in the great tasks of nation building: fighting illiteracy and poverty, building a political consciousness, assisting in economic development. Implicit here is the Social Responsibility view that the government must step in and provide adequate media service when the private sector is unable to do so, as is the case in many poor nations.

- The Media therefore should support authority, not challenge it. Dissent or criticism has no place, in part because the alternative to the ruling government would be chaos, it is argued. Freedom of the press, then, can be restricted according to the development needs of the society.
- Information (or truth) thus becomes the property of the state: the flow of power (and truth) between the governors and the governed works from the top down as in traditional authoritarianism. Information or news is a scarce national resource; it must be utilized to further the national goals.
- Implied but not often articulated is the view that individual rights of expression and other civil liberties are somewhat irrelevant in the face of the overwhelming problems of poverty, disease, illiteracy, and ethnicity that face a majority of these nations. (Critics argue that the concept provides a palatable rationale for old-fashioned authoritarianism.)
- This concept of a guided press further implies that in international news each nation has a sovereign right to control both foreign journalists and the flow of news back and forth across its borders.

Some critics argue that central to the Developmental concept is a rejection of the Western view. As British journalist Rosemary Righter wrote, there is a growing feeling that the Western model of the press is undesirable in itself. Instead of backing diversity and free flow, the mass media must adopt a didactic, even ideological, role of explaining to the people their part in forging a new social order.[11]

Western news media are attacked on several scores. To begin with, some critics say that the Western international media are too monopolistic and powerful; they penetrate too widely and effectively. The world news organizations—AP (Associated Press), CNN, Reuters, BBC, and AFP (Agence France-Presse)—are particular targets, charged with creating a clear imbalance, a one-way flow, and a near monopoly of news that favors the affluent North. Furthermore, Western media represent an alien viewpoint, which they impose on nations trying to build independent modern identities. Traditional cultures, it is charged, have been threatened by the inundation of news and mass culture—television programs, pop music, movies, videocassettes, and audiocassettes—principally from America and Britain. Such domination, it is argued, amounts to cultural aggression.

Finally, a few proponents of the Developmental concept charge that the Western media are part of an international conspiracy by which the economic and political interests of the capitalist nations are using global mass communication to dominate, even subjugate, the developing nations. Some advocates of this concept argue that the world needs a "new international information order" to redress these imbalances.

The Developmental concept is a view of mass communication from the many nations of the former Third World where most citizens are people of color, poor, ill-nourished, and illiterate, and it reflects resentments against the West where people are mainly Caucasians (except in Japan), affluent, and literate. The concept is related as well to what some feel is the major problem facing the world today: the widening gap between the rich and the poor, debt-ridden, "failed" nations. The same nations that decry the trade and GNP (gross national product) imbalances between North and South also excoriate the Western news media. Echoes of the Developmental concept are being heard in current protests and demonstrations against globalization.

By the mid-1990s, the Developmental concept appeared to be losing momentum among developing nations. The current global trends toward more democracy and market economies appear to have boosted the Western press concept, but the odds that many of the new democracies will succeed are not good. At the same time, the Communist press concept appears to have disappeared as a viable press theory. Communist regimes persist in North Korea, Cuba, and the People's Republic of China, but the ideological fervor and justification seems to have waned—only police states remain.

China has jettisoned Marxist economic theory while holding onto centralized, totalitarian controls over its people. The resulting mix has been called market Leninism, which has produced a rapidly growing economy and seems to have something in common with the corporate capitalism or neoauthoritarianism of its Asian neighbors, South Korea, Singapore, and Malaysia. The Chinese people have been prospering economically but enjoy little freedom of expression. President Jiang Zemin presides over the world's most elaborate system of media control.

The controversies engendered by these conflicting concepts of mass communication have long been marked by rancor, but this, too, has shown some signs of abating. As of 2002, ideological conflict between press systems seems to have clearly subsided, if only temporarily. Some would argue that in today's world only two concepts of the press are viable: the Authoritarian approach, which insists on its right to control news and information and restrict its circulation, and the Western concept, which argues that news and information, like knowledge itself, belong to all people and that journalists have the right to pursue and report news wherever it can be found.

Yet there remain valid arguments on all sides of these political and cultural confrontations, each reflecting differing social and political traditions that are difficult to reconcile. But as the international news system becomes more integrated and interdependent, the conflicts over how news and information are to be controlled may diminsh. Although few if any nations fit neatly into any of these five normative concepts of the press, the concepts are still useful in illustrating some of the divergent perceptions of the nature of news and how it should be disseminated.

Despite the variety of news and views refracted through the world news prism, the great bulk of foreign news is gathered and disseminated by Western news media. In recent years, two clear trends have emerged: the triumph of the Western concept of the press and the reality that many more millions of people, mostly in the Eurasian landmass, have joined the vast world audience of international communication. Both trends are integral aspects of the globalization of the media.

Notes

1. For this analysis, the authors owe a debt to the classic book by Fred Siebert, Theodore Peterson, and Wilbur Schramm, *Four Theories of the Press* (Urbana: University of Illinois Press, 1956).
2. "Indonesian Government Bans Correspondent for the Times," *New York Times*, November 27, 1990, sec. A, 7.
3. *Associated Press v. United States*, 52 F. Supp. 362, 372 (1943).
4. See Vincent Blasi, "The Checking Value in First Amendment Theory," *ABA Research Journal* no. 3, Summer 1977, 521–649.
5. Robert Picard, "Revisions of Four Theories of the Press," *Mass Comm Review*, Winter/Spring, 1982–83, 27.
6. Denis McQuail, *Mass Communication Theory: An Introduction* (Beverly Hills: Sage, 1983), 96–97.
7. Mark Hopkins, *Mass Media in the Soviet Union* (New York: Pegasus, 1970), 55.

8. McQuail, *Mass Communication Theory*, 93–94.
9. Roger Cohen, "Propaganda to Journalism: Europe's Latest Revolution," *New York Times*, December 27, 1992, sec. A, 15.
10. Anthony Sampson, "Rebel Poli-Techs," *New York Times*, May 6, 1979, sec. A, 15.
11. Rosemary Righter, *Whose News: Politics, the Press and the Third World* (New York: Times Books, 1978), 14–15.

CHAPTER 12
Western Media to World Media

> Western values and assumptions have been internalized to a remarkable degree in almost every other major culture. ... What the West has done to the rest of the world has been done indelibly. Nothing can be the same again. History has been changed by the West, which has made the world One World. ... What seems to be clear is that the story of the western civilization is now the story of mankind, its influence so diffused that old oppositions and antitheses are now meaningless. "The West" is hardly now a meaningful term, except to historians.
>
> —J.M. Roberts

Modern mass communications, from newspapers and television sets to communication satellites and videocassette recorders, are among the many devices and cultural artifacts of Western society that have so inexorably spread throughout the world since 1945. Words on paper, electronic impulses, and images on tape, film, and recordings have penetrated the minds and cultures of non-Western peoples with tremendous impact. Along with pop and classical music, Hollywood movies, television programs, and youthful lifestyles have come ideas and ideology: equality, human rights, democracy, freedom of expression, individual autonomy, and free enterprise. John Locke, Thomas Jefferson, John Stuart Mill, Abraham Lincoln, and Adam Smith were Westerners, as was Karl Marx.

International communication, travel, industrialization, commerce, and trade have all participated in this Westernizing process, that is, globalization, which perhaps should be termed the *modernization* of the world because so many non-Western societies now contribute to the process. The practices of Western mass communication have been so widely dispersed and accepted by people everywhere that the adjective *Western* perhaps should be reserved for historians, as Professor Roberts has suggested.[1] The September 11 events and their aftermath showed the crucial role that professional journalism, free of government controls, plays at a time of crisis by supplying reliable and verifiable news to the world. In America, the

167

familiar anchors of network television, Jennings, Brokaw, and Rather, not only reported the news but also reassured, steadied, and consoled millions of viewers. When national security is endangered, Americans and others were reminded how important it is to know and understand the greater world.

Checklist of Global News Impact

To summarize the main points of this book, we list some ways that the new global journalism has influenced and, yes, even changed our world, for high-speed, international news communication is something new and different—in matters of degree if not in kind. Some of these effects have been global or geopolitical, others have directly influenced the media themselves, and some effects have been felt mostly by individuals.

- *Triumph of Western journalism.* Since the fall of the communist "second" world, the Western concept of journalism and mass communication has become the dominant model throughout the world and is widely emulated. In journalism, many non-Western nations have adopted not only the equipment and gadgets of the Western press and broadcasting but also its practices, norms, ethical standards, and ideology. Throughout the developing and former communist nations, print and broadcast journalists today increasingly seek editorial autonomy and freedom from government interference. These journalists understand and aspire to the professional values of fairness, objectivity, and responsibility as well as the "checking effect"— the role of the press as a watchdog of government and authority. They want to report the news as they see it—not some government's version of events. But, of course, many autocratic nations still have controlled media.
- *Globalization of media.* The internationalization of mass communication has grown hand in hand with the globalization of the world's economy. In fact, the expanding international business media play a key role in "servicing" the world economy by supplying rapid, reliable economic and financial news. Globalization has its negative traits and independent news media provide forums for dissent and complaints.
- *Mass culture accepted.* For better or worse, Western mass media also have conditioned much of the world to use media for

entertainment and leisure. (Political indoctrination by media has been rejected by many people. But with the war on terrorism, political persuasion, that is, propaganda, has increased on global media.) Ever-growing audiences accept and enjoy the movies, television, pop music, and even the ever-present commercials. Today, the most traditional of parents find it almost impossible to prevent the influence on their children of that most powerful engine of mass education the West has yet produced, commercial advertising. Parents and others over thirty years old almost everywhere must be offended and repelled by the noisy, brassy music videos of MTV, but there is no doubting their appeal to teenagers literally everywhere. Yet in lands under the sway of religious fundamentalism, opposition to Western mass culture remains strong.

- *Impact on Cold War.* Today many experts agree that news and mass culture from the West contributed to the demise of the USSR and the communist regimes in Eastern Europe. Western media provided news not available otherwise and served the "forbidden fruit" of Western movies, rock music, lifestyles, and the promise of a better life—democracy, market economies, and a higher standard of living.

- *Global audiences growing.* Each year, literally millions more people are being drawn into the global audience mainly through competing satellite and cable services, computers, and shortwave radio. With satellite dishes and antennas sprouting everywhere, the lands of Asia, particularly China and India, are flocking to join the global village. The events of September 11 saw a tremendous surge of interest for global television news. Some Asian nations welcome global television but others see it as a threat to their cultural identity and political stability. Across the former Third World, governments have had only limited success in blocking satellite services. Governments are finding it nearly impossible to prevent people from getting news and entertainment from the skies. Satellite dishes, which are growing smaller, cheaper, and more powerful, are easily put together from imported kits.

- *Vast audiences for global events.* Great events—the terror attack on the World Trade Center and Pentagon, or the quadrennial Olympic Games—can attract significant parts of the global audience. About 3.5 billion people watched some of the 1996 Olympics in Atlanta. The biggest share of that audience was in China because more than

900 million Chinese had access to television sets, and three channels broadcast events there all day long.

- *History speeded up.* Nations and people react faster to important events because information moves so quickly and widely. A bomb explodes in an airliner and security measures tighten up in airports everywhere. War breaks out in the Middle East and the price of gas at the pump goes up everywhere. Actions that would have been taken later are now taken sooner, thus accelerating the pace of change.

- *"The whole world is watching"* The reality that many millions can watch on television as tanks rumble across borders, troops storm ashore in a distant land, or police fire on peaceful protesters gives much greater import and consequences to news reports. A camcorder's report of Los Angeles police beating a man named Rodney King set off repercussions lasting for years. A discarded "home videocassette" showing Osama bin Laden rejoicing over the New York City terror attacks provided what many considered the "smoking gun" that proved his complicity in the attacks.

- *Diplomacy changed.* Foreign relations and the ways that nations react to each other are clearly influenced by public (and world) opinion formed by global communication. Television viewers concerned by watching starving children in Somalia can exert pressures on their government to intervene with military force in a place they later regret going to. Media discussions and debate between diplomats and leaders can clarify policy and influence nations or alliances to act. Nonstop coverage by CNN and BBC provides the opportunity to monitor news events constantly and disseminate timely diplomatic information. But some politicians are more concerned than elated by global, real-time broadcasting, fearing a loss of control and the absence of quiet time to make deliberate choices, reach private agreements, and mold the public's understanding of events.

- *Autocrats' loss of controls.* Authoritarian regimes can no longer maintain a monopoly over news and censor what their people know. They cannot stop news from coming into their nation or getting out. Shortwave radio, fax, Internet, cell and video telephones, and communication satellites have changed all that and blunted the power of state censorship. During times of crisis, dictators can no longer seal their borders and control information. The news will get out.

- *"Revolution" by personalized media.* Internet, desktop publishing, videocassettes, and VCRs have turned individuals into communicators who can reach out to their own audiences. Photocopiers and audiocassettes have shown that they can facilitate political upheavals or revolution.
- *Surrogate media for fettered people.* Independent media from outside now provide news and information for people who are captives of their own governments. By publicizing human-rights violations, torture, and political imprisonment, independent media help those victims to survive. It has been argued that a famine never occurs in a nation with a free press because the press, by reporting incipient food shortages, will bring pressures on its government to act before people begin dying. Western reporting of the harsh and brutal life of Afghans living under the Taliban augmented the argument for U.S. intervention.
- *Reporting pariah states.* The foreign press's persistent reporting about pariah states, such as South Africa under apartheid or the Philippines under Marcos, can apparently help to facilitate political change by forming world public opinion, which in turn can lead to actions by governments. Persistent American and European press reporting of the civil war in Bosnia and growing evidence of genocide by Bosnian Serbs undoubtedly pushed the Clinton administration and NATO to intervene and impose a cease-fire.
- *"Copycat" effect.* With global news so pervasive and widely available, sometimes imitative acts occur that have unexpected consequences. A terrorist's car bombing in one country, widely shown on television, is replicated three thousand miles away. Somali clansmen defy U.S. soldiers in Mogadishu, and a few days later, Haitian thugs are encouraged to stage a near-riot as U.S. troops try to land at Port au Prince, causing the U.S. forces to withdraw.
- *Profit-driven media.* The international communication system has grown and expanded so rapidly because there was money to be made by globalization of the world economy. The profit motive is, of course, a powerful force for technological change. The INTELSAT system, a crucial early component in expanding the reach of global news, expanded so rapidly and effectively because there were real profits from a more efficient and cost-effective way to make international telephone calls. Other innovations in media

technology, such as interactive television, have failed so far to become widely adopted because they are not (yet) profitable. Whatever their faults, the "media barons"—Rupert Murdoch and Ted Turner, among others—are entrepreneurs who will take risks and are willing to innovate. When Turner proposed a twenty-four–hour global news channel, many thought he was crazy. Of course, news media have followed, and profited from, the expanding world economy as it has become increasingly globalized.

- *Globalization of advertising and public relations.* The two persuasive arms of Western mass communications, advertising and public relations, have become globalized as well. Here again, the Anglo-American model, speaking English, is the world standard. Though often criticized, advertising and public relations are necessary and inevitable components of market economies and open societies. Moreover, advertising and public relations often make news and are, in fact, an aspect of news.

The Downside of Global Media Effects

Rapid change causes dislocations and inequities, and global communication certainly has its negative impacts as well.

- *Fragility of democracy and open societies.* The worldwide surge of the late 1980s toward democracy and market economies—from Eastern Europe to Tropical Africa and South Asia—provided the promise and possibility of press freedom and independent media in nations long under one-party or military rule. Recently, more than half, or 99 out of 191, countries held competitive elections with promising various guarantees of political and individual rights. Yet most efforts to move from authoritarianism to democracy have failed more often than not after most revolutions, according to Seymour Martin Lipset. He wrote that cultural factors appear more important than economic ones. Some of the factors that have promoted democracy in the past are capitalism, economic growth, a moderate opposition, British influences, and Protestantism.[2] As a result of ethnic and nationalistic clashes, the democratic outlook for many nations in Eastern Europe, the Middle East, and Africa today is not promising. The "failed states" of the Arab world, which have been unable to modernize economically or to acquire democratic rule, have been a major breeding ground for terrorists.

The failure to relieve economic misery in the newly democratic governments in Africa has led to discouragement with democracy, and this may lead to new military or civilian dictators. L. Gray Cowan said, "In most of the African countries where they have had elected democratic governments, the fundamental problem is that they are left with precisely the same economic and social problems they had before."[3]

The rise of democracy and a free press has been associated with market economies, but market economies do not guarantee democratic societies. Currently, the capitalist nations of Indonesia, Thailand, and Malaysia have modern media systems and rising standards of living but are not yet fully democratic and are facing financial difficulties as well.

Even the robust and successful Western nations have proved vulnerable to sneak terrorist attacks. The chief characteristics of globalization—open borders, lenient immigration policies, individual freedoms including privacy protection, and ample free trade—has made the United States and Europe particularly vulnerable to terrorist attacks. Terrorism has been rightly called the dark side of globalization. And when thousands of civilians are killed or endangered, national security becomes a dominant imperative and government controls are tightened.

- *Poor nations lag in the information age.* Optimism about the trends in global communication is based mainly on what is happening in the prosperous societies of the United States, Europe, and Japan. Among the poorer nations of the Southern Hemisphere, especially in Africa, development and growth of media and their audiences have been painfully slow in large part because the stubborn problems of poverty, overpopulation, poor health, illiteracy, and economic underdevelopment still defy solution. African countries and some other nations are not acquiring the technology and infrastructure needed to travel on the information superhighway. In absolute terms, the poorer nations are falling further behind and becoming further marginalized. In addition, the onrush of rapid technological change is further widening the gap between rich and poor nations. The lack of skilled workers, an industrial base (including investment capital), and a literate and educated middle class precludes the poor nations from participating fully in the information revolution, particularly the Internet. When most of a country's population still lives as illiterate peasants on subsistence agriculture, as in much of Africa, Asia, and parts of Latin America, terms such as "transnational data flows," "free flow of information," or "logging on" have little practical meaning. Further, deep political and cultural differences still contribute to hatred, envy, and animosities among many millions toward affluent Westerners. The communication revolution has been coming about through education, communications, technology, and dynamic free-market economies—regrettably all in short supply in too many developing countries.

- *Trends toward media monopoly.* The financial activities of the big players in international communication—Murdoch, NBC, AOL Time Warner, Disney/ABC, BBC, Sony, Vivendi, Viacom, Bertelsmann—are moving generally in one direction: toward consolidation and monopoly of the main structures of international communication. Bigger conglomerates and fewer competitors mean greater profits but less variety and diversity. Problems of regulating these transnational entities are already proving formidable, especially in light of recent megamergers among U.S. media giants. (The U.S. government today has been backing off from anti-trust regulation of media giants.) Primarily involved with profitable entertainment enterprises, these conglomerates show slight concern with quality news dissemination. Critics fear that consolidation means a loss of diverse opinions and less competition among competing news media.

- *Declining standards.* Some critics ask, where in this commercial scramble for profits and power is the concern for serious journalism and quality entertainment? Europeans, for example, lament the decline of public service broadcasting and of quality drama and entertainment. Serious international news is often pushed aside for stories that are more sensational and celebrity oriented. Entertainment values are degrading news values. Before September 11, the U.S. news media carried a lot less serious news from abroad in part because the public seemed less interested. Such apathy reflected the fact that before the terrorist attacks, most Americans felt safe and prosperous. No one can predict how long the revived interest in foreign news, especially as it relates to the war on terrorism, will continue.

• *Shortcomings of audiences.* In the affluent West, the majority of people attending to mass media have only a superficial interest and knowledge of world affairs. They may know that Russia is having economic problems, but they do not understand the reasons. Most Americans were deeply shocked by the September 11 attacks, in part because the news media, as well as the U.S. government, had paid scant attention earlier to the possibilities of surprise terror attacks on America. In less affluent nations, most people lack the education and standard of living to pay attention to world events. In many cases, their own inadequate media are incapable of providing significant foreign news.

Indications of Improvement

The expanding capacity to communicate information rapidly around a world that has become ever more interdependent has begun to erase some differences and perhaps improve understanding among diverse societies. The better educated and more affluent people of most nations—the media users—know more about the outside world and have access to more information than ever before. The educated elites of the developing nations, though small in number, travel more and are more conversant with world affairs than were their predecessors under colonialism. However, the euphoric reaction of some in the Islamic world to the September 11 attacks were sobering reminders to Westerners of the widespread hatred and anti-Americanism and anti-Westernism found abroad. Americans, who like to be liked, were shocked that so many do not like them.

The international news system, despite its inadequacies, moves a great deal of information, data, and pictures much faster than ever before, and there is every indication that this flow will expand in the years ahead. Walter Goodman, a frequent critic of television, had some good things to say recently about the little box: "Television, that product of the West, is by its nature on the West's side when it comes to freedom of information. Censors may hedge it in and manipulate it, but they cannot contain it; the content flows across boundaries and over the globe. When Communism fell, television, which every East bloc country boss thought was his to run for purposes of celebrating himself and suppressing his critics, was among the forces that gave it a shove. ... Television's natural impulse is to reveal, not conceal."[4]

These are some of the reasons that the West's version of world news and events, largely gathered and disseminated by American and West

European journalists, often antagonizes and annoys non-Western governments and peoples, despite their reliance on these sources of information.

To assist governments in dealing with their formidable problems of poverty, massive debt, economic stagnation, disease, and sometimes famine, some leaders would harness mass communications—a clear invocation of the Developmental concept of the press. But under the Western concept, the press must be free of government to maintain liberty, to make democracy possible, and to provide reliable and objective news. Liberty is not the same as social justice or economic equality. History shows that when press freedom is sacrificed for some "greater good," political liberty and human rights usually disappear.

To the Western journalist, the press must be independent of authority, not an instrument of government, so that it can report the news and expose the abuses of governments at home and abroad. Now more than ever, governments (and corporations) need watching. For whether democratic or authoritarian, only governments—not multinational corporations or media conglomerates—have the power to start wars, nuclear or conventional; to conscript soldiers and send them off to dubious wars; to punish dissidents; to establish gulags; to "ethnically cleanse" people with a different religion— or to deal with terrorists. Media in both North and South must contend with governments that try and often succeed in controlling, manipulating, and suppressing what the news media wish to report. Democratic government and private ownership give the press a better chance of resisting government control and serving the public interest, but they are no guarantee of independence. (But also it should be remembered that when national security is threatened, as after September 11, people quickly turn to government for help to counter subversive terrorism.)

Modern history is replete with regimes marred by incompetence, venality, corruption, and brutality. Some journalists believe that the world's free press has done far too little, rather than too much, critical reporting about economic failures and political abuses, especially among developing nations. This basic impasse over the proper purpose of international news communication and the relations between the press and government will continue. But the greater the threat from abroad, the greater will be the interest and need for foreign news.

What Can Be Done

Improvements in international news communication must come from several quarters. Western journalists and mass communicators can do much to improve their own effectiveness. And governments and journalists of the communications-poor developing nations can do more to involve themselves in transnational news, both as senders and receivers. Much can be accomplished as well by nations and journalists working together through international organizations to arrive at some consensus on policy questions and proposals for improved news communication. But it should be remembered that most journalism is essentially local and parochial—it serves the interests and needs of its own audiences. Therefore, the front pages of the leading papers in Japan, Turkey, Norway, and Nigeria will always feature quite different stories. And yet, high-quality foreign news is still essential and does bring diverse peoples closer together.

Western Intitiatives

Western media, with their greater resources, should gather and report more news of the non-Western world and do it with more understanding of the problems and concerns of those nations. The coups, the economic disasters, the civil wars, the famines, and other disasters must be reported, of course, but the press also should provide more sustained, comprehensive coverage of social and cultural aspects in a historical perspective. The public requires more general knowledge of the greater world so that if, say, Algeria or Pakistan suddenly dominates the news, readers can react more knowledgeably.

Even in noncrisis times, television news needs to expand its foreign coverage and, furthermore, do more than provide blanket coverage of a single running story, such as the O.J. Simpson trial, while virtually ignoring other important stories elsewhere. CNN's round-the-clock coverage of the Persian Gulf War revealed the inadequacies of the major networks' formats. Commercial networks should revive the hour-long news documentary, which has almost disappeared from television screens, and not leave it entirely to public television. News media in general need to show more responsibility and sense of public service—and to cover foreign news even when no crisis looms.

More Western media should invest more money and human resources in covering foreign news and not leave the immense task to the few media groups that do maintain correspondents abroad. And newspapers and broadcasters without their own reporters abroad should do a better job of using the considerable amount of foreign news available from news services and syndicates.

Foreign-news editors could make much more use, as well, of academic sources. Hundreds of area specialists who have current and reliable information about every corner of the world are to be found throughout American universities.

Programs to train journalists from abroad should be continued and expanded. Western news organizations have helped to establish national news agencies and trained personnel to run them. For years, a steady stream of journalists and broadcasters has come to Europe and America for training and internships, but training journalists in their home countries or regions still has merit and perhaps priority.

Western media organizations might also consider selectively establishing newspapers in non-Western countries. Although fraught with political risks, some previous ventures have markedly raised the level of journalism in those countries. Two of the best newspapers in black Africa, the *Daily Times* of Nigeria and the *Daily Nation* of Kenya (now both African owned) were started by foreign publishers as commercial ventures. India has a number of vigorous newspapers today because British interests started newspapers there during colonial rule. Since independence, these papers have been managed completely by Indians and have served that nation well.

Closer Western ties can be established between journalists of different nationalities through professional groups such as the International Press Institute and Inter-American Press Association. This can lead to better understanding and cooperation. These organizations and others, such as Amnesty International and the Committee to Protect Journalists, often come to the aid of journalists who have become victims of political repression and violence. Journalists of various nations working together in professional organizations can assist developing nations in such practical matters as subsidies for expensive newsprint, which is almost entirely produced in northern nations, obtaining media equipment such as used presses and broadcast electronics from Western media, and helping to obtain cheaper preferential rates for news transmissions via Comsats and cable.

Non-Western Initiatives

To balance the flow of information better, the news media in developing nations must be improved and expanded, but this will not be easy, because any nation's mass media grow and expand along with general economic and social development and the modernization of individuals. Educated and informed individuals are required for media jobs as well as for media audiences. Although training and technical assistance from outside can be helpful, the impetus for media improvement must come from within.

A few Western news agencies and other media ideally should not dominate global news gathering as they do now, but they themselves are incapable of correcting the inequities of the system—nor should it be expected they can. Newspapers and broadcasters in Africa or South Asia should not have to rely upon a news agency based in London or New York City to find out what is happening in their own region. A much greater diversity of news sources for the world's media to draw upon is needed. For that reason alone, the persistent efforts in Asia, Africa, and Latin America to establish regional news agencies and broadcasting exchange agreements should be encouraged, despite the difficulties involved. Happily, some regions are producing more and more of their own movies, television programs, and popular music. The rise of the Al-Jazeera satellite television news service in Qatar, heard in Arabic all over the Middle East, was an important addition to news diversity in a region of government-controlled news.

How soon and how effectively developing nations can improve their news media may well depend on how their governments respond to the following policy questions.

1. Will non-Western nations cooperate effectively in developing regional and continental telecommunications and news exchange?

   In Africa, for example, long-distance telecommunications can have a revolutionary potential for the sub-Sahara by providing a truly continental system of telecommunications where none has previously existed. An integrated system of regional satellites, Internet connections, cable systems, ground stations, improved AM and FM broadcasting, and microwave relays can have important implications for intra-African exchanges of news, educational broadcasting, telephone service, television programming, and high-speed data transfers. Effectiveness of the Pan African News Agency would be greatly enhanced by improved telecommunications.

2. Will non-Western governments show more concern both for their own peoples' right to know and for an unimpeded flow of information throughout the world?

Too much of the world news controversy has involved the claims
of professional journalists versus the claims of governments over
regulation of news and information. In today's world, any person,
whether born in Pakistan, Norway, Peru, or Tanzania, has the right,
at least in theory, to acquire information that affects his or her
own welfare and future. And the government under which that person lives should respect that right. A hopeless ideal, some will say,
because the overwhelming majority of the world's peoples live under authoritarianism and are far removed from information sources.
Nevertheless, that is the direction in which the world has been
moving.

   To participate in global news flow requires that information,
news, technical data, and cultural fare be permitted to move unimpeded across borders. It also requires that journalists be protected by
law from government intrusion in their activities.

3. Will non-Western nations encourage more diversity and freedom in
   news and information?

Regional and alternative news agencies can be helpful and should be
actively fostered. A key question is whether the governments will
provide their own journalists and broadcasters with greater autonomy and independence. Journalism flourishes best in an atmosphere
of freedom from authority and corporate interference, but few journalists in non-Western nations enjoy such latitude. Too many, unfortunately, either work for autocratic governments or are at the mercy
of arbitrary political interference. Too few governments in the world
today permit their own journalists the freedom to probe serious
internal problems, much less allow them to criticize even mildly the
performance of those in authority. In general, these nations will continue to lag behind the information societies of the West until they
evolve into constitutional, democratic societies with market
economies. That will take time, and some nations obviously will not
opt for that path to development. But to date, few one-party nations
have shown the flexibility and dynamism to join the information
societies.

   In conclusion, what has happened to international news communication in the past quarter-century is, of course, only one aspect of the broad
trend of the revolution in information processing and diffusion that has

been transforming the modern world and its economy. The frictions we have seen between various concepts of journalism—Western, Developmental, Revolutionary, Authoritarian, and Communist—are just aspects of broader issues of international relations.

For the foreseeable future, the current system of international communication will probably retain its present basic structure with the flow of information and news steadily expanding and audiences steadily increasing. Modifications will come mainly from the adoption of more technological and economic innovations in the media themselves. In the late twentieth century, communication technology and economic forces have proved powerful forces for change.

But more than that, a reliable flow of global news and other essential information is an absolute necessity for our interdependent world, and the "closed" nations that try to block out that flow will find themselves unable to compete and prosper. Global politics and wars influence and shape international communication, and in the uncertain and danger-fraught era of terrorism ahead, the world's news media will play central roles in helping people everywhere understand the world beyond their borders.

Notes

1. J.M. Roberts, *The Triumph of the West* (Boston: Little, Brown, 1985), 278, 290–91.
2. "New Democracies Face Long Odds for Survival," *Stanford Alumni Review*, September 1993, 5.
3. Howard W. French, "African Democracies Fear Aid Will Dry Up," *New York Times*, March 19, 1995, sec. A, 1.
4. Walter Goodman, "Even If Used As a Weapon, TV is True to Its Nature," *New York Times*, January 20, 1998, sec. B, 3.

Selected Bibliography

(Related books published since 1990.)

Alleyne, Mark D. *News Revolution: Political and Economic Decisions About Global Information.* New York: St. Martin's, 1997.

Blumler, Jay (ed.). *Television and the Public Interest.* Newbury Park, Calif.: Sage, 1992.

Boyd, Douglas A. *Broadcasting in the Arab World.* 2d ed. Ames: Iowa State University Press, 1993.

Boyd-Barrett, Oliver, and Daya Kishan Thussu. *Contra-Flow in Global News.* London: John Libbey, 1992.

Cole, Richard R. (ed.). *Communication in Latin America: Journalism, Mass Media and Society.* Wilmington, Del.: Scholarly Resources, 1996.

Demers, David. *Global Media: Menace or Messiah?* Cresshill, NJ: Hampton Press, 1999.

Dizard, Wilson P. *Meganet: How the Global Communications Network Will Connect Everyone on Earth.* Boulder, Colo.: Westview, 1997.

————. *Old Media New Media.* New York: Longman, 1994.

Dordick, Herbert, and Georgette Wang. *The Information Society.* Newbury Park, Calif.: Sage, 1993.

Flournoy, Don M. *CNN World Report: Ted Turner's International News Coup.* London: Jon Libbey, 1992.

Flournoy, Don M., and Robert K. Stewart. *Making News in the Global Market.* Luton, U.K.: University of Luton, 1997.

Fortner, Robert S. *International Communication.* Belmont, Calif.: Wadsworth, 1992.

Frederick, Howard H. *Global Communication and International Relations.* Belmont, Calif.: Wadsworth, 1992.

Friedland, Lewis A. *Covering the World: International Television News Services.* New York: Twentieth Century Fund, 1992.

Friedman, Thomas L. *The Lexus and the Olive Tree: Understanding Globalization*. New York: Anchor Books, 2000.

Geyer, Georgie Anne. *Buying the Night Flight*. Washington, D.C.: Brassey's, 1996.

Gwertzman, Bernard, and Michael T. Kaufman (eds.). *The Collapse of Communism*. New York: St. Martin's, 1990.

Hachten, William A. *Growth of Media in the Third World: African Failures, Asian Successes*. Ames: Iowa State University Press, 1991.

————. *The Troubles of Journalism: A Critical Look at What's Right and Wrong with the Press*. 2d ed. Mahwah, N.J.: Lawrence Erlbaum, 2000.

Harasim, Linda. *Global Networks: Computers and International Communication*. Cambridge, Mass.: MIT Press, 1993.

Hawk, Beverly G. *Africa's Media Image*. New York: Praeger, 1992.

Herman, Edward S., and Robert W. McChesney. *The Global Media: The New Missionaries of Corporate Capitalism*. London: Cassell, 1997.

Hess, Stephen. *International News & Foreign Correspondents*. Washington, D.C.: Brookings Institution, 1996.

Kaplan, Robert D. *The Ends of the Earth*. New York: Vintage, 1996.

McQuail, Denis. *Mass Communication Theory*. 3d ed. Newbury Park, Calif.: Sage, 1994.

Merrill, John C. *Global Journalism: Survey of International Communication*. 3d ed. New York: Longman, 1995.

Mickiewicz, Ellen. *Changing Channels: Television and the Struggle for Power in Russia*. New York: Oxford University Press, 1997.

Mueller, Barbara. *International Advertising: Communicating Across Cultures*. Belmont, Calif.: Wadsworth, 1996.

Mytton, Graham. *Global Audiences: Research for World Broadcasting, 1993*. London: BBC World Service/John Libbey, 1993.

Naisbitt, John, and Patricia Aburdene. *Megatrends 2000*. New York: Avon, 1990.

Nelson, Michael. *War of the Black Heavens: The Battle of Western Broadcasting in the Cold War*. Syracuse: Syracuse University Press, 1997.

Pavlik, John V. *Journalism and New Media*. New York: Columbia University Press, 2000.

Rosenblum, Mort. *Who Stole the News?* New York: John Wiley & Sons, 1993.

Seib, Philip. *Headline Diplomacy: How News Coverage Affects Foreign Policy.* Westport, Conn.: Praeger, 1997.

Shenk, David. *Data Smog: Surviving the Information Glut.* New York: Harper Edge/Harper Collins, 1997.

Smith, Anthony. *The Age of Behemoths: The Globalization of Mass Media Firms.* New York: Priority, 1991.

Stevenson, Robert L. *Global Communication in the Twenty-first Century.* New York: Longman, 1994.

Strobel, Warren. *Late-Breaking Foreign Policy: The News Media's Influence on Peace Operations.* Washington, D.C.: U.S. Institute of Peace Press, 1997.

Sussman, Gerald, and John Lent. *Transnational Communications: Wiring the Third World.* Newbury Park, Calif.: Sage, 1991.

Thussu, Daya K. *International Communication: Continuity and Change.* London: University of North London, 2000.

Toffler, Alvin. *PowerShift.* New York: Bantam, 1990.

Van Ginneken, Jaap. *Understanding Global News.* Thousand Oaks, Calif.: Sage, 1998.

Walker, Andrew. *A Skyfull of Freedom: Sixty Years of the BBC World Service.* London: Broadside, 1992.

Wilhelm, Donald. *Global Communication and Political Power.* New Brunswick, N.J.: Transaction, 1990.

Wolfsfeld, Gadi. *Media and Political Conflict: News from the Middle East.* New York: Cambridge University Press, 1997.

Zhou, He, and Jian Hua Zhu. *The 'Voice of America' and China.* Journalism Monographs, no. 143, February 1994.

Index

A

Abacha, Sani, 98
ABC, 39, 121
ABC Radio, 121
Abel, Elie, 120
Advertising
  globalization of, 172
  influence of, 169
  online, 51
  transnational agencies, 78–79
Afghanistan
  propaganda efforts within, 26
  videophones in, 141–142
  violence against journalists, 126
AFP, 33, 119
Africa
  anticolonial movements in, 12
  civil war in, xv
  democracy in, 173
  fertility rate in, 6
  illiteracy in, 9
  Internet capabilities, 51
  journalists in, 98–99
  media in, 97–100
  reporting on, 99
  telecommunications in, 179
Africa's Media Image, 97
Age, effect on news interests, 11
Agence France-Presse, xix
Airliners, hijackings, 67
Ajami, Fouad, 92

Albania, 117, 129
Algeria
  civil war in, xi
  press control in, 150
  violence against journalists, 126
Al-Jazeera, 19–20, 91–92, 179
  anti-Israel/anti-American bias, 25
"All Things Considered," 40
Amanpour, Christiane, 121
America, hatred for, 16, 175
Americans, world view of, xvi, 7,
  11, 123
America Online, xii, 38
Amnesty International, 178
ANSA, 33, 119
Anthrax scare, 20
  exaggeration of, 67–68
Anti-Americanism, 16, 175
Anticolonialism, 12
  West Africa, 159
Anti-Westernism, 175
AOL Time Warner, 54, 74
  Chinese programming, 64
  European-based programming,
  80
  revenues of, 81–82
AP, xix, 77, 119
Apollo 11 mission, 5
Approval ratings, 20
Aquino, Benigno, 8
Aquino, Corazon, 8
Arabic, 86

Arab world
  Al-Jazeera and, 91–92
  "failed states," 172–173
  opinions of, 19–20
Argentina, 152
Argumenti i Kakti, 157
Armstrong, Neil, xix
Arnett, Peter, 134
Asahi, 34
Asia
  anticolonial movements in, 12
  cell phones in, 93
  satellite television in, 64–65
Asian Wall Street Journal, The, xix,
  46, 76
Associated Press. *See* AP
Audiences, 47, 54
  global, 169–170
  interest in world affairs, 175
  targeting, 108–109
Audiocassettes, 160, 171
Auletta, Ken, 82
Australia, 151
Austria, 151
Authoritarian press theory,
  148–151
Awolowo, 159
Azikiwe, 159

B

Baghdad, 132, 134
Baltimore Sun, 34, 121
Bantam, Doubleday, Dell, 83
Barnathan, Julius, 55
Bates, Ted Worldwide, 78
Bazoft, Farzad, 148
BBC, 9/11 coverage, 19
BBC World Services, 25, 37–38,
  105–106
  Arabic-language broadcasts, 107
  in China, 62

internationalization of, 13
  Mandarin-language
    programming, 62, 110
  objectivity of, 107
  official communications,
    103
  Russian-language programming,
    61
  in USSR, 156
BBDO International, 78
Beers, Charlotte, 25
Beijing, 62
Beirut, 69–70
Belarus, 150
Belgium, 151
Benin, 95, 98
Bennet, James Gordon, 75
Berlin, uprisings in, 8
Berliner Zeitung, 158
Berlusconi, Silvio, 74, 84
Bertelsmann, 54, 74, 81, 83
Bhangra pop, 4
Bhutan, 90
Bias
  Al-Jazeera and, 92
  in reporting, xxi
Bigotry, 12
bin Laden, Osama, ix, 16, 170
Bioterrorism, 20, 67
Black, Hugo, 143
Blair, Tony, 26, 92
Bombay, cable television in, 96
Bombings
  aerial, 134
  suicide, 65
  terrorist, ix
Bombs, smart, 133
Bosnia, x–xi, 138, 171
Boston Globe, 34, 121
Botswana, 97–98
Brazil, 152

Bridge News, 34
Bright Star, 92
Britain, response to Muslim
   propaganda, 25
British Council, 108
British Empire, anticolonialist
   movements, 159–160
British Information Services,
   103, 108
Broadcasters, international, xx
Broadcasting
   direct, xi
   English-language, 86
Broadcast television, 18, 34
Brokaw, Tom, 19, 134
Browne, Malcolm, 135
Brown, Lester, 6
Burkina Faso, 98
Burma, 110
Burundi, xi, 98
Bush, George, 133, 139
Bush, George W., 20, 130
"Business Plus," 90

C

Cable News Network. See CNN
Cable television, 41
   India versus China, 95–96
   satellites and, 44
   24–hour war coverage, 129
   24/7 news, 37–38, 83
Cambodia, 110
Camcorders, xviii, 91
Camus, Albert, xxi
Canada, 151
Capital, flow of, 12
Capital Cities/ABC, 81
Carter, Hodding, 124–125
Cassette recorders, 48
Castro, Fidel, 150
Casualties, reporting, 134

CBS, xii, 82
   foreign bureaus, 39, 118, 121
CBS Radio, 121
Cell phones, xii, 92–94
Censorship
   and authoritarian press theory,
      148–151
   the Internet and, 52
   in Saudi Arabia, 90
   wartime, 21–24, 129–132, 135
Chad, 98
Challenger, 45
Chancellor, John, 108
Chechnya, war in, 158
Cheney, Dick, 137
Chernobyl, 157
Cherry, Colin, 30–31
Chicago Tribune, 34
   foreign reporting, 40, 121
Chile, 152
China
   anti-Communist uprising in,
      62–65
   cable television in, 95–96
   cell phones in, 93
   control of radio broadcasting, 110
   dissidents in, 161
   Internet use in, 63
   newspapers in, 64
   press control in, 150
China Daily, 47
Christian Science Monitor, 40, 121
Chronicle of Gibraltar, 87
Civil law, and press freedom, 151
Clarke, Arthur C., 13, 43
Clinton, Bill, 97, 111, 124
   Lewinsky scandal, 17
CNB India, 96
CNN, 25, 36–39
   coverage of Yugoslav conflict, 140
   foreign bureaus, 121

CNN (*cont.*)
  global audience, xix
  Gulf War coverage, 132,
    134, 136
  impact on diplomacy, 37
  internationalization of, 13
  and news hyping, 20
  9/11 coverage, 18
CNN.com, 9/11 page views, 16
CNN effect, 132
CNN Interactive, 49–50
CNN International, 36–37
  in China, 64
Coalition Coordination Center, 26
Cohen, Roger, 158
Cold War
  end of, x, 58
  impact of Western media on,
    156–158, 169
  and public diplomacy, 102,
    109–113
Colombia, 152
Columbia Journalism Review,
    69–70
Combat reports, spinning, 129
Commentaries, online, 50
Commercialization, of media,
    4, 154
Committee to Protect Journalists,
    126, 150, 178
Common law, and press freedom,
    151
Communication
  illegal, 159
  machine-to-machine, 44
  subversive, 159
Communication explosion, 31–32
Communications
  benchmarks of, 7
  cost of, 53

instant, 7
  Marxist/Leninist, xiv-xv
  modernization of, 167–168
  official, 103
  private, 103
  satellite, use in Yugoslav
    conflict, 140
  technology and, 38–39
  Western, xiv-xv
Communications Decency Act, 52
Communism
  American response to, 21
  collapse of, x, xiv, 58–60
  journalism and, x
Communist press theory, 148,
    155–159
Compunication, 53
CompuServe, 52
Computers, 4
  communication and, 7
  laptop. *See* Laptops
Comstats, 43–47
Condit, Gary, 39
  Chandra Levy story, 17
Conglomerates
  entertainment, 4
  and journalistic freedom, 153
  media, 174
Copycat effect, news and, 171
Cordiant, 78
Correspondents, foreign. *See*
    Foreign correspondents
Cosmopolitan, 76
Coups d'état, and radio
    broadcasting, 160
Cowan, L. Gray, 173
Cox Cable, European-based
    programming, 80
Crime, cross-border, 11
Crises, global, 5

Cronkite, Walter, 131, 142
Crossette, Barbara, 121
Cruise missile, 134
Cuba, 109, 150
Culture
  blending/diffusion of, 3–4,
    84–85
  effect on journalism, 147
  Western, 168–169
Cybernews, 48–51
  international concerns, 51–52

D

Dailies, English-language, 87
Daily Mail (London), 75
Daily Nation (Kenya), 178
Daily Telegraph (London), 34, 75
Daily Times (Nigeria), 178
Dallas News, 34
Dar es Salaam, embassy
    bombing, 67
Dari, 26
Databases, 46
Data Smog: Surviving the
    Information Glut, 54–55
Defense Department, 132
de Gaulle, Charles, 150
Democracy
  factors promoting, 1
  and independent news media, 10
  and press control, 151
Democratic Participant
    concept, 154
Democratic Socialist concept, 154
Denmark, 151
Depth News, 96
Deregulation
  of European media, 80
  of telecommunications system, 3
Deutsche Presse Agentur, 33, 78

Deutsche Welle, 103, 106
Deutschland Funk, 106
Developing nations
  and access to information,
    173–174
  media in, 89
  population growth in, 46
  press in, 161–164
Developmental press theory, xx,
    148, 161–164
Diana, Princess, death of, 39
Dictators, censorship by, 170
Digitalization, 4
Diller, Barry, 84
Diplomacy, impact of news media
    on, 170
Dish antennas, xii
Dishes, satellite, 64
Disney Company, 54, 74
  acquisitions, xii, 81–83
  European-based programming,
    80
Dissidents, political, 159
Diversity, loss of, 85
Divisiveness, global, 12
Djibouti, 98
Doordarshan, 125
Dot.coms, 51
Doyle Dane Bernbach Group, 78
dpa, 119
Drug trafficking, 11

E

Early Bird, 31, 45
Earnshaw, Graham, 63
Eastern Europe
  collapse of Communism, x,
    58–60
  journalism in, 157–158
Economist, 34, 47

Economy
  global, 31, 168
  world. *See* World economy
Education, effect on news
  interests, 11
efe, 33, 119
Egypt, radio broadcasting,
  104–105
Eisner, Michael, 82
Elections, media coverage of, 41
Emerson, Gloria, 120–121
Energy, 9
Engels, 155
English, as media language, xix,
  86–87, 120
Enron, collapse of, 24
Entertainment, conglomerates, 4
Environment, 11
Erlanger, Steven, 150
Escorts, military, 138
Espionage
  economic, 102
  and journalism, 148
  political, 102
ESPN, 64, 83
Esquire, 76
Ethics, in journalism, xiv
Ethiopia, 98, 150
Ethnic conflicts, 12
Europe, media changes in, 79–80
European-based programming, 80
European Community, 79–80
Eurovision, 35
Events, global, 169–170
Excellence, journalistic, 153
Exchange agreements, between
  news services, 35
Exclusives, 69
Exports, world, 3
Express, L', 34, 76
Exxon, 33

F

Facsimile production. *See* Fax
  production
Falkland Islands, 131
Fallaci, Oriana, 120
Fax, 118
Fax production, 46–48
Financial Times, 34, 74
Fininvest, 54, 84
First Amendment, 52, 143–144
Flyaway dish, 46
FM radio, and political change,
  94–95
Food, 9
Foreign bureaus
  cost of, 119–120
  newspapers, 34
Foreign correspondents, 115
  and authoritarian regimes, 151
  distribution of, 122
  female, 120–121
  freedom of access, 117
  freelancers, 120
  salaries of, 121
  violence against, 125–127
Foreign news
  importance of, 9–11
  increased interest in, 116
Foreign policy
  influence of television on, 42
  multilateral, 17
Foreign reporting
  expansion of, 177
  and technology, xiii-xiv
Fox News, 38
  coverage of Yugoslav conflict, 140
  and news hyping, 20
Fox television network, 80
France, 80, 151
Frankel, Max, 39
Frankfurter Allgemeine, 34, 75

Freelancers, 120
Free press, xxi
  values of, 152–153
Free speech, 148–149, 151
  Internet and, 52
Friedman, Thomas, 4
Friendly, Fred, 69
Fujisankei, 74
Fullbright grants, 111

G

Gazeta, 157
Gazprom corporation, 158
Gellhorn, Martha, 120
Gemini, 96
Gender, effect on news interests, 11
Genocide, xi
Gergen, David, 97
German, 86
Germany, 151
Getler, Michael, 24, 133
Geyer, Georgie Ann, 121
Ghana, 94–95, 97
Gibbons, Floyd, 130
Giornale, Il, 84
Glasnost, 61, 157
Global electronic village, 42
Globalization, 73–87
  criticisms of, 3–4, 172–175
  impact of, 168–172
  positive aspects, 4
  start of, x
  and telecommunications, 7
  trends in, 12–14
Global sell theory, 79
Global society, xvii
Goddess of Liberty, 62
Goebbels, Joseph, 105
Good Housekeeping, 76
Goodman, Walter, 175
Gorbachev, Mikhail, 61, 157

Governments
  non-Western, and growth of
    media, 179–180
  press control by, 148, 155–159
Greece, 152
Grenada, 21, 131
Griffith, Thomas, 8
Guardian, 34, 75
Guinea, 98
Gulf War, 21, 123, 129, 132–136
  BBC World Services coverage
    of, 107
  CNN coverage of, 136

H

Hackworth, David, 138
Haiti, 93, 138
Halberstam, David, 140
Hand, Learned, 152
Harding, Richard, 130
HarperCollins, 65
Havel, Václav, 110
Hawk, Beverly, 97
Headline News, 36
Health, threats to, 11
Hearst Magazines International,
  75–76
Henry, William E., 60
Hess, Stephen, 11, 120–121
Higgins, Marguerite, 120
Hijackings
  airliners, 67
  terrorist, ix
  TWA Flight 847, 69
Hindu fundamentalists, 65
Hispanics, 86
Hoagland, Jim, 97
Hoge, James, 139
Holliman, John, 134
Homeland security, 20, 24
Honecker, Erich, 158

Hostage crisis
  Beirut, 69–70
  Iran, 68–69

I

IBS, 47
Iceland, 151
Ideas, sharing, 50
Illiteracy, 9
Immigration, 7, 11
Imports, quotas on, 80
Independent, 34, 75
India, 152
  cable television in, 95–96
  cell phone sales, 93
  news censorship in, 125
  satellite television in, 65
  video newsmagazines, 90
Indian MTV, 95
Indian National Satellite, 45
Indonesia, satellite television in, 65
Infobahn, 48
Information
  access to, 135, 179–180
  classified, 22
  combat-related, 129–130
  control of, 21–24
  free flow of, 153
  leaks, 142
  rapid transmission of, 8
  revolution, 42
  societies, 9
  specialized, 11
  speed of, 170
  superhighway, 48
  withheld by military, 129–130
Information Age, 89
Information Telegraph Agency of
    Russia, 33
Infotainment, xvi
Insat 1–B, 45

INTELSAT, 31, 43–45, 55, 171
Inter-American Press Association,
    178
Interdependence, global, xviii, 5
Interfax, 61
International affairs, Americans
    and, xvi, 7, 11, 123
International Broadcasting Act, 111
International Broadcasting
    Bureau, 111
International Herald Tribune, 59
  distribution of, 75
  fax production methods, 47
  Indonesian bar against, 150
  libel suit, 150
  readership of, xix
International news system, 32–36
International political
    communication (IPC),
    103–105
International Press Institute, 178
Internet
  censorship, 52
  and free speech, 52
  journalism and, 48–51
  9/11 audience, 16
  war coverage, 129
Inter Press Service Third World, 96
Investment
  domestic, 3
  foreign, 3
Iran
  conflict with Iraq, 125
  hostage crisis in, 68–69
  revolution in, 160
  satellite television in, 65
Iraq, 133
  conflict with Iran, 125
  press control in, 150
  violence against journalists, 148
Ireland, 151

Irwin, Will, 130
Islam
    conflict with West, xvi
    propaganda, 27
    radical, 16, 20, 25
    response to 9/11 attacks, 16, 24
    terrorists and, 67
Israel, xi, 151
Italy, 84, 151
ITAR-TASS, 33

J

Japan, 152
Jefferson, Thomas, 152, 167
Jennings, Peter, 19, 133
Jiang Zemin, 150, 163
Journalism
    Communist concept of, x
    cultural differences and, 147
    education, 49
    and espionage, 148
    ethics in, xiv
    independent, 151
    international, trends in, 53–55
    and the Internet, 48–51
    libertarian, 152
    and military security, 21–24
    parachute, 98, 122
    standards in, 174
    technology and, 53–55
    transnational, role/function
        of, 148
    Western
        dominance of, 168
        ethic of, 32
        political impact of, 58–60
Journalism of exception, 125
Journalists
    in Africa, 98–99
    foreign, 120
    freelance, 135

independence of, xx
violence against, 19, 125–126,
    148
Junge Welt, 158

K

Kaiser, Robert, 120
Kakutani, Michiko, 85
Kamikaze pilots, 15
Kanyatta, 160
Kaplan, Robert, 99
Karnow, Stanley, 120
Kaufman, Michael T., 59–60
"Kaun Banega Crorepati," 96
Kaunda, 159
Kaus, Mickey, 50
KDKA (Pittsburgh), 41
Keller, Bill, 21
Kennan, George, 118
Kerala (India), 93
Khomeini, Ayatollah, 150, 160
Kifner, John, 136
King, Rodney, 170
Knight-Ridder, 34
Kohut, Andrew, 10
Kondracke, Mort, 110
Korean War, 130
Kosovo, xvi, 124, 129, 139
Krasner, Stephen, 11
Kremlin, censorship by, 158
Kristof, Nicholas, 63
Kuchma, Leonid, 150
Kufuor, J.A., 94
Kurtz, Howard, 138
Kuwait, 65
Kyodo News Service, 33

L

Labor, flow of, 12
Languages, 86
    radio broadcasting, 106

Laos, 110
Laptops, 53, 118
    and foreign reporting, 45
Laqueur, Walter, 112–113
Lasswell, Harold, 7
Latin America
    American newspapers/magazines
        in, 77
    cell phones in, 94
Lebanon, 69
    Marine barracks bombing, 67
Lee Kuan Yew, 76–77
Lenin, 159, 161
Leninist theory, 64, 155–156
Lerner, Daniel, 161
Lesotho, 98
Liberalism, 148
Liberia, 98
Libertarian journalism, 152
Liberty, and press freedom, 176
Lincoln, Abraham, 167
Li Peng, 62
Lipset, Seymour Martin, 172
Live events, broadcast of, 45
Locke, John, 152, 167
Long, Gerald, 125
Loory, Stuart, 42
Los Angeles Times
    African reporting, 99
    foreign bureaus, 34, 121
Los Angeles Times/Washington
    Post News Service, 78

M
Magazines, Spanish-language
    editions, 77
Malaysia, 150, 163, 173
    satellite dish ban, 65
Mali, 95, 98
Mandarin Chinese, 86

Marcos, Ferdinand, 8, 171
Market economy, and democracy,
    173
Marxist/Leninist doctrine,
    155–156
Marx, Karl, 155–156, 167
Mass culture, diffusion of, 3–4,
    84–85
Matsushita Electric Industrial
    Company, 84
MCA/Universal, 84
McLuhan, Marshall, 42, 79
McQuail, Denis, 154–155
Media
    accuracy of, 23
    centralization of power, 4
    conglomerates, 54, 74,
        80–83, 174
    globalization of, 73–87
    independent, 32
    monopolization of, 162–163
    personalized, xi, 47–48, 155, 171
    profit-driven, 171
    transnational, 32
Media, Western, 25, 89
    capabilities of, 32
    needed improvements, 177–178
    resentment of, xx
Meese, Edwin, 69
Megamergers, 81–82, 174
Memory chips, 31
Mena, 33
Merrick, Thomas, 6
Middle East
    and Al-Jazeera, 91
    American's interest in, 123
    conflicts, 67
    views of, 25
Mideast Media and Research
    Institute, 49

Military
  censorship by, 129–132, 135
  expenditure, 9
  and new media technology, 141
  security, and journalism, 21–24
Military Intelligence Service, 130
Mill, John Stuart, 152, 167
Milosevic, Slobodan, 129, 139
Milton, John, 152
Ministry of Defence, 131
Misinformation, 133
Missiles, 133–134
Mitsubishi, 33
Modernization, of mass
  communications, 167–168
Mogadishu, xv, 139
Monde, Le, 34, 74
Monetary system, world, 9
Monopolization, of media,
  154, 174
Moon walk, coverage of, xix
"Morning Edition," 40
Moscow, failed coup, 60–61
Movies, pirated, 102
Moynihan, Daniel Patrick,
  126–127
MSNBC, 38
  coverage of Yugoslav conflict, 140
  and news hyping, 20
MTV, 85
  Indian, 95
MTV Asia, 64–65
Mugabe, Robert, 150
Murdoch, Rupert, 38, 54, 74, 172
  and News Corporation, 80–81
  and Star TV, 65
Murphy, Caryle, 120–121
Murrow, Edward R., 108
Muslim world, response to 9/11,
  ix, 16, 24

Mutual Radio/NBC, foreign
  bureaus, 121
Myanmar, satellite television
  in, 65
My Lai Massacre, 131

N

Nairobi, embassy bombing, 67
Naisbitt, John, 42–43
Nationalism, 6
National Public Radio, 40, 121
National security, 23
Nations
  developing. See Developing
    nations
  interdependence of, xviii
NATO, xv–xvi
  Yugoslavia and, 139–141
Navy SEALS, 138
NBC, 54
  foreign reporting, 39, 121
NBC News, Iranian hostage
  interview, 69
Needham Harper Worldwide, 78
Needs, global, 5–6
Nelson, Michael, 110
Netherlands, 151
Neues Deutschland, 158
Neue Zürcher Zeitung, 34, 75
News
  authenticity of, 122
  broadcast versus cable, 116
  distribution of, xxi
  foreign. See Foreign news
  global, xvii
  instantaneous, xvii, 32
  international, needed
    improvements, 176–177
  manipulating, 118
  non-Western, 96

News (*cont.*)
    online, 49–50
    packages, 45
    security review of, 138
    sources, diversity of, 179
    syndicated, 34, 121
    transmission of, xiv
    24–hour, 36, 136–138
    24/7 coverage, 130
News agencies
    national, 33–34
    use of locals, 120
    Western, 32
    world, 32–36
News Corporation, 80–82
Newsday, 34
Newsmagazines
    foreign editions, 76–77
    video, 90
    and world news, 34
News media
    approval rating, 20
    creating public fear/panic, 20
    influence on international
        politics, 8
    internationalization of, 7, 13
    neutrality of, 22
    response to 9/11, 19
    topics of interest, 10
    U.S., 17
    Western, political impact of,
        58–60
News of the World, 81
Newspapers
    Chinese, 64
    foreign bureaus of, 34
    and foreign reporting, 177
    Gulf War coverage, 137
    hotel copies, 47, 73
    9/11 headlines, 29

online, 48
    "prestige," 74–75
    response to 9/11, 19
News system, international, 32–36
"Newstrack," 90
Newsweek, xix, 34
    fax production methods, 47
    foreign readership, 76
    foreign reporting, 39–40, 119
    on failed Moscow coup, 61
    response to 9/11, 19
Newsweek International, 76
New York Herald, 75
New York Post, 81
New York Times, 75
    African reporting, 99
    foreign reporting, 34, 39–40, 121
    response to 9/11, 19
New York Times News Service, 78
New Zealand, 151
Niger, 98
"Night letters," 160
9/11, 3, 15
    cost of, 16
    coverage of, 16
    effect on foreign news coverage,
        115
    global coverage of, 66–68
    initial coverage of, 29–30
    media response to, ix
    newspaper headlines, 29
1989, major events of, x
1990s, x-xi
Nkrumah, 159
Non-Aligned News Agencies
    Pool, 96
North America, terrorist attacks
    in, 15
North Korea, 110, 163
    radio broadcasting, 104–105

Norway, 151, 154
NTV (Russia), 158
Nuclear threats, 20

O

Office of Censorship, 130
Olgilvy and Mather, 79
Olympic Games, 169

P

Pahlavi, Shah Mohammad Reza, 68
Pakistan
   press control in, 150
   U.S. interest in, 112
Palestine, conflict with Israel, xi
Panama, 21, 132
Parachute journalism, 98, 122
Paramount Communications, 82
Pariah states, 171
Pashto, 26
Patriot missiles, 133
Patten, Chris, 65
Pavlik, John V., 50
Pearl, Daniel, 126
Pearl Harbor, 15
Pelton, Joseph, 43–55
Pentagon
   attack on, 5, 15, 66–68.
      See also 9/11
   press briefing room, 141
Pentagon Papers case, 143
Perestroika, 159
Persian Gulf War, 21, 123,
   132–136
   media coverage of, 107, 129, 136
Pfaff, William, 99
Philippines, 171
Phones
   cell. See Cell phones
   mobile, 53, 92–94

Photocopiers, 160, 171
Pirating, 102
Plaza y Jane, 83
Poland, collapse of communism,
   59
Political warfare, and radio,
   101–102
Politicians, news manipulation
   by, 118
Politics, international, news media
   and, 8
Pollution, 9
Pond, Elizabeth, 120
Popular culture, 4, 84–85, 89
Popular Mechanics, 76
Population
   growth of, 9
   stabilization, 6
   world's, 6
Population Reference Bureau, 6
Portugal, 152
Postal service, 41
Postman, Neil, 124
Poverty, 9, 173–174
Powell, Colin, 20, 92, 132,
   134
Prague, 8, 158
Pravda, 159
Press
   critics, 17
   freedom of, xxi
   independence of, 176
   one-party, 156
   political concepts of, 148–164
   regulation of, 148
   right to information, 143–144
   self-discipline of, 138
   underground, 159
   unpatriotic, 20
   watchdog role, 168

Press control
  authoritarianism, 148–151
  communist, 148, 155–159
  developmental, 148, 161–164
  revolutionary, 148, 159–161
  Western, 148, 151–155
Price, Byron, 130
Privatization, of European
  media, 80
Profitability, and press control,
  153
Project for Excellence in
  Journalism, 23
Propaganda, xx, 104
  definition of, 102
  Islamic, 27
  terrorist, 22
  wartime, 133
Propaganda of the deed, 66
Propaganda War, 24–27
Provincialism, 7
Public diplomacy, 103–105
  post-Cold War, 109–113
  and radio, 101–102
  U.S. activities in, 108–109
Public relations, globalization
  of, 172
Public service, 154
Public service broadcasting
  decline in, 174
  European, 80
Publishers
  establishing foreign newspapers,
    178
  ownership of, 83
Putin, Vladimir, 150, 158

Q

Qatar, 91
Quint, Bert, 122

R

Radio Beijing, 106
Radio broadcasting, 41
  Cold War and, 110
  during political crises, 160
  international, 105–108
  largest operators, 106
  and political change, 94–95
  and political warfare,
    101–102
  and public diplomacy,
    101–102
  shortwave, 59, 62
  transnational, 102
  Western, 61
Radio Cairo, 106
Radio France Internationale,
  106, 111
Radio Free Afghanistan, 26
Radio Free Asia, 110–111
Radio Free Europe, 26, 59, 106,
  108, 110–113
  in USSR, 157
Radio Havana, 103
Radio Liberty, 59, 106, 108,
  110–113
  in USSR, 157
Radio Marti, 109
Radio Moscow, 103, 106
Radios
  shortwave, xix-xx
  transistor, xviii
Random House, 83
Rather, Dan, 19, 39, 118–119
Rawlings, Jerry, 94
RCA/Ariola, 83
Reader's Digest, 76–77
Reagan, Ronald, 108–109
Relief organizations, 103
Reporters, pools, 133, 135

Reporting
  biased, xxi
  instantaneous, 140
  videophone, 142
Resource depletion, 11
Reuters, xix, 33, 119
  foreign bureaus, 34
  online news delivery, 49
Reuters Television, 34–35, 78
Revolutionary press theory, 148,
  159–161
Righter, Rosemary, 162
Riyadh, 132
Rosenblum, Mort, 119
Rosenthal, Andrew, 140
Rowan, Carl, 108
Rumsfeld, Donald, 21–22, 142
Russia
  collapse of communism, 58–60
  violence against journalists
    in, 158
Russian, 86
Rwanda, 97–98
  genocide in, xi

S

Saatchi & Saatchi, 78
Samizdat, 157, 159
Sampson, Anthony, 160
Satellite dishes, Chinese ban
  on, 64
Satellites, xii, 4
  communication, xvii, 13, 31
  cost of, 115
  role of, 42–47
Satellite uplinks, 46
Saudi Arabia
  Air Force quarters bombing, 67
  satellite dish ban, 65
  television censorship in, 90

Sawyer, Forrest, 136
Scandals, 17
Schramm, Wilbur, 161
Schuster, Scott, 120
Schwarzkopf, Norman, 132
Sciolino, Elaine, 121
Scud missiles, 133
Seagram, 84
Seditious libel, 151
Self-censorship
  and authoritarianism, 149–150
  of foreign journalists, 99
  terrorist incidents and, 68–70
Senegal, 95, 97
September 11th. See 9/11
Serbia, xvi, 124, 129, 138
Services, global trade of, 5
Shah of Iran, 160
Shaw, Bernard, 134
Shell, 33
Shenk, David, 54
Shorr, Daniel, 120
Simpson, O.J., 17, 39, 123
Singapore, 150, 163
  censorship in, 52
  satellite dish ban, 65
Sky Channel, 81
Smart bombs, 133
Smartertimes.com, 50
Smiley, Ian, 99
Smith, Adam, 167
Social Responsibility, 154, 162
Software, pirated, 102
Solidarity, 59
Somalia, 98, 138–139
Sony, 74, 84
Sources
  use of, 178
  verifying, xiv
South Africa, 97, 171

South-North News Service, 96
Soviet Union, x
Spain, 152
Spanish, 86
Spanish-language editions,
    magazines, 77
Specialists, as sources, 178
Spiegel, Der, 34, 76
Star TV, 65, 96
    in China, 64
Stealth bomber, 134
Steiner, George, 58
Stoll, Ira, 50
Stories, sensational, 17
Stringers, 117, 120
Sudan, 98, 117
Sudan News Agency, 117
Suharto, xi, 8
Suicide bombings, 65
Sun (London), 81
Sunday Times (London), 81
Sweden, 117, 151, 154
Switzerland, 151
Syria, press control in, 150

T

Tanter, Raymond, 68
TAS, 33
Taylor, Charles, 150
Technology
    effect on censorship, 170
    foreign reporting and, xiii-xiv
    journalism and, 53–55
    news reporting and, 41–42
Tehran, 68–69
Tel Aviv, 132
Telecommunications
    cost of, 4
    deregulation of, 3
    globalization and, 7

interactive, 53
satellite, 42–47
Telegraph, 41
Telephones, 41
    impact on communication, 43
    portable wireless, 46
satellite, 19, 118, 129
    cost of, 142
    in Yugoslav conflict, 140
video, 19, 46
Television
    emotional impact of, 140
    foreign news coverage, 10
    foreign policy and, 42
    interactive, 171
    live, 136
    networks, and foreign reporting,
        177
    news
        manipulation by terrorists, 66
        syndicated, 78
    patriotism in response to 9/11, 19
    and public's perceptions of
        war, 30
    satellites and, 45, 64–65
    terrorism and, 65–70
Television Marti, 109
Terrorism
    American response to, 21
    coverage of, 68
    international, 12, 65–70
    media self-censorship and,
        68–70
    and security concerns, 102
    and television, 65–70
    vulnerability to, 173
    war against, 16, 113
        cost of covering, 115
        opening of, 141–142
Terrorists, Islamic, 67

Tet offensive, 131
Thailand, 64–65, 173
Thatcher, Margaret, 69, 107
Thompson, Dorothy, 120
Thompson, J. Walter, 79
Tiananmen Square, 8, 62–65
Mandarin-language reporting
during, 110
Tibet, 111
Time, 34
fax production methods, 47
foreign reporting, 39–40, 119
readership of, xix
response to 9/11, 19
Times (London), 32, 34, 81
Time Warner, xii, 38
Tipson, Frederick, 4
TIUPIL, 44
Toffler, Alvin, 79
Togo, 98
Trade, volume of, 12
Trade negotiations, impact of, 11
Transistor, first, 31
Transmission, of information, 8
Transmitters, portable, xi
Travel, and newspaper access,
47, 73
Tribalism, modern, 6
Tunstull, Jeremy, 87
Turkey, 150, 152
Turner Broadcasting, xii, 38
Turner, Ted, 36, 172
TV-6 (Moscow), 159
TV Guide, 81
TWA Flight 847, 69
20th Century Fox Broadcasting, 81

U

Uganda, 97
Underclass, permanent, 6

UNESCO, 9
Ungar, Sanford, 26, 113
United Kingdom, 151
United Nations (UN), 7, 11
United States
international news reporting
in, 123
news media, 17
public diplomacy, 108
response to Muslim
propaganda, 25
Western press in, 151
U.S. Armed Forces Radio and
Television Network, 103
U.S. Census Bureau, 6
U.S. Information Agency, 103, 108
U.S. Information Service, 108
U.S. Marines, in Somalia, 138
U.S. News, international news
coverage, 119
U.S. News and World Report,
foreign reporting, 39–40
U.S. Supreme Court, 143
UPI, 33, 119
USA Today, 75
fax production methods, 46
foreign bureaus, 34
USS Cole, attack on, 67
USSR, press control in, 155–159

V

VCRs, 89–91
Venezuela, 94, 152
Viacom, xii, 74, 81–82
European-based programming,
80
Victims, and independent
media, 171
Videocassettes, 89–91
Videoconferencing, 142

Videophones, xii, 118
  in Afghanistan, 141–142
  "Videophone war," 141
Videos, pirated, 102
Videotapes, and viewer
    freedom, 90
Vietnam, 110
Vietnam War, 123, 131
  access to information during, 22
Views, diversity of, 149, 152
Visnews, 34–35
Vivendi, 54
Vivendi/Universal, 74, 81, 84
Vivendi Universal Entertainment,
    84
Voice of America, 25, 61, 106
  in Arab world, 112
  audience, 26
  Mandarin-language
      programming, 62, 110
  official communications, 103
  public diplomacy and, 110–113
  start of, 108
  in USSR, 156–157
  Web page, 112
Voice-overs, 122

W

Walcott, John, 118
Walesa, Lech, 110
Wall Street Journal, The
  European edition, 77
  fax production methods, 46
  foreign reporting, 34, 39–40,
    121
War
  authoritarian press control
      during, 150–151
  news sources, 116

  real time, 132
  reporting, 21–24
Washington Post
  African reporting, 99
  foreign reporting, 34, 39–40, 121
  response to 9/11, 19
Watergate, 123
Watson, James, 4
Web sites
  commentary/single issue, 50
  top ten for news, 50
West
  conflict with Islam, xvi
  media in, 89
  news agencies, 32
  popular culture of, 4
West Africa, 99
Western media. See Media,
    Western
Western press theory, 148,
    151–155
Western Sahara, 98
Westinghouse, xii, 82
What Is to be Done?, 159
"Who Wants to Be a
    Millionaire?," 96
Wick, Charles, 109
Wicker, Tom, 70
Wolzien, Tom, 122
Women, as foreign
    correspondents, 120–121
World community, organization
    of, 9
World economy, two-tiered, 6
World events, coverage of, 57, 70
Worldnet, 109
World news services, 32–36
  personnel, 77
  scope of, 77–78

World problems, 9
World Service Television (WST),
    37, 136
World Television News, 78
World trade, value of, 3
World Trade Center attacks, 5, 10,
    15. *See also* 9/11
    global coverage of, 66–68
    media response to, ix
World War I, 130
World War II, 130
Worldwide Television News
    (WTN), 34–35

WPP Agency, 78–79
Wright, Robin, 121
Wriston, Walter B., 8

Y

Yeltsin, Boris, 61
Yemen, 67
Yugoslavia, xvi, 139–141

Z

Zee, 96
Zeit, Die, 47
Zorthian, Barry, 22